Breakfast in Bridgetown

Breakfast in Bridgetown

The definitive guide to Portland's favorite meal
2nd serving

Paul Gerald

Bacon and Eggs Press
Portland, Oregon

Bacon and Eggs Press
PO Box 9243
Portland, OR 97207-9243
www.breakfastinbridgetown.com

ISBN: 978-0-9797350-1-1
Library of Congress Control Number: 2010915011

Photo credits:
    Front cover photos by Paul Gerald
    Back cover photo by Veronica Vadakan
    Restaurant photos on pages 45, 57, 91, 200, 213, 232, 253, and 277 by
        Veronica Vadakan
    Restaurant photos on pages 131 and 227 by Jacob Grove
    Other restaurant photos by Paul Gerald

Editing by www.IndigoEditing.com
Design by www.ALLPublications.com

Dedication

This book is dedicated, with immense admiration and gratitude, to everybody who grows it, delivers it, preps it, cooks it, brings it out, and cleans it up.

Also to my star researcher and fine friend, Linda Faino.

And finally, in loving and grateful memory of Trina, "Funny Story" Mike, and "Wharf Rat" John. I'll see you all at the top of the falls.

Contents

CONTENTS

Acknowledgments

I wrote and published this book myself, and I can't recommend that process highly enough. In fact, I'm not sure I can recommend it at all.

Write a book for a publisher, which I've done, and you do a big chunk of work and then get a few scraps of money—but almost no headaches or risk, other than poverty. Ah, but commit to publishing it yourself and you get all the risk, all the control, all the work, and (you hope) all the rewards. You are also going to need a *lot* of help.

At least 90 percent of what I have learned about publishing books was taught to me by the fine folks at the Northwest Association of Book Publishers. They meet once a month for the sole purpose of helping people market and publish their own books. Check them out at *nwabp.org*. It was there I found the book's editor, Ali McCart of Indigo Editing & Publications; its designer, Jennifer Omner of ALL Publications; and the indispensable Bob Smith of BookPrinters Network, who knows everything and everybody involved in printing books. Special thanks to NWABP President Paul Gerhards, just for being a great guy. And to Mike Jones for his many forms of generosity.

But before all of that, I needed to know where to eat breakfast. That information came from a constant stream of sources, but special mention must go to Linda Faino, who seemed to send me a clipping or e-mail weekly, to the extent that in the final weeks before publication I had to ask her to stop. I thank her immensely, nonetheless.

Next, of course, were all those meals, the dozens of breakfast outings ranging from private to intimate to large-scale wacky. With the possible exception of my expanded understanding of French toast, the finest thing about writing this book has been going out to breakfast with various combinations of these people while writing this second edition:

Trisa Alemany, Lori Ashberg, Joe Bianco, Jenny Boyce, Chela Zini Caban, Rich Chouinard, Eriana Cistis, Dave Cohen, Amaren Colosi, Corky Corcoran, Maureen Culligan, Debi Danielson, Jan Dance, Lori Davis, Kerri Dee, Christie Dewey, Tom Eggers, Jennifer Fields, Rey Franco, Craig Frerichs, Jane Garbisch, Jeri Gedrose, Signe Geneser,

Lee Gerald, Patrick Gihring, Brandi Gilroy, Joseph Grabeal, Ken Hallenius, Robin Healy, Bevan Hurd, Kerry Jeffrey, Maria Garner Jeffrey, Erica Jensen, Marie Johns, Juliet Johnson, Cheryl Juetten, Mona Kate, Erin Kelly, Mindie Kniss, Amy Kuntz, Rebecca Luedloff, Anna Long, Jeannette Lyons, Bob Malone, Jerry Martin, Shari Melton, Brian McGinty, Megan McMorris, Beth McNeil, Barbara Meyer, Tricia Montoya, Mick Mortlock, Anne Marie Moss, Brian Murray, Donna Ramsey, Elida Ramsey, Kelly Rodgers, Kelley Webb Roy, Steven Schechterman, Craig Schuhmann, Maria Shindler, Al Stern, Alice Sufka, Marshall Talley, Marcella Tancreti, Cathy Steele Tappel, Jean Tuller, Rick Vazquez, Paul Vorvick, Phil Wentz, Caleb Winter, Leslie Woods, Robb and Whitney Wynhausen, Elena Yingling, Jeff Young, and Al Zimmerman.

With all that done, it was, of course, time to write. During that time I had the loving support of many friends, as well as the nice folks at the ActivSpace on Lovejoy and their coffee shop, Modern Love. I also thank Joe and Vonne Williams for letting me live in the coolest house in town, and the Cascade Locks Motel for a great writing retreat I had there.

This time, though, I didn't even write the whole thing. I needed Brett Burmeister of *foodcartsportland.com* and Nick Zukin of Kenny and Zuke's Delicatessen to help out, and I appreciate their great work. Thanks, as well, to Scott Bronson for creating the cool maps in this edition.

Thanks to the Food Dude of *portlandfoodanddrink.com* for his support, as well as to Kacey Montoya of KOIN TV and Rick Sebak of PBS and WQED for showing an interest and putting me on television, for better or worse.

Thanks to Juliet for being such a sweetie. Let's go camping soon! And to Roman Dominguez for being such a cool little brother.

And finally there's the nutty and wonderful crew at *cascadia.fm*, where my podcast goes out each week from the "Penthouse Studios." Thank you to Robert Wagner and Sabrina Miller for letting me join the fun, and to Emily Gibson for making it so all I have to do is show up and run my mouth.

Introduction

Where Do You Like to Go for Breakfast?

It all started with that question. And soon I figured out that I had no idea what I was getting into with this book.

It started with a simple idea: describe all the breakfast places in Portland. That quaint notion was shattered as I came to realize how many such places there are. It's insane. So I decided to keep it to places within the city limits that serve an honest-to-goodness breakfast. So, no coffee shops or doughnut shops or local taverns with an egg sandwich special.

For this edition, I am throwing in a collection of out-of-town places, and I've brought on two experts, Brett Burmeister and Nick Zukin, to write about food carts and ethnic breakfasts.

Even then, I can't get them all. I'm sure many of you have a favorite you won't see here, and all I can say is I'm sorry. It may be that they opened too late (roughly the start of 2010) to make it in this time. Or maybe they fell between categories. Or maybe I'm just an idiot. Either way, 117 restaurants—plus several pages each on carts and ethnic food—is all I'm capable of at this point.

The basic idea is to describe Portland by how and where its people eat breakfast—kind of a breakfast tour of the city—while also giving folks a whole mess of options to check out. And yes, I've eaten in every one of the restaurants described. And yes, I weigh more than I used to.

The seed of this idea lies in my 14-year (and counting) career as a travel writer for the *Memphis Flyer*, where I used to be a staffer. In the process of writing some 300 articles, a theme developed: describe a place by describing a meal eaten there, usually breakfast, which I did for Las Vegas, an Amtrak train, Hong Kong, Santa Barbara, Skykomish, and so on. To read how that seed took root in my brain, read the chapter on Beaterville Cafe.

What This Book Isn't (or, Why No Stars?)

I am neither a critic nor a foodie, and I don't have a sophisticated palate or any inside scoop on what's happening behind the scenes—mainly because I am lazy, unsophisticated, and don't care about such things. I do have this going for me: I am certain I've eaten breakfast in more Portland restaurants than any other human being. I'm just not sure how I feel about that.

Anyway, no ratings. I honestly believe that my opinion of a place, which is based on my preferences and perhaps only one visit, almost certainly has no connection to your opinion of a place. Some of these places I don't care for, some I love, but I think they're all interesting in some way, so that's what I shoot for. Besides, how do you have the same rating system for, say, Tosis and the Tasty n Sons? If you really care, I listed my 12 favorites in the back.

I should let you know that with very few exceptions (when I was profiling places for *livepdx.com* or doing an interview for my podcast) my experiences were not influenced by restaurant staff; none knew I was writing a book when I visited, and none paid for my meals.

My Cry for Help

I still find out about breakfast places every week, and I'm usually not happy about it, because I could work on this %^!&$#! book forever! But I do want to know about them, and also how I can make the book better and more suited to your needs. What ideas do you have for organization, information, and presentation? Do you have any news tips I should know about? Is something out of date or just plain wrong?

Even if you just want to bitch at me, you are strongly encouraged to get in touch. I'm blogging regularly at *breakfastinbridgetown.com*, my email address is paul@baconandeggspress.com, and I look forward to hearing from you.

I'll see you at breakfast.

Paul

Paul Gerald

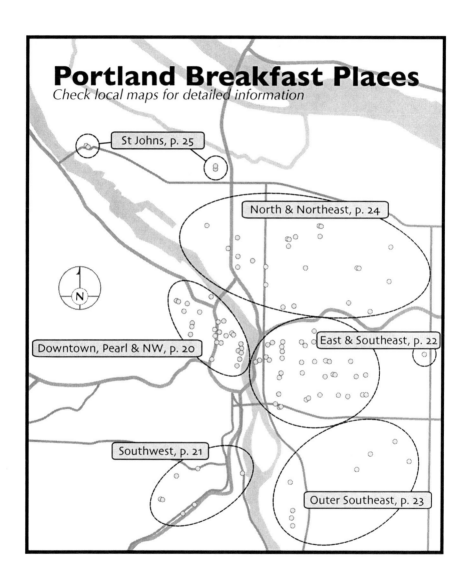

Portland Breakfast Places
Check local maps for detailed information

St Johns, p. 25

North & Northeast, p. 24

N

Downtown, Pearl & NW, p. 20

East & Southeast, p. 22

Southwest, p. 21

Outer Southeast, p. 23

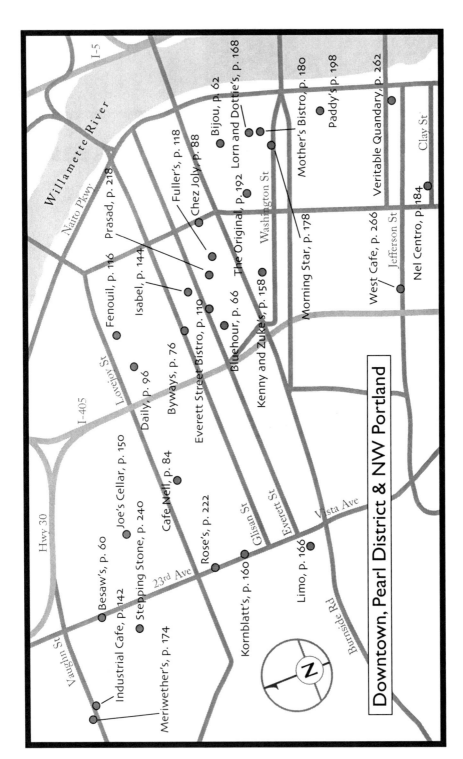

I-5

Willamette River

Naito Pkwy

Bijou, p. 62

Lorn and Dottie's, p. 168

Mother's Bistro, p. 180

Paddy's, p. 198

Veritable Quandary, p. 262

Clay St

Fuller's, p. 118

Chez Joly, p. 88

Prasad, p. 218

The Original, p. 192

Washington St

Morning Star, p. 178

West Cafe, p. 266

Jefferson St

Nel Centro, p. 184

Fenouil, p. 116

Isabel, p. 144

Bluehour, p. 66

Kenny and Zuke's, p. 158

Everett Street Bistro, p. 110

Daily, p. 96

Byways, p. 76

Lovejoy St

I-405

Hwy 30

Joe's Cellar, p. 150

Stepping Stone, p. 240

Cafe Nell, p. 84

Rose's, p. 222

Glisan St

Everett St

Vista Ave

Limo, p. 166

Besaw's, p. 60

Industrial Cafe, p. 142

Meriwether's, p. 174

Vaughn St

23rd Ave

Kornblatt's, p. 160

Burnside Rd

N

Downtown, Pearl District & NW Portland

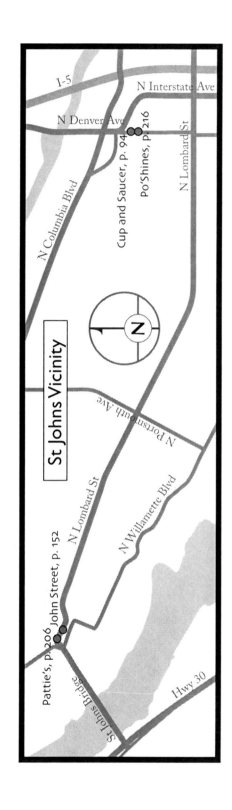

St Johns Vicinity

I-5

N Interstate Ave

N Denver Ave

Cup and Saucer, p. 94

Po'Shines, p. 216

N Lombard St

N Columbia Blvd

N

N Portsmouth Ave

N Lombard St

N Willamette Blvd

Pattie's, p. 206

John Street, p. 152

St Johns Bridge

Hwy 30

Categories

I've created categories to give you a quick take on what kind of place each restaurant is. I have also put places into more than one category, some of which probably make no sense. To try to explain things a little, here's what I'm thinking when I assign each category:

New doesn't mean it recently opened. The category is more like New Portland and refers to a place that has the hippie/yuppie/foodie feel to it, serves Asiago cheese and whatnot, and generally represents the changes Portland's food scene has undergone in the last, say, 20 years. Examples: Simpatica, Zell's, Tin Shed.

Old School places have generally been around awhile, though not necessarily any longer than a New Portland place. A lot of folks would call them diners, but that's too narrow for my purposes. When an Old School place says cheese and coffee, it probably means Tillamook cheddar and Farmer Brothers. Examples: Patti's Homeplate, Fat City, Original Pancake House.

Mom & Pop places are often Old School as well. But where the Original Pancake House is clearly Old School, you're not likely to meet the owner when you're there, and the food wasn't cooked by Dad and brought out by Mom. *That's* a Mom & Pop place. Examples: Johnny B's, Beaterville, Hollywood Burger Bar.

Classy doesn't necessarily mean crazy expensive, though these places do run more expensive than average. At the very least, Classy means a place has tablecloths, the staff is in black and white, candles or flowers are on the tables, and an omelet may be $10 or more. Examples: Cafe du Berry, Simpatica, Fenouil.

Hip probably sounds like I'm stereotyping. But Hip means it's the kind of place where you can chill for a while and the people generally known as hipsters often eat there—a hipster being identified by the trademark thick-rimmed glasses, vintage clothing, upturned pants, sideburns, sneakers, and late rising hour. And if you're offended by that description, you're probably a hipster. Examples: Junior's, Cricket Café, Stepping Stone.

Weekend means breakfast (many call it brunch) is served only on weekends. Or, in some cases a Weekend designation means breakfast is served all week but staff does something special on weekends—often a buffet or fancy brunch. Examples: Screen Door, Petite Provence, Accanto.

Kiddie means the place goes out of its way to accommodate kids. I can't think of a place that doesn't want kids, but these places have a play area or extensive kids' menus or just generally a kid-friendly vibe about them. Some even have kids working there. Examples: Old Wives' Tales, New Deal Café, Bumblekiss.

Veggie, as you might imagine, means the place is particularly friendly to nonmeat-eaters. Most places have a vegetarian omelet, but Veggie here means vegetarians and vegans will have more than a couple of choices. A few places really hang their hat on this category. Examples: Vita, Paradox Café, Prasad.

Late-Night Breakfasts

A common question over the years has been, where can I get breakfast late at night?

Well, here you go. And by late-night, I mean dinnertime and on.

Name	Category	Location	Page
Golden Touch	Old School	SW/Inner	124
Hotcake House	Old School	SE/Inner	138
Hungry Tiger Too	Hip/Veggie	SE/Inner	140
Kenny and Zuke's	Hip/Old School	Downtown	158
Kornblatt's	Old School	NW	160
Marco's Cafe	Classy	SW/Inner	172
Overlook	Old School	N/Inner	196
Paradox Café	Hip/Veggie	SE/Belmont	204
Po'Shines (weekends)	Mom and Pop	N/Outer	216
Stepping Stone	Hip/Mom and Pop	NW	240
Tosis	Old School	NE/Hollywood	256

Let's Eat Out(side)!

Feel like dining under the, um, legendary Portland sun? Here are your options for outdoor seating among the places covered in the book.

Name	Location	Page	Scene
Alameda Cafe	NE/Fremont	40	Umbrella sidewalk tables
Bertie Lou's Cafe	SE/Sellwood	58	Picnic tables on the street
Besaw's Cafe	NW	60	Covered patio
Bridges Cafe	NE/MLK	70	Uncovered tables near MLK
Bumblekiss	NE/Fremont	74	Umbrellas on a quiet patio
Cafe Nell	NW	84	Sidewalk tables, no cover
Cameo Cafe East	NE/Outer	86	Deck with some cover
Cricket Café	SE/Belmont	92	Uncovered sidewalk tables
Cup and Saucer	NE/Alberta	94	Uncovered sidewalk tables
Daily Cafe	Pearl	96	Sidewalk tables with umbrellas
Detour Cafe	SE/Division	100	Shady, covered patio
EaT Oyster Bar	N/Inner	106	Covered patio
Equinox	N/Inner	108	Uncovered patio
Fenouil	Pearl	116	Uncovered patio next to park
FlavourSpot	N/Inner	276	Both locations no cover
Fuller's Coffee Shop	Pearl	118	Open tables on the street
Hands On Cafe	SW/Inner	128	Lovely garden patio
Hawthorne Street Cafe	SE/Hawthorne	132	Patio above street
Helser's	NE/Alberta	134	Uncovered sidewalk tables
Industrial Cafe	NW	142	Uncovered patio
Isabel	Pearl	144	Uncovered patio
John Street Café	N/Outer	152	Shady, quiet garden patio
Kenny and Zuke's	Downtown	158	Uncovered sidewalk tables
Kornblatt's	NW	160	Uncovered sidewalk tables
Limo	NW	166	Small patio
Meriwether's	NW	174	Quiet patio with some cover
New Deal Café	NE/Hollywood	186	Open tables on the street
Pambiche	E/Burnside	200	Covered tables, heat lamps
Papa Haydn	SE/Sellwood	202	Garden patio

Veggie-Friendly Places

For you non-carnivores out there, congratulations. You live in a great place for breakfast.

While I am not one of you, I've tried to keep you in mind as I checked out all these restaurants. Each place in the book has its own little listing at the end for how I think you'll do there, but these particularly stand out as places where vegetarians and/or vegans would have more options than the ol' Spinach Omelet.

Am I full of it? Get in touch and let me know.

Name	Category	Location	Page
Bakery Bar	Hip/Weekend	NE/Hollywood	46
Bar Carlo	New/Hip	SE/Outer	48
Beaterville Cafe	Hip/Mom & Pop	N/Inner	52
bloop! Oatmeal	Cart	Downtown	275
Buddha Bites	Cart	Downtown	276
Bumblekiss	New/Kiddie	NE/Fremont	74
Cricket Café	Hip	SE/Belmont	92
Cup and Saucer Cafe	Hip	Several	94
Delta Cafe Bar	Hip/Weekend	SE/Outer	98
Equinox	New/Weekend	N/Inner	108
Flavour Spot	Cart	North	276
Hawthorne Street Cafe	New/Hip	SE/Hawthorne	132
Hungry Tiger Too	Hip	SE/Inner	140
J&M Cafe	New/Classy	SE/Inner	146
Jam on Hawthorne	New/Hip	SE/Hawthorne	148
Junior's Cafe	Hip	SE/Inner	156
Old Wives' Tales	New/Kiddie	E Burnside	190
Moxie Rx	Cart	N/Inner	278
Paradox Café	Hip	SE/Belmont	204
Parkers Waffles	Cart	Downtown	277
Perierra Crêperie	Cart	SE/Hawthorne	274
Ruby Dragon	Cart	N/Inner	273
Slappy Cakes	Kiddie	SE/Belmont	238

Kid-Friendly Places

Parents make up a category like vegetarians and vegans: I am not among your number, but I try to keep you in mind, and I ask some of you for input.

I've only heard of a few places that seem to not dig kids, but the places listed here make a particular effort to welcome our littlest friends.

Name	Category	Location	Page
Bakery Bar	Hip/Veggie/Weekend	NE/Hollywood	46
Bumblekiss	New	NE/Fremont	74
New Deal Café	New	NE/Hollywood	186
Old Wives' Tales	New/Veggie	E Burnside	190
Po'Shines	Mom & Pop/Old School	N/Outer	216
Sckavone's	Weekend	SE/Division	230
Slappy Cakes	Veggie	SE/Belmont	238
Sub Rosa	Weekend/Classy	SE/Division	242
Vita Cafe	Hip/Veggie	NE/Alberta	264

It's Waffle Time!

by Nikki Harding

It's a wonderfully cold and drizzly Portland morning. My son awakes and shuffles into my room, rubbing the sleep from his eyes.

"Good morning, Mommy. Waffles?"

This is his daily salutation. Once every couple of weeks, I indulge him. We dress quickly and warmly to make our way to "Happy Waffles" or more commonly known as FlavourSpot. He runs to the window and immediately places his order.

"Hot chocolate, please?"

We argue over what we want in our waffle. He is two and a half and has impeccable persuasion skills. He wants sausage, I want bacon. He tells me he loves sausage more than Bubba (our dog) does. We order a sausage waffle.

At this point it's raining. Drinking our coffee and chocolate in the rain, smelling the griddle as it creates our masterpiece, I suggest we eat it at home.

"No. It tastes better in the rain."

We grab our order. The incessant giggling begins. Profuse thank-yous are given. More giggling. He sits on the wet bench with his napkin and in a maniacally excited voice screams, "I'm ready!"

We eat in silence for a minute. In between bites he giggles and tells me he is so happy. He sings to his waffle. He tells it how delicious it is. He asks if he can give some to the dog when we get home. He takes one carefully selected bite, wraps it up in the leftover paper, and we head back to the car. On the car ride home, he tells me he loves me more than waffles. I tell him I love him more than waffles. We get out of the car, get inside the toasty house, and call to Bubba for his treat. I tell my son to hand it over. He looks at me, smiles, and says, "I ate it."

This was the winning entry in a writing contest I had on my podcast in early 2010.

The Restaurants

Accanto

New/Classy/Weekend

The Legend's casual sibling.
2838 SE Belmont St. (SE/Belmont) ~ 503-235-4900 ~ *accantopdx.com*
Brunch weekends 9 a.m. to 2 p.m.
$13–$15 (all major cards, no checks)

———◆•◆———

On my freelance writer's budget, a restaurant like Genoa is saved for once a year—maybe. If the folks are in town, or some magazine is paying, or I'm desperately trying to impress somebody, I can see it. Otherwise I leave it to rich folks and serious restaurant people.

Well, there are a lot more of me than them. And the owners of Genoa know this. So in late 2009 the new owners, having renovated and reopened the legendary restaurant, did the same to the storage area next door and opened Accanto, which their website calls "a slice of Italian café life" and "a friendly place to share an espresso, a glass of wine, or stuffed focaccia warm from the oven."

For once, a website has undersold a place. I'm writing this a few months after the Breakfast Crew descended upon Accanto—10 of us, with notice, at 11 on a Sunday—and some of them are still asking when we're going back. Or they're just going back on their own.

I don't know about "a slice of Italian café life," but I do know that it shares a kitchen and some staff with Genoa (*accanto* is Italian for "next to"), as well as the same philosophy—and some amazing food. The service was top-notch, the atmosphere both classy and casual, and the brunch entrées all priced at $8–$10. It's like the serious restaurant world opened a little brunch door for the rest of us to come through.

Once through that door, you can sit in a spacious, naturally lit room with wood floors, an open kitchen, and a seating area filled with Italian cookbooks. The menu has eight main dishes, seven sides (like fennel bacon and a sage biscuit), four sandwiches, and three cocktails—most of these are a classy, Italian twist on an old favorite.

Consider the salmon scramble: hardly unique in Portland, but this one comes with fennel, red onion, and *crème fraîche* for only $9.

There's a frittata with mushrooms, arugula, mascarpone, and truffles ($9); poached eggs over polenta and pancetta hash with leeks, fennel, and piquillo peppers ($10); and panetonne French toast with amaretto syrup, blueberry compote, and whipped cream ($9). No one in the Crew can describe that French toast, because I ran off and hid with it.

If you don't know what panetonne is, here's a little education. It's a sweet bread, traditionally made with candied oranges, citron, lemon zest, and raisins. It's made to rise over 20 or more hours, which makes it so fluffy, you have to hold it on the table, and in Italy it's a big deal around Christmastime. I mention all of this for two reasons: one is to try to tell you how good Accanto's French toast is—although I can't—and the other is to point out that Accanto isn't just a great brunch without a huge line. It's a place to sample Italian culture for a bit, have a nice meal, and even learn something.

Wait: A little, not so far—brunch is new. **Large groups:** With notice; no official reservations. **Coffee:** World Cup. **Other drinks:** Cocktails, espresso, very good Bloody Marys, carrot cocktail (picante carrotini). **Feel-goods:** Eggs are fresh from Sweet Briar Farms; bacon, sausage, pancetta, quick breads, and panetonne are all house made. **Health options:** Vegetarian friendly. **WiFi:** Yes.

Alameda Cafe

New/Classy

The French invade New Mexico.

4641 NE Fremont Ave. (NE/Fremont) ~ 503-284-5314 ~
thealamedacafe.com

Breakfast weekdays 8 to 11 a.m., Saturday 8 to 1:30 p.m., Sunday 8 a.m. to 2 p.m.

$12–$14 (Visa, MasterCard, no checks)

———————◆●◆———————

When I see white tablecloths, paintings of flowers on the walls, the staff wearing black, and bottles of wine in a display on the counter, I might think, "Great, welcome to Pompous Valley." Had I looked at the Alameda's menu and seen an omelet with blue cheese, eggs Benedict with chili-infused hollandaise, and French toast named for Santa Fe, I might have left.

But at Alameda, on top of the white tablecloth is paper for kids to draw on; they're even given crayons. All the omelets, scrambles, and even the eggs Benedict, are less than $9. When I saw all this, I thought, "Hey, being kid-friendly and serving big portions for reasonable prices isn't pompous!"

The Alameda suits its neighborhood perfectly. Is the neighborhood defined by grand homes along Alameda Ridge? Or is it the streets north of Fremont without sidewalks? Yes and yes. Is it Stanich's old-

school burgers? Or is it Starbucks and the Alameda Brew Pub? Yes and yes, again.

Such is this café's food, which is part stylish (the Southwestern Benedict also comes with sweet and spicy cornbread) and part, well, kind of down-home. You can, for example, build your own omelet with any three ingredients for $8.95, and it's served with potatoes and toast.

The Alameda has new-agey stuff like the Klickitat Omelet with blue cheese, apples, and bacon. And there's a braised mushroom omelet with spinach, sweet onions, and Swiss cheese, which you should stay away from unless you really love mushrooms. And the hollandaise is prepared with par-cooked eggs (I don't even know what that means).

But then there is a Belgian waffle that's only $4.95; oatmeal with bananas, raisins, and brown sugar for $4.95; and granola or yogurt with fruit for $5 or $6.

And the French toast. Giving in to their elegant, stylish side, the Alameda chefs couldn't just do French toast; they had to fancy it up. And yet they didn't do anything *too* fancy. They make it with thick baguette bread, dipped just enough to hold a crust of cinnamon-and-sugar crushed corn flakes, then fried. As my friend Beth said, it looks like pieces of cod in fish and chips. It's called Santa Fe Railroad French Toast because, apparently, the recipe originated on the old Santa Fe Railway.

The first time I had it, I wasn't sure what to make of it. I like my French toast soaked, and this was dry in the middle. The second time? Well, now I'm thinking that the cinnamon is a nice touch, the crunch of the crust plays well with the soft bread, the syrup takes care of the moisture, and it reminds me simultaneously of Navajo fry bread and breakfast cereal with Saturday morning cartoons. Clearly, more research is required.

Wait: Can be bad on Sunday, mostly outside with some cover. **Large groups:** With notice. **Coffee:** Stumptown. **Other drinks:** Mimosas, homemade Bloody Marys, tea, fresh-squeezed juice. **Feel-goods:** Some veggie options, tofu. **Health options:** Soy and 2% milk. **WiFi:** From Starbucks next door.

Arleta Library Bakery and Cafe

New/Mom & Pop

Almost hate to pass it on . . .
5513 SE 72nd (SE/Outer) ~ 503-774-4470 ~ *arletalibrary.com*
Tuesday through Friday 8 a.m. to 2:30 p.m., weekends 8:30 a.m. to
2:30 p.m.
$11–$15 (Visa, MasterCard)

At first, all I heard about this place was "outer Woodstock" and "library." I had visions of stale croissants over by the periodicals.

Undeterred, out I went, and I took a friend. How was it? The short answer is that my friend, who lives in Northeast, now takes her boyfriend there all the time. And when I was looking for a place to live, I seriously looked in that neighborhood so I could walk to Arleta every day.

So first, it's not in a library; it's named for a former library in the neighborhood. It's also just about the least pretentious place you'll ever walk into; in fact, much of the décor is recycled doors, and the walls remain unadorned.

It is, however, a bakery. When I was there, they had a moist date scone, morning glory muffins, almond anise biscotti, triple ginger snaps, coconut macaroons with bittersweet chocolate, and sour cream coffee cake. There's always something new. My favorite is the coffee cake, which uses various fruits, mostly those in season. One day it was pineapple, another time blueberries, and without exception the crust was perfectly crunchy and the inside moist but light. Just what you want, along with the French-press Stumptown, while waiting for your order.

If the cake doesn't make you feel good, then you can bask in the mission of the place, which, according to the website, includes the ambitious hope that the restaurant "will continue the trend toward revitalization in the area." Arleta is also committed to "sustaining its neighborhood and foodshed by purchasing as much organic food from local farmers and producers as possible and by paying its employees an equitable, living wage."

Such innovation would be admirable even if the chefs weren't fantastic. Everything I've eaten has been not only delicious but also cooked just right, whether it's the roasted red peppers in the Tuscan scramble (with spicy sausage and Romano cheese) or the Library Fries, which are like big Jo-Jos done right: soft inside but just crunchy outside, with a light dose of salt and rosemary. A special scramble with Swiss chard, mustard greens, collard greens, red and white Russian kale, and spinach was a spicy trip through the shades of green, like walking through an old-growth forest. (The Florentine, a version with ricotta and Parmesan, is on the weekend brunch menu.) The sweet potato biscuits and rosemary sausage gravy come with a thin slice of slow-roasted pork loin that our server said had been in a brine "for a few days."

Topping everything off is a shot-glass-sized addition of wonderful jam of the day; once it was apricot-pineapple-ginger, another time roasted nectarine with rosemary.

These days, the line can get a bit nuts, especially on weekends. I've also been told they don't have any high chairs, so maybe kids are better eating elsewhere. I already feel sentimental about its small, charming old days, back in foggy 2007 when only a devoted few of us knew and the rest were wondering why we ate in a library.

Wait: Quite long on weekends; summertime patio helps. **Large groups:** Yes, a heads up is good. **Coffee:** French-press Stumptown. **Other drinks:** Fresh juice, homemade lemonade (seasonally), organic OJ. **Feel-goods:** Most ingredients are local and organic. **Health options:** Good for veggies. **WiFi:** Possibly from a coffee shop next door.

Autentica

New/Classy/Weekend

Mexican sophistication, Portland relaxation.
5507 NE 30th Ave. (NE/Alberta) ~ 503-287-7555 ~ *autenticaportland.com*
Brunch weekends 10 a.m. to 3 p.m.
$15–$20 (all major cards, maximum of two per table)

———————◆•◆———————

Among the many signs that a neighborhood is changing, one that will really catch your eye is a man doing tai chi in the middle of the street. That's what we found when we arrived at the corner of NE 30th and Killingsworth in search of Autentica and found a wellness fair in full swing, featuring booths from local yoga classes and meditation programs. "Yep," I thought, "this end of Killingsworth ain't what it used to be!"

From what I had been reading online, a Mexican brunch ain't what I thought it was, either. Autentica is a serious restaurant that happens to serve dishes from the owner's hometown of Guerrero, Mexico.

The owner, Oswaldo Bibiano, has cooked in restaurants like Basilico, South Park, and Pazzo, and he uses local meats and produce, features vegetarian and vegan options as well as freshly made tortillas—a treat, if you don't know that already.

Eager to check this out, the Breakfast Crew headed out for what the real estate world calls the Upscale Killingsworth Strip. At 10:30 on a lovely Saturday morning, we perused the fair, shot a curious glance at the line outside Cup and Saucer, and walked into the half-filled Autentica.

Long before Alice uttered the day's first astonished "damn!" upon biting into her *sope*, we knew we had found something pleasantly out of the ordinary. I had spotted huevos rancheros on the menu but told the server I wanted something I can't get anywhere else. Her response was, "Everything here is something you can't get anywhere else."

Some of the items, I was familiar with—like enchiladas. I had no idea people ate enchiladas for breakfast, but after trying these (stuffed with chicken and a red mole sauce, topped with iceberg

lettuce, avocado, radishes, and Oaxacan cream), I would have eaten them at any time of day. As for the *sope*, which elicited Alice's "damn," it was a little like an open-faced soft taco with refried beans, cheese, onions, salsa, and your choice of meat. We were amazed at the number of flavors in that little thing!

It sounds like the Mexican food you know, right? Well, how about this: a cactus salad with crispy pork skin, onions, tomatoes, avocado, and fresh cheese. Or a crispy tortilla shell filled with octopus and prawns, topped with spicy cabbage salad. Or a *torta* (sandwich) that features pickled jalapeños. Or *huevos ahogados*, which is eggs poached in a traditional chicken broth with cilantro, lime, onions, and serrano peppers. I'm telling you, Autentica is a culinary tour of the Mexican countryside!

Alice, Rick, and I ordered four dishes among us, shared them all, and then kicked back and had a long, rambling discussion without ever feeling pressured to leave. We admired the down-to-earth nature of the menu and the place, with its ceramic dishes and its photos of families on earth-tone walls.

You'll pay a few more dollars at Autentica than, say, Cup and Saucer, but the food is so much better and the scene so much more chilled out that when you leave, you'll see all the folks waiting across the street and be glad that you, too, found out about Autentica.

Wait: Average. **Large groups:** Yes, groups of 10 in party room, but some notice would help. **Coffee:** Caffè Umbria. **Other drinks:** Cocktails, juice, homemade sangria, Bloody Marys. **Feel-goods:** Only free-range organic eggs and local ingredients are used. **Health options:** Many vegetarian options, and some dishes can be made vegan. **WiFi:** No.

Bakery Bar

Hip/Veggie/Weekend

More, and less, than it sounds like.

2935 NE Glisan St. (NE/Hollywood) ~ 503-477-7779 ~ *bakerybar.com*

Weekdays 7 a.m. to 3 p.m., weekends 8 a.m. to 2 p.m.

$10–$14 (Visa, MasterCard, no checks)

———◆—•—◆———

Let's get a couple of things straight, because I was briefly confused on these points: Bakery Bar isn't a bar, and it isn't just a bakery.

Now, this must also be said: a bakery is a magical place, anyway. Technically, baking is just chemistry, but the whole, historical development of it—like, who figured out cornstarch?—plus the precision required to get it right, and the creativity available, and all of it resulting in the amazing, decorative cakes and pastries at Bakery Bar . . . well, I'd encourage you to go there even if there was no breakfast.

Don't let the exterior drive you off, either. The patio can look pretty stark, and the door looks like the entrance to a warehouse of some sort. But inside is a nice mix of casual, clean, and family-friendly. It's order-from-the-counter during the week and sit-down service on weekends. And I'll say this about the staff: they trend young, and I've read many online comments ranging from "They're so friendly and cute!" to "They're so slow!" As you may imagine, it's entirely possible that both of those will often be true.

Speaking of friendly, my first visit there was with a friend and her eight-year-old daughter; we lounged and surfed the web while I noshed on apple-walnut brown butter streusel coffee cake, and the two of them split a piece of blueberry-almond pound cake with cream cheese glaze. Especially during the week, Bakery Bar has that vibe about it: a place to hang out as long as you like and get either some pastries, cupcakes, or cookies.

Another time I was headed out for a hike and filled up on a frittata of Yukon gold potatoes, tomatoes, red onions, grain mustard, and cheddar. It's served with your choice of English muffin or biscuit, and you can add bacon or house-made turkey-apple sausage. And for a little trail snack to go, I ordered a carrot five-spice cupcake with cinnamon, fennel seed, cardamom, nutmeg, and ginger topped with orange zest buttercream. Did I mention that baking is magical?

The menu goes well beyond pastries, although the thread of house-baked goodness is woven throughout. The French toast is made with pumpkin-cinnamon brioche, orange bourbon custard, and bourbon caramel. There's a bacon and cheddar corncake topped with braised greens. Seven breakfast sandwiches—ranging from simple eggs and cheddar to a Reuben to one with fried egg, pimento cheese, bacon, and tomatoes—are served on house-made English muffins or black pepper buttermilk biscuits.

Vegetarians can also do well here. For example, the Migas (eggs scrambled with pickled jalapeños, red onions, and fried tortillas, topped with tomatillo salsa and cotija cheese) can be served with or without house-made chorizo. There's also a veggie hash (and a house-made pastrami hash), oatmeal with seasonal fruit compote, and granola with oats, pecans, almonds, wheat germ, flax seeds, pumpkin seeds, sunflower seeds, golden raisins, dried cranberries, crystallized ginger, orange zest, and orange blossom honey. Dang!

On the weekends, Bakery Bar transforms into a more traditional breakfast restaurant, with table service as of early 2010. I've heard that the lines get long. Yet it retains the casual feel, especially with the picnic tables outside. And as long as you're not in a hurry or hung up on fanciness—or looking for a bar—you'll probably dig it.

Wait: Medium on weekends. **Large groups:** No. **Coffee:** Stumptown. **Other drinks:** Espresso, beer, and cocktails. **Feel-goods:** Cage-free eggs, and everything is house-made. **Health options:** Not much for vegans. **WiFi:** Yes.

Bar Carlo

New/Hip/Veggie

Decent breakfast, or frontier outpost?
6433 SE Foster Blvd. (SE/Outer) ~ 503-771-1664 ~ *barcarlo.com*
Weekdays 7:30 a.m. to 3 p.m., weekends 8 a.m. to 3 p.m.
$12–$15 (all major cards, no checks)

When Bar Carlo opened in 2007, lots of folks took the opportunity to make socioeconomic statements about its neighborhood. Local media ran articles that read like reports from the land of savages, telling us there are actual reasons to go "out there." "My gosh," they collectively exclaimed, "healthy, tasty food on Foster!"

Think I'm exaggerating?

The *Mercury*'s blog: "Foster: not just for felons. . . . SE Foster is starting to get some attention (and this time it's the good kind)."

The *Mercury*'s (mostly positive) review: "I probably wouldn't make the trip out to SE 64th and Foster for lunch alone."

A *Willamette Week* review of new restaurants in the area referred to it as a "fast-food vortex" and a "dusty, urban frontier." The only other preexisting businesses mentioned were a strip club, a tobacco shack, a "variety store selling windup toys," and a gun shop.

That *Willamette Week* story set off quite a discussion in its online comments area, with readers lobbing grenades like "gentrification," "meth houses," and "white trash." Others ridiculed the area's new name, FoPo (for Foster-Powell). Purely entertaining—and none of it had anything to do with the food at Bar Carlo.

Other than its (irrelevant) location, what set Bar Carlo apart was a wide variety of egg-based dishes—four sandwiches, six scrambles, and three omelets, plus daily specials and two Benedicts every weekend—in addition to French toast and waffles. Prices are generally around $8 per dish, which is reasonable, but portions are not exactly gut-busters, either.

It's been open since 2007, yet still has kind of an unfinished feel. In 2010, work seems to have stopped on the room next to the dining area, which they used to say would offer nighttime dining with kind of a pub feel. We had to walk through that big, empty space to reach the restroom. And the main room itself was still a bit raw—or maybe it was finished and we had just expected more decoration. (Of course, it's an outpost on a "dusty frontier.")

My girlfriend and I went there twice and found no lines, friendly staff, strong tasty coffee, and food that made us shrug. Like I said, in any other neighborhood this would be a fairly run-of-the-mill place, with loyal followers and others who find it disappointing. And Bar Carlo does have both.

A smoked salmon scramble was long on salmon and had a nice combination of grilled red onions and fresh dill, but the eggs were a smidge overdone. The King Melt sandwich (eggs, bacon, mild peppers, mascarpone, tomato, and basil on a butter bun) lacked zing and was on a rapidly wilting roll. On the weekends crepes are added, and although I had one with mascarpone and pears soaked in champagne and orange juice that was not tasty at all, other diners have said good things.

All in all, it sounds like a pretty decent breakfast place, right? That's what Bar Carlo is to these eyes: a pretty standard Portland breakfast place that a lot of folks like. It just happens to also be in the crosshairs of some weird sociological energy.

Wait: Mostly on Sundays, with the side room to be available for waiting soon. **Large groups:** Yes, though can be difficult—no brunch reservations. **Coffee:** Self-serve Stumptown. **Other drinks:** Tea, espresso, DragonFly Chai, juice, and soda, cocktails. **Feel-goods:** Ingredients are local and organic whenever possible. **Health options:** More for vegans on the weekends, but plenty for vegetarians. **WiFi:** Yes.

Beast

New/Classy/Weekend

They don't care. They just cook.
5425 NE 30th Ave. (NE/Alberta) ~ 503-841-6968 ~ *beastpdx.com*
Brunch seating Sunday at 10 a.m. *or* noon
$28 plus beverages (all major cards, no checks)

———————————◆•◆———————————

Beast just doesn't care.

For one thing, they don't care what you want to eat. It's four courses, and you'll find out what you're getting when you get there. It's on the little menu, right above "SUBSTITUTIONS POLITELY DECLINED."

They also celebrate meat, and serve lots of it. There's a famous picture of the chef hugging a dead pig in a field. If that's a problem for you, well, they don't care. There are plenty of places in town.

They're expensive—as in $28 per person. See above.

Their chairs are uncomfortable and are apparently well-known carryovers from another restaurant. They crank '70s rock. They make you sit with folks you don't know. See above.

But they also "don't care" in the way my friend John T. means it. You don't know John T., which is a shame, but when he gets all worked up about something he likes, be it John Irving's writing or the Arkansas football team or Arlo Guthrie's version of "The Gates of Eden," he will pronounce that his current hero "doesn't care!" As in, dude just hammers out the good stuff like he knows how, the Big Magic Way, and *does . . . not . . . care* what folks think.

That's how they cook over at Beast. They don't care.

Here's the magic they threw at the Crew and me one time. We sat down, got a French press, and they laid out a brioche and baguette bread pudding with maple bourbon sauce, candied hazelnuts, and glazed bacon. Right there, on that plate, was a breakfast not to be messed with. It was course number one. Of four.

Next up, the hash: duck confit, prosciutto, sweet potatoes, brussels sprouts, rapini, and market potatoes with a poached farm egg and hollandaise. Don't know what confit or rapini are? Me, neither. You won't care.

They had us on our heels now, could have thrown anything at us. "I eat like this in my dreams," I thought. They gave us a break with a selection from the Cheese Bar. I don't remember what they were, because I think in all the excitement I ate my notes. But just think four or five cheeses that you've never heard of, come from all over, are several different kinds of amazing, and come with some greens and a sherry vinaigrette.

Did I mention that there's a wine pairing available for every course? That's right, imagine eating this way *and drinking*.

For closers, what do you think about a chocolate truffle cake and a cream puff with soft vanilla whipped cream? I'm still thinking about it. Consider it a nice, sweet kiss after a . . . um, no, can't say that here. The staff at Beast sure is hot, though. Did I mention that? Adds a certain something.

I guess the chef was involved in some weird restaurant drama that I probably should know about. Changed the restaurant scene, blew the foodies' minds, fell from the throne, relationship ended, rose from the ashes . . . honestly, I don't care. Beast almost killed me, and I thank them for it. Go there if you dare.

Either way, they don't care.

Wait: Reservations strongly advised. **Large groups:** Reservations required. **Coffee:** French-press Stumptown. **Other drinks:** Mimosas, wine pairings available with each course ($20), juice. **Feel-goods:** None that they tout. **Health options:** Vegetarians beware! **WiFi:** No.

Beaterville Cafe

Hip/Mom & Pop/Veggie

They put the fun *in* funky.
2201 N Killingsworth St. (N/Inner) ~ 503-735-4652
Weekdays 6 a.m. to 2 p.m., weekends 7 a.m. to 2 p.m.
$9–$13 (Visa, MasterCard, no checks)

———————————◆●◆———————————

Folks often ask how I got the idea for a book about breakfast in Portland. Well, in my 14+ years as a travel writer for the *Memphis Flyer*, I have often described a place by describing a meal I ate there, because a place's essence shines through its restaurants. Generally, that meal was breakfast.

One day a few years back, I was sitting at the Beaterville Cafe with my friend Craig, who's also an author. Already that morning, the front room of the cafe had come to a standstill because a regular had come in with photos from a vacation in France. I also noticed a stream of UPS drivers heading for the back room. The server told me the drivers were a regular Bible-study group, and I told Craig, "See, friends coming in from a trip and people meeting every week to get religion: *that's* the kind of thing you write about when you write about breakfast." Then Craig asked if I'd ever written about breakfast in Portland, and I said, "Man, I could write a whole book about places to eat break-

fast in Portland!" We looked at each other, and that moment, this book was born.

So the short answer to the birth of this book is, "I got the idea sitting in Beaterville," and I couldn't think of a more appropriate place for that to happen. It's hard for me to think of the Beaterville and not have the phrase "perfect Portland breakfast place" come to mind. Maybe not the best or most innovative, but the most Portland, like a drizzly day is perfect Portland weather or like Bud Clark was our perfect mayor. Beaterville is a little strange, really friendly, colorful in both the paint way and the people way, and in a part of town that is seeing both grassroots changes and intensive urban planning.

It has a good story, as well. A *beater*, you may know, is an old, beat-up car that is street-legal but barely runs. And, of course, our fair city has a club—people who are into this kind of thing—and, of course, they occasionally parade their beaters, which is a perfect Portland thing to do. Beaterville's owner is one of these folks, and he still keeps some of his beaters out back, as well as who knows what assortment of automotive parts on the walls. And an odd collection of art. And a backwards clock.

Oh, and the food is solid and consistent. The car theme is carried into the menu, which includes up to eight yummy, filling scramblers (get it, like Ramblers?) such as the the Onassis (tomatoes, spinach, red onions, garlic, Greek olives, and feta cheese). There are also eight omelets and hashes, several combos, and plenty of vegetarian options. (Tofu and egg substitutes are available in all the scrambles and omelets at no extra charge.) The French toast has a little crispiness to it and comes slathered with blueberries.

None of this stuff is likely to knock your socks off, but it's all solid and consistent, and there's no more relaxed, fun place to hang out than Beaterville.

Wait: Long-ish on weekends, with space inside and some cover outside. **Large groups:** Best on weekends. **Coffee:** Portland Roasting. **Other drinks:** Numi Tea, espresso, fruit smoothies. **Feel-goods:** Humane cage-free eggs. **Health options:** Egg substitutes, tofu, veggie sausage. **WiFi:** Yes.

Belly

New/Classy/Weekend

Nice place, no wait, good food.

3500 NE MLK Blvd. (NE/MLK) ~ 503-249-9764 ~ *bellyrestaurant.com*

Brunch Sunday 10 a.m. to 2 p.m.

$14–$16 (all major cards, no checks)

It was a beautiful spring Sunday, with birds chirping and flowers blooming. I was up early, felt refreshed, had coverage at work, dressed up a little, went to church for some singin' and preachin' . . . in short, a good morning. With friends coming to meet me for brunch, I was primed for joy.

I arrived at Belly and immediately felt comfortable. It's simple but elegant and yet casual, if that makes sense. Kind of dressed up like I was, but also relaxed, with lots of wood and light. I had an excellent cappuccino before the Crew arrived, and we had a fine chat. I ordered cinnamon pancakes with a side of sausage. Jean and Jerry had the duck confit hash with whole grain mustard aioli. Shari had a wild mushroom and chèvre scramble. With the weather, the scene, the company, my attitude about the world, and the promised yumminess to come, we were anticipating a great meal.

And then every first bite produced a shrug. It's just a fact. The pancakes seemed doughy. The sausage had a lot of spice going on but didn't really please anybody (I liked it more than the others did, but to me there's no such thing as too garlicky). The hash was long on potatoes and short on taste; the duck seemed a little lost in all those taters.

Across the board, we thought it lacked taste and excitement. The potatoes were good, coffee excellent, service and scene wonderful. My pancakes with sausage and a cappuccino came out to $14 pre-tip. I feel like there are better meals available for that money.

On the plus side, all the food was good, there was no line, and usually isn't. There's also a small seating area outside—but it's right next to Fremont Street and alongside a bus stop. And plenty of folks like it, enough to keep Belly open despite the corner's reputation as a black hole for restaurants.

At times like this, questioning my feeble palette, I turn to the "experts." Over on *portlandfood.org*, I found a similar reaction—along with a lot of discussion about the name and location. Most people thought it was . . . okay. There were also no reviews posted from February 2009 to May 2010, which might be because no one on the site is eating there.

The *Oregonian* called it "a reasonably priced, satisfying neighborhood hangout" and gave it a B, but the *Willamette Week* thought more of it. Yelp reviews ranged from decent to best-ever. And if somebody told me it was one of their favorite places, I wouldn't think they were nuts. In fact, it would probably inspire me to go check it out again. You can do a lot worse than a pleasant place with no wait and a menu that changes with the seasons. And who knows? You just might find that you click with the place.

Wait: Between 10 and 11 a.m. **Large groups:** With notice; they do take reservations. **Coffee:** Stumptown. **Other drinks:** Lots of cocktails. **Feel-goods:** Most ingredients are local. **Health options:** Vegetarians can sub veggies for meat. **WiFi:** Yes

Berlin Inn

Weekend

Authentic German food, I suppose.
3131 SE 12th Ave. (SE/Inner) ~ 503-236-6761 ~ *berlininn.com*
Brunch weekends 10 a.m. to 2:30 p.m.
$10–$17 (all major cards, no checks)

━━━━━━◆━•━━◆━━━━━━

Trying to write about the Berlin Inn reminds me of writing about the Paradox Café. That isn't because a place loaded with sausages and schnitzels reminds me of a hipstered-out organic joint with tofu and tempeh. It's because in both cases, I am wandering into a cuisine which I know nothing about. I am left to eat, wonder, and ask the experts.

I have had German food many times, including in Germany. But I was there as a 23-year-old backpacking youth hosteler; I ate Wiener schnitzel wherever I went and was drunk for 10 days straight. So that wasn't much help—though it sure was fun. Ask me about the Rosenmontag parade in Mainz someday. Whew Nelly!

Okay, back to Portland now. The *Mercury* wrote a positive review of Berlin Inn in 2010—a review which included assertions like it's in an "incongruous cottage" that "feels older than its years" and is "located in what must be one of the worst restaurant locations I can think of—the inner Southeast Portland wasteland near SE Powell and Milwaukie." Never mind that many of the *Mercury*'s readers probably live in that "wasteland"; I couldn't figure out if the guy was about to trash the place or not.

The rest of the review confused me even further. He said one dish was "not much to write home about" but had good gravy. Another was "fantastically light despite the heavy ingredients and a pool of cheese sauce." And he liked the place! So, for the record, do most online reviewers.

So I am baffled by Berlin Inn. For one thing, I cannot imagine one human eating an entire portion of, say, the Alpine. That's the one I tackled: pork-chicken sausage patties, two poached eggs, gouda and garlic fondue sauce with blue cheese crumbles, dried cranberries, and toasted almonds, served with two potato pancakes. I'm no light-weight, but that thing almost killed me. And you should see the size of the omelets! There's one with spicy beer sausage, one with Black Forest ham and Gouda, and one with veggies finished with white wine and spinach. You can also take on a Black Forest ham Benedict with smoked Gouda sauce or another Benedict with smoked salmon

and enough dill to produce a peck of pickles.

So, here's the thing. I ate there once and thought it was both bowl-ing-ball heavy and pillow-filling plain. But maybe that's just German food. Even folks that like Berlin Inn confess, even proclaim, that there's nothing fancy about it. Many say it's authentic German food, and maybe it is. I showed the menu to my German friends Claudia and Alexander, and they insisted (among other mostly mild objec-tions) that Germans don't eat pancakes at breakfast. I know it will fill you up, probably twice, unless you're drunk too. I know it's like eating in an old house, because it *is* an old house. And I know that you won't have to wait at all to get in, even though it's been popular for almost 20 years.

Other than that, all I know is that it's far and away the best German brunch in town.

Wait: Occasionally. **Large groups:** With notice. **Coffee:** K&F. **Other drinks:** Mimosas and Sparkling Gewurztraminer, which is a sweet wine. **Feel-goods:** Use only Canola oil and no MSG. **Health options:** Vegan and gluten-free options available. **WiFi:** No.

Bertie Lou's Cafe

Mom & Pop

1940s diner with a dash of goofiness.
8051 SE 17th Ave. (SE/Sellwood) ~ 503-239-1177
Weekdays 7 a.m. to 2 p.m., weekends 7:30 a.m. to 3 p.m.
$7–$11 (Visa, MasterCard, Discover, checks)

———————◆—•—◆———————

There's a sign on the wall in Bertie Lou's that captures the essence of the place: "Unattended children will be given a shot of espresso and a free puppy." It conveys both the reasonable (control your kids) and the whimsical. Think about it: is there anything cuter than a wound-up kid with a puppy? That would be *fun*, right?

Another item on the wall is a picture of Bertie and Lou standing at the same counter in the 1940s. Though they are long gone, their presence brings in an added depth: if there's an old-time Portland breakfast place in nearly original condition and still in its original neighborhood, it's Bertie Lou's. The only major change is that the second room, which was a barber shop also owned by Bertie and Lou, now has eighteen seats at tables to go along with the six at the counter.

Well, that and the 1940s menu probably didn't say, "Parties of 24 or more require a reservation and 80% gratuity." Probably also didn't say you could get a half-order of biscuits and gravy that's "no biscuits . . . or no gravy." Or that you can get a signed copy of the menu for $10 . . . plus $50 for framing, $25 for packaging, and $50 for delivery.

Get the picture? There's definitely a sense of humor about Bertie Lou's as well as a very friendly vibe. Sit at the counter and join in the conversation with the regulars and the staff, because at Bertie Lou's, about 25 percent of the diners at any given time can reach out and touch the cook.

There's nothing fancy about the food—seven omelets and scrambles, four Benedicts, a couple of breakfast sandwiches, waffles, a burrito—but it's all solid. Egg Beaters and soy bacon are available for non-meat eaters, as is a veggie scramble "made with one, some, or all of the following, depending on what we have at the time you order: mushrooms, eggplant, zucchini, spinach, tomatoes, peppers, onions, and provolone."

Two items do stand out, if only for their difference: the potatoes are deep-fried reds, golden brown on the outside and soft on the inside, just about perfect to this Southern palette. In one dish, they're grilled with onions and peppers and laid over a bed of sautéed spinach. The other standout is the French toast, which they make with two croissants sliced lengthwise and serve with fruit and thick maple syrup. If that isn't enough sugar for you (and if it isn't, I'd like to meet you), usually there are cinnamon rolls and bear claws.

So sit back, chat with the folks at the counter, have some sugar and locally roasted coffee, then look at that old picture on the wall and ask yourself how much has really changed. Oh, and control your kids or else you might take home more than a full belly.

Wait: Long on weekends, entirely outside. **Large groups:** Not good. Would be a hassle. **Coffee:** Mudworks. **Other drinks:** Tazo Tea, fresh OJ, fresh-squeezed grapefruit. **Feel-goods:** Bear claws feel good, right? **Health options:** Egg Beaters, soy bacon and Morningstar sausage patties, some veggie options. **WiFi:** No, can steal from bar across street if outside.

Besaw's Cafe

New/Old School/Classy
Where new cuisine meets Old Portland.
2301 NW Savier St. (NW) ~ 503-228-2619 ~ *besaws.com*
Breakfast weekdays 7 a.m. to 3 p.m., weekends 8 a.m. to 3 p.m.
$10–$17 (all major cards)

My personal history of breakfast in Portland began with Besaw's. I was staying with a friend who lived on the edge of Forest Park, and each morning we'd stumble down to Besaw's to warm up. I'd get the Farmer's Hash, apple-cranberry juice, and coffee, and Chip and I would sit for hours, read the paper, and marvel at our new home. Anyplace where a guy could get good food and friendly service, chill out with the paper, then go walking in a 4,000-acre forest was a place to call home.

And why should you care? Well, it's impossible to discuss breakfast and Portland history without getting Besaw's into the mix. It's been there since 1903, when two French-Canadian loggers got seed money from Henry Weinhard to start a tavern. In fact, back in the corner on the right, there's a photo that shows Besaw's with a steeple on top, before a 1922 fire took out the second floor.

So when you sit at or near the 18th-century oak bar to enjoy your classic Portland breakfast dishes—Wild Salmon Scramble, Forest Mushroom Omelette—you're literally surrounded by Portland history. You'll even see Cousin Maurice's Eggs on the menu, a brie-scallion-tomato dish that used to be a staple at Zell's; the two restaurants have swapped ownership and staff over the years.

The weekend wait can be historic as well, but the staff serves coffee outside, and it's quite a social scene out there. Inside you'll find the perfectly Portland combination of class and chill. The staff is in black and makes a fine Bloody Mary, but many are actors, hired for their charm and wit. The clientele is as likely to be mountain bikers in from Forest Park as high-end shoppers ready to cruise Northwest 23rd Avenue. You can sit inside under the ceiling fans or out back on the covered patio, and you'll find the menu extensive and the dishes full of fresh, local ingredients.

The salmon scramble is spiced with dill and smoothed by cream cheese. The potatoes are big chunks of reds tossed with garlic and rosemary. The mushroom omelet has shitake, portobello, and button mushrooms. The Farmer's Hash, a longtime favorite, is three eggs scrambled with potatoes, roasted garlic cloves, bacon, onions, peppers, and cheddar cheese.

The priciest entrée (two eggs, potatoes, and either grilled wild salmon or chicken-basil sausage) is only $14, so it's not a budget-busting place. And for $6.50 or less, you can get organic oatmeal, organic homemade granola, buttermilk pancakes, or a big, tasty Belgian waffle.

And, sitting under the twirling fans listening to the creaking wood floor, you can try to decide (as my friends Linda and Rich and I once did) if Northwest Portland reminds you more of a relaxed San Francisco or a hilly Back Bay in Boston. Then you can hop the streetcar to go downtown, stroll the scene on Northwest 23rd, or head up to Forest Park for a woodsy walk. In other words, you can relax, eat well, and feel right at home.

Wait: Way long on weekends after about 9 a.m. **Large groups:** A mild hassle on weekends. **Coffee:** Stumptown. **Other drinks:** Espresso, Tao of Tea, fresh juice, Italian soda, DragonFly Chai, mimosas, and Bloody Marys. **Feel-goods:** The menu says, "Fresh, local and organic ingredients whenever possible." **Health options:** Egg substitute for $1.50, some gluten-free options. **WiFi:** Yes, but you have to ask for the passcode.

Bijou, Cafe

New/Classy/Veggie

You can be healthy/progressive and be a "real" restaurant!

132 SW 3rd Ave. (Downtown) ~ 503-222-3187

Weekdays 7 a.m. to 2 p.m., weekends 8 a.m. to 2 p.m.

$14–$17 (Visa, MasterCard, local checks)

Consider the Willapa Bay Fresh Oyster Hash, one of my favorite plates in Portland. Four or five cornmeal-dredged grilled oysters sit on thin strips of onion and potatoes with parsley and a dash of lemon. Sorting through all this for variations on the perfect bite might be the highlight of your day. It's serious food. It's also $14.95, with no toast or other sides.

The Bijou's old brick walls and exposed wood beams say history; the modern art on the walls say style; the coat racks on each booth actually host coats and say utility; the blue-and-white checkered tablecloths, old-timey sugar pourers, and muffins in a basket say down-home. You'll see businesspeople going over charts, friends planning a wedding, tourists poring over maps, conventioneers reuniting, and regulars chatting with the staff.

The Bijou is darn near the prototypical Portland breakfast place. It's not necessarily the best, and it's certainly not the cheapest, but it's perhaps the one place you'd take your parents or other visitors who want a nice, safe dose of Portland's organic, progressive, friendly, homey culture without the tattoos, hairy armpits, and all-out vegan fare. Your server might be wearing rainbow stockings, though.

Another telling tidbit: They serve Heritage Farms bacon, Bravo sharp cheddar cheese, Nancy's yogurt, Tracy's Small Batch granola, Kookoolan Farms chicken, and Holy Kakow hot chocolate, and they don't offer a word of explanation regarding what these ingredients are. It's like what was once a radical idea—using artisan and (presumably) local ingredients raised in a healthy way—now doesn't even need an explanation.

It's also true that a lot of folks in town think this is all very uppity and just an excuse to charge $8.95 for bacon and eggs or $11.50 for a cheese-and-mushroom omelet (ah, but they're *cremini* mushrooms!). And grilled orange-anise bread "baked for us by Pearl Bakery" and called *gibassier?* Please.

It's not a slacker, stumble in hungover and surf the web for two hours kind of place. It's like a grown-up restaurant—but a relaxed, Portland breakfast restaurant. The Roast Beef Hash is made with vegetarian-fed beef ($12.25). Daily-special muffins (I had banana-hazelnut) are made fresh. Brioche, French, or whole wheat toast; cornmeal, buckwheat, or buttermilk pancakes, all with real maple syrup.

Maybe the place just grew up. And maybe the new Portland is doing the same.

Wait: Long on weekends; sometimes a wait during the week. Small indoor waiting area. **Large groups:** Could be a seriously long wait. No reservations. **Coffee:** Cafe Femenino (organic). **Other drinks:** Illy espresso, Holy Kakow hot chocolate, Tao of Tea, fresh organic orange and grapefruit juices, Knudsen's organic vegetable juice. **Feelgoods:** Heavy emphasis on organic and local ingredients. **Health options:** Tofu, granola. **WiFi:** No, but you can pick it up from next door.

Blue Pig Café

Mom and Pop

Plenty of basic, local yumminess.
5026 SE Division St. (SE/Division) ~ 503-231-2775 ~ *bluepigpdx.com*
Weekdays 8 a.m. to 3 p.m, weekends 8 a.m. to 4 p.m.
$10–14 (all major cards, no checks); cheaper early bird menu before 9 a.m.

———————◆ • ◆———————

I confess a certain sadness upon the closing of Gramma Lucy's Cafe on Southeast Division. It was far from the best food, or the best-looking place, in town. But it was possibly the most entertaining place to eat breakfast, mainly because it was run by a certifiable nut job—and I mean that in a good way—who wowed everyone with his loud charms.

So when I heard he had ridden his motorcycle off into the sunset, I was a little bummed—until I met the new owners, who promised they would redesign the place and "take the food up a notch or two."

Well, they've accomplished both tasks. The space is nicer, the food is better, and the place is now called the Blue Pig Café.

The outside still doesn't look like much, but that's fine. It's a casual little neighborhood place. One owner had his wife help with décor, which was a good idea; two of my female friends once described the old place as "looking like a dude decorated it." The Blue Pig has a subtle flower theme, and my gardener friend Maureen loved it; they stripped pieces of floral fabric over wooden frames, bought some new chairs and light fixtures, turned the old booths into banquettes for a more open feel, and repainted the walls "butter color" and the ceiling "a deep, rusty terra cotta." So said Maureen. I'm a dude; I only know that the place seems clean and open.

They use, as much as possible, local and what you might call "politically correct" ingredients (free-range, hormone-free, sustainable, etc.), though they make some concessions for out-of-season stuff. You can even recycle your to-go containers and compost your coffee cups.

The menu covers all the classics, like a two-egg breakfast ($7.95), Chicken Fried Steak with two eggs ($9.95), and Corned Beef Hash ($9.95). One time I even had a Tofu Scramble with curry, ginger and garlic ($7.95). You can also get more than filled up with a breakfast burrito, huevos rancheros, and biscuits and gravy. And with plenty of sides and a massive build-your-own omelet/scramble section ($9.95 for unlimited ingredients!), you can pretty much piece together whatever meal you want.

From what I've seen, though, the griddle is where the action is. Of course, I have a mouth full of sweet teeth. They have a Waffle Breakfast, a French Toast Breakfast, and a Flapjack Breakfast, each of which comes with two eggs and two pieces of bacon, sausage, or ham for $8.95. All three options are basic and non-flashy, but quite good.

So maybe the Blue Pig really is two steps up from Gramma Lucy's: one for the décor and one for the food. And they've added quite a few cocktails. And even if it might be one step down on the wackiness scale, it's still a gentle, welcome change.

Wait: Medium on weekends, with some space inside. **Large groups:** Not great. **Coffee:** Portland Roasting. **Other drinks:** A couple dozen cocktails. **Feel-goods:** Abundant. **Health options:** Can do tofu in the scrambles. **WiFi:** Yes.

Bluehour

Weekend/New/Classy

Approachable sophistication.

250 NW 13th Ave. (Pearl) ~ 503-226-3394 ~ *bluehouronline.com*

Brunch Sunday 10 a.m. to 2:30 p.m.

$15–$23 (all major cards, no checks)

I can offer but one table's opinion on brunch at Bluehour: It felt like listening to a famous recording by Miles Davis. I became immensely comfortable, felt sophisticated, concentrated hard, and believed that something good and impressive was happening. In both jazz and fine cuisine, however, I must depend on the opinions of experts. To my ears Miles Davis sounds nice and is obviously talented, but the experts tell me he's also important, influential, monumental, and historic. Bluehour is a beautiful restaurant with very good food and excellent service, but the experts tell me it's a lot more than that.

They tell me that its owner, Bruce Carey, changed the Portland dining scene forever with his previous place, Zefiro. After Zefiro closed, Carey opened Bluehour, with its million-dollar interior featuring Italian space-defining curtains, supremely tall windows, and leather Bellini chairs. (Note: I don't know what a Bellini chair is.)

So Bluehour is important, as (I am told) was Davis's album *Kind of Blue*. Accordingly, I figured the lowly Breakfast Crew would need reservations, and maybe a loan from the World Bank. Neither was true; half the restaurant is saved for walk-ins and, as an example, the eggs Benedict (with house-smoked pork loin) is $12.

But first you have to *see* the place! The ceilings soar, the curtains ripple, and various nooks are adorned with large sprigs from flowering trees. Visiting movie stars eat at Bluehour, probably because it's the only place that reminds them of L.A. or New York. I don't know that we saw anybody famous, but one good candidate was a guy in jeans, black boots, wrinkled white shirt, sport coat, and a perfect three-day beard stylishly sprawled at a corner table.

The staff is everywhere and nice looking, in sleek white aprons held together in back by metal clips. We found the service to be phenomenal. When Jerry dropped a knife, in the time it took me to crack a joke about his lack of grace, somebody was standing next to him with a new, clean knife . . . on a platter. Shari had a pancake that was a little overdone, and it took about two minutes to bring out another, perfectly done and with a new complement of huckleberry sauce. Or maybe it was compote. Or coulis. I can never tell.

Ah, yes, the food. We all thought the food was good, and Jerry loved his French omelet with its smoky truffle flavor. Our waitstaff brought us yummy almond tea cakes as an *amuse-bouche*, certainly the only one I've seen at breakfast. The rest of the items, at least the titles, are quite common; it's a true brunch, with sandwiches and salads in addition to breakfast stuff like omelets, Benedicts, hashes, pancakes, and waffles. None of us were as blown away by what was on the plate as we were by what was going on around us. But we sure had fun eating whatever was there, if that makes sense.

I mean, this isn't just a breakfast place, right? It's an institution, a landmark, a breakthrough, a *scene*! It's nice of them to let us common folks in too.

Wait: Little to none, but they do take reservations. **Large groups:** Absolutely, but easiest to call for reservations. **Coffee:** Café Vita, French press available. **Other drinks:** Espresso, cocktails, juice, latte in a bowl. **Feel-goods:** Local ingredients, including organic eggs. **Health options:** Not a whole lot for vegetarians. **WiFi:** Yes.

Bread and Ink Cafe

New/Classy/Kiddie

A classy old lady down on Hawthorne.

3610 SE Hawthorne Blvd. (SE/Hawthorne) ~ 503-239-4756 ~
breadandinkcafe.com

Breakfast weekdays 8 a.m. to 11:30 a.m., Saturday 8 a.m. to 12:30 p.m.,
Sunday 8 a.m. to 2 p.m.

$12–$16 (all major cards, checks)

———————————◆———————————

Down in New Orleans there are restaurants called old line. They
aren't cutting edge, and a lot of folks consider them stuffy, but they are
immensely popular and traditional. The Grand Dame is 100-year-old
Galatoire's, with its tuxedoed staff twirling under massive chandeliers,
and the debauchery of Bourbon Street right outside the door.

Bread and Ink Cafe may be the Galatoire's of the Portland breakfast
scene. It opened "way back" in 1983, and was sort of a pioneer on then
run-down Hawthorne; it was one of the first places in town to commit
to buying from local farmers.

To this day, it's definitely aiming for the area between classy and
casual. It has fresh flowers to greet you and high-backed green chairs
with armrests. Its white-tablecloth reputation has labeled it as a high-
end, expensive place—but the drawing paper on the tables marks it as

kid-friendly. And when you walk out
of Bread and Ink, you have a decent
chance of hearing drums or seeing
somebody in a Guatemalan skirt.

I should tell you that in my research,
no other place got quite the negative
online reviews for service like Bread
and Ink. The reviews spanned several
years and may or may not have been
the result of Southeast Portland slack-
erness running into high expectations
that come with a $10 eggs Benedict.

Among the more serious food-oriented sites and blogs, it's often damned with the "ain't what it used to be" designation. On the other hand, it's packed every weekend.

Now you can even get a little something on the street. Inspired by an owner's son's trip to Holland, they opened the Waffle Window (8 a.m. to 5 p.m. seven days a week; until 9 p.m. in summer) with a wide range of sweet waffle flavors like chocolate dipped, apple pie, and banana Nutella waffle. All of these run from $2 to $6.

Inside, the menu changes regularly. Some of the things I've had or seen include the basic B&I Scramble (red onions, herbed potatoes, Italian sausage, spinach, and cheddar cheese with a side of fresh fruit) to the more sophisticated Smoked Trout Scramble with onions, pepper bacon, spinach, and jack cheese topped with horseradish sour cream. There's also an omelet unique to Portland, as far as I know: the Apple Omelet of Granny Smiths with caramelized onions, pepper bacon, and Gruyère cheese. They sometimes do a Brioche French Toast, a whopping four slices of super-moist raisin bread soaked in a cinnamon-vanilla custard. In my experience only the over-the-top offering at Cafe du Berry is less in need of maple syrup.

I ate there once on a weekday with my girlfriend at the time, and when I looked around, I realized (this was at 11 a.m. on a Friday) that I was the only male! Seven tables were occupied, two of them with kids, and they were girls, too. I had gone through the looking glass, transcended the pseudo-hippie Hawthorne, and arrived in the land of the leisurely. Me and all the ladies, having a late breakfast!

Still caught up in the moment and feeling a bit old line, I took Jenny's hand and said, "I wonder what all the employed folk are doing today?"

Wait: Long on weekends. **Large groups:** Sure. **Coffee:** Kobos. **Other drinks:** Espresso, tea, fresh juice. **Feel-goods:** Local ingredients. **Health options:** Sub fruit for potatoes for $1. **WiFi:** Yes.

Bridges Cafe

New/Hip/Veggie
It was cool before MLK was cool.
2716 NE MLK Jr. Blvd. (NE/MLK) ~ 503-288-4169 ~
bridgescafeandcatering.net
Weekdays 7 a.m. to 2 p.m., weekends 8 a.m. to 3 p.m.
$9–$15 (all major cards)

————————◆•◆————————

Everything happening these days on Martin Luther King Jr. Boulevard—all the new construction, redevelopment, and old homes getting fixed up—was only a twinkle in some city planner's eye when Bridges Cafe first opened in 1994. In fact, when Bridges opened, it was one of only two restaurants in almost two miles along MLK.

What happened next was a classic example of the effect a little neighborhood restaurant can have. A crowd of regulars formed, and the new owner teamed up with the owner of another business to start events called Saturday Stroll and the Dog Days of Summer to get people walking around and noticing the neighborhood's businesses.

Word spread around the city: there's this cool place to eat breakfast up on MLK! From the beginning Bridges was known for a laid-back atmosphere, good Benedicts, local organic ingredients, and the best mimosas around. And believe me, in the mid- to late-1990s this was exciting news in pretty much any Portland neighborhood, let alone MLK.

All these years later, Bridges hasn't changed that much. It still has the same tile tables, the same big windows, the same staff that can seem alternately goofy or surly, and the same down-to-earth menu Portland-style: four Benedicts (Carlton Farms Canadian bacon, smoked wild salmon, Florentine, and a seasonal); four omelet or scramble options; a wide range of basics like oatmeal, granola, and biscuits and gravy; and seven specialties that range from waffles and challah French toast to catfish hash, a breakfast burrito, and Eggs Fiesta, a Mexi-mix served on cornbread.

Bridges' star has faded somewhat while the rest of the neighborhood has blossomed and countless other breakfast places have spread like moss throughout the city. A typical modern take on the place was a review on the website *altportland.com*, which called it a "sunny little breakfast joint" and started out, "I hate to damn Bridges with faint praise, but it's a neighborhood joint . . . reasonably friendly, generous with the food . . . consistently not bad."

Since I have fond memories of Bridges (I'm fairly sure I saw my first hipster there), I went back to check it out. I walked in at about 10:30 a.m. on a weekday, just like the old days, and saw a guy hunched over his computer, two contractors talking shop, an older couple looking around as if they'd never been there, and four young women talking about their favorite teacher.

The specials that day, each about $8 or $9, were old standards: a bacon-onion-mushroom-cheddar scramble and another scramble with garlic, spinach, roasted red peppers, and jack cheese. I ordered my old favorite, the Catfish Hash, and the rest was a trip down memory lane. It's still a big pile of potatoes with grilled onions and peppers and chunks of fried catfish in a stiff batter spotted with sesame seeds, topped with two perfectly poached eggs and something called Creole Hollandaise, which is a spicy version, still one of my favorite sauces in town. It's still served with big slices of yummy toast that somehow play perfectly with the savory festival on the plate and the house-made marionberry jam on the table. And all this for $10.95!

Neighborhood joint, indeed. An old friend in a rapidly changing neighborhood, I say.

Wait: Pretty long on weekends after about 10 a.m., with limited space inside and cover outside. **Large groups:** Yes, but not the best place for it. **Coffee:** K&F. **Other drinks:** Soda, apple juice, espresso, DragonFly Chai, cocktails, mimosas, bottled beer. **Feel-goods:** Many ingredients are local and organic. **Health options:** Good options for vegetarians. **WiFi:** No.

Broder

New

Absolutely the best Swedish breakfast in town.
2508 SE Clinton St. (SE/Division) ~ 503-736-3333 ~ *broderpdx.com*
Breakfast daily 9 a.m. to 3 p.m.
$12–$15 (Visa, MasterCard)

When Broder opened in 2007, so many people wrote about it that it was a little overwhelming. Allow me, then, to summarize what every review had in common: Broder is a cute, popular place that serves authentic Swedish cuisine—the reviewer knows because of various Swedish connections or experiences—that, when you eat it, will make you want to ride a reindeer or something.

Some folks think it's great food at a good price; others think it's a novelty restaurant with bland food. The *Oregonian*, in a generally positive review, wondered why the food couldn't be more interesting, even if a little less authentic. The *Mercury* said, "Breakfast at Broder is a dainty affair, with modest portions and an emphasis on adorability. But the preciousness wears off if you realize you've ordered the most expensive breakfast item and you're still hungry."

So Broder is not a gut-bomb place, it's not greasy, and breakfast is served on boards. The latter, I must admit, is what Elena and I were excited about when we went to check it out. We wanted something on a board. And I wanted to eat there with Elena because she's a tall, attractive blonde, which I thought would accentuate my Scandinavian experience.

Broder aims for a cross between old-timey (dark wood and light fixtures that everyone compares to antlers) and the sleek-modern-Euro feel, with white tiles, stainless steel, and lots of powder blue that reminded me of flying on KLM. Handwritten specials on a mirror offer AM Booze called Damenel Dansk (whatever that is) and desserts like Swedish cream, Danish butter cream, applesauce cake, and bread pudding.

The menu is surprisingly close to what you're used to seeing, just with little twists and different names. *Aebleskivers* are Danish pancakes, tasty little fried balls of dough served with lingonberry jam, lemon curd, and syrup on the side. Options for baked scrambles (served with walnut toast and a choice of roasted tomatoes, green salad, or potato pancake) include smoked trout and red onion, wild mushroom and caramelized onion, or duroc ham and homemade ricotta. (Duroc is a type of pig, prized for its marbled meat.) And yes, everything is served on a board, which is spelled *bord*. Cute, huh?

The signature dish is the Swedish Breakfast Bord, a sampler plate of rye crisp, walnut toast, salami, smoked trout, grapefruit, yogurt and honey, lingonberry jam, and hard cheese, for $12. The rest of the menu is close to standard American fare. There's Pytti Panna (Swedish hash) with potatoes, peppers, green onions, ham, and roast beef topped with baked eggs and served with walnut toast ($9.50). Swedish Waffles come with butter, syrup, and seasonal fruit. The Breakfast Sandwich has duroc ham, Gruyère, marjoram cream, and roasted tomatoes topped with baked eggs ($9).

Elena and I were not blown away by the food, which means either we didn't know and appreciate the subtleties of Scandinavian cuisine or they were really more novelty than taste. But Broder is fun and cute, and if you can avoid the lines, and maybe bring a cute, tall blonde with you, it's a charming little place to eat breakfast.

Wait: Pretty long on weekends, but coffee is available, Most waiting is outside, but they do open up the inside seating area when it's cold. **Large groups:** Yes, but no reservations. **Coffee:** Stumptown. **Other drinks:** Fresh lemonade, orange juice, and grapefruit juice; wine and beer, cocktails. **Feel-goods:** Menu says, "We always use cage-free eggs and organic produce and meats whenever possible." **Health options:** They can sub out meat in many dishes. **WiFi:** Yes.

Bumblekiss

New/Kiddie

Sweet, happy, sunny day!
3517 NE 46th Ave. (NE/Fremont) ~ 503-282-6313 ~ *bumblekiss.org*
Weekdays 8 a.m. to 2:30 p.m., weekends 8 a.m. to 3:30 p.m.
$10–$14 (Visa, MasterCard, no checks)

———————◆—•—◆———————

While Bumblekiss is not a "kids' restaurant," the name practically screams, "Bring your young'uns!" And when you want to evaluate how a place does with kids, there's no better way than to call in the Play Group.

The Play Group is a group of moms who meet weekly to get the kids together, share the work and play, and have some adult time. And when you see the group doing its thing at Bumblekiss, you realize the two were made for each other.

Bumblekiss is in an old orange-painted house with a Ping-Pong table in the garage and a driveway filled with tables under umbrellas. In the single room inside, you're greeted with orange plastic chairs (cheerful and unbreakable), yellow walls with a constellation of mirrors, and an orange ceiling from which hangs a collection of coloring-book pages.

When our group announced itself as a party of 11—that's out of 20 seats inside—the server didn't even flinch. And I'll say that out of more than 100 breakfasts I ate for this book, no server did more with less help and in a more cheerful manner than our heroine at Bumblekiss. We ordered in three waves, asked for changes, and paid with about four cards; she was happy and efficient the whole time.

The food fit the mix of adult and kiddie that Play Group is all about. A little basket of yummy mini-muffins (blueberry-banana and lavender-coconut plus a third flavor that changes daily) included oat-based options for protein and health and an apple-pecan special that was sweet enough to send a kid bouncing around the room. The kids' menu (with room for scribbling) features four items at $4.25 each: pancakes with chocolate sauce and maple syrup for dipping, an egg-French toast combo, Chicken-Apple (sausage) in a Blanket, and Green Eggs and Ham, the color courtesy of some blueberry extract. Although the adults agreed that the kid portions were too big, the youngsters offered up such feedback as Porter's "mmmmm." Lily, who was by now wearing some of the Little Dipper's chocolate sauce, added, "This is good!"

The moms talked of hair and shopping and trips to the zoo; I sampled the oatmeal (a slight berry flavor), one of four Benedicts (this was a veggie version with a nice light sauce and a big slice of tomato), the French toast (cinnamon-swirl with berries all over it), the fantastic pancakes (moist and rich), and the pepper bacon, which I'm happy to say was both tasty and a little too spicy for the kids. Hence, more for me.

The *Willamette Week*, soon after Bumblekiss opened, wrote a review that called it "an adorable neighborhood place" but suggested that maybe the chefs were trying to do too much, especially with the number of ingredients in some of their dishes. The Sweet Stuff Scramble, for example, has chicken apple sausage, yellow onions, diced green apple, mozzarella, and blue cheese. The Farmer's Benedict has a tomato slice, basil pesto, feta cheese, and hollandaise sauce. Some of these tastes might kind of run together; then again, they're all well cooked and tasty.

My theory, as the Play Group's trip to Bumblekiss suggested, is that a little managed chaos can be fun, especially when it's playful and colorful and cute.

Wait: Up to a half-hour, but you can play Ping-Pong. **Large groups:** Yes; no reservations. **Coffee:** Organic, shade-grown, farmer direct Tanager's Song Coffee from Portland Roasting Company (also for sale at $12.50 a pound). **Other drinks:** Mighty Leaf Tea. **Feel-goods:** They use "organic and local ingredients whenever possible," as well as free-range meats and cage-free eggs. **Health options:** Egg whites and tofu available for scrambles. They use no hydrogenated oils and say they have neither a fryer nor a microwave. Vegan and gluten-free options. **WiFi:** No.

Byways Cafe

Hip/Old School

Can you resist the kitsch? What about the French toast?
1212 NW Glisan St. (Pearl) ~ 503-221-0011 ~ *bywayscafe.com*
Breakfast weekdays 7 to 11 a.m., weekends 7:30 a.m. to 2 p.m. (breakfast only on weekends, no lunches)
$8–$11 (Visa, MasterCard, no checks)

———————————◆•◆———————————

Dan and Amy are self-proclaimed foodies. They actually met at the Culinary Institute of America, ran a restaurant, and spent most of a year at a restaurant school in Bologna, Italy. So I took them to Byways Cafe to get their impression. I think it might have been like taking a classical musician to a Grateful Dead concert.

Byways isn't as wacky as a Dead show, and Dan and Amy are not snooty by any means. But seeing these two fairly serious people sit in a springy booth that makes the table a little too high, under a collection of national park pennants, and with their coffee in a House of Mystery–Oregon Vortex mug . . . well, I had to chuckle.

When Amy said the amaretto-infused French toast with honey-pecan butter probably wasn't on real brioche, and Dan grudgingly admitted that his omelet was at least well cooked, it was a little like a non-Deadhead pointing out that Bob Weir forgot the words to "Truckin'." I wanted to say, "Yeah, but it was still fun, right?"

Maybe I'm just a sucker for kitsch, particularly of the travel variety. (I once made out with my girlfriend while watching a PBS documentary about the Lincoln Highway.) When I see a place decorated with souvenirs from the 1910s to the '70s—plates from various tourist sites, luggage, a globe, postcards, View-Masters—on the tables, the cases along the walls filled with trinkets, and Roger Miller on the stereo, it could smother previously frozen semi-brioche with butter and syrup and still make me happy.

The place even has a history of kitsch. It used to be Shakers, a similar breakfast place with, instead of all the travel knickknacks, the biggest, freakiest collection of salt and pepper shakers you'll ever see.

It's funny: My notes from three research trips to Byways include phrases like "chic greasy-spoon: just a marketing theme?" and "down-home feel, food not exceptional." And yet I kind of like the place; hell, I kept going back to "research" it! It's like listening to a tape of a Dead show I had a good time at and finding out they repeated verses and missed solos and all the other stoner stuff they did. Does it even matter? Maybe I'm just a rube.

So now I think back on the meals I've had at Byways. One time I had eggs, sausage, and mushy-yummy blue corn pancakes, topped with honey-pecan butter and organic maple syrup. But were those 'cakes supposed to be mushy? Another time, while waiting for a friend who was late, I had a blueberry crumble muffin that my notes say was "more crumble than blueberry, but good. Dry and sweet." Of course I ate the whole thing.

Now I'm confused. The rest of the menu is just classic stuff—hashes, scrambles, taters, and so on—and I have always enjoyed chatting up the staff. I guess I'm just a little more slacker than foodie, just like I'm a lot more Deadhead than symphony. And Byways seems to fit all that: it's a casual place in the middle of the foodie-infused Pearl, and I'm glad it's there, even if I don't know if it's any good.

Wait: Can get long on weekends, almost entirely outside and uncovered. **Large groups:** Would be a hassle on weekends. **Coffee:** Stumptown. **Other drinks:** Various brands of teas, including Tazo, Stash, and some British teas; hand-packed milkshakes. **Feel-goods:** House-made baked goods. **Health options:** Egg whites and tofu available for $1. **WiFi:** No.

Cadillac Cafe

Old School/Classy

The one place everybody knows about.
1801 NE Broadway (NE/Broadway) ~ 503-287-4750
Weekdays 6 a.m. to 2:30 p.m., weekends 7 a.m. to 3 p.m.
$12–$18 (all major cards, no checks)

Whenever I visit my hometown of Memphis, certain traditions must be observed—one of which is to stuff myself with barbecued pork. And when Memphians think of *tradition* and *barbecue* together, one place always springs to mind: Charlie Vergos's Rendezvous. When visiting the Bluff City, you pretty much *have* to eat there, after which you have a drink at the Peabody Hotel and then go boogie to the blues and R&B down on Beale Street.

But the lines at the Rendezvous are insane, sometimes up to two hours. Old-timers rue the massive expansion that happened in the 1990s, and not many locals actually think it's the best barbecue in town. It's just the place to go. In fact, part of the reason everybody goes there is that, well, everybody goes there.

Well, the Cadillac Cafe is the Rendezvous of Portland's breakfast scene. The lines are insane, it isn't often considered the best in town, some folks say it used to be cooler in the old location . . . but seemingly everybody has been there.

Folks do flip over the size of the portions and the variety of choices: eight specialties like Filet Mignon Steak and Eggs, Cajun Catfish, and a breakfast burrito in addition to seven omelets and eight items listed as "Simple Fare," including basic egg plates, granola, porridge, pancakes, and French toast.

About that French toast: it's the Cadillac's calling card, and I add my voice to its chorus of praise. It's done two ways: three pieces soaked in custard egg batter for $7.50 (or $9 with seasonal fruit and roasted hazelnuts) or Hazelnut French Custard Toast, which is covered in hazelnuts and powdered sugar and served with one egg and either bacon or chicken apple sausage for $9. You can also get a slice of either kind as part of the Bunkhouse Vittles, a terrific combo plate with sausage, potatoes, and two eggs ($9.25). A waiter told me the French toast bread was developed specifically for the Cadillac.

The main gripes against the Cadillac boil down to either "Why would I wait 90 minutes for breakfast?" or "It's more of a suburban chain feel than a 'real' Portland breakfast place." On the former, I have to agree. If you're standing in line for an hour and a half, it's because you've already decided you love it, you're determined to check it out, or you're entertaining some out-of-town guest who just *has* to experience the tradition.

To the "real Portland" argument, well, that just depends on your style. The Cadillac definitely has an upscale, cosmopolitan, flowers-on-the-tables vibe, made a little theme-y by the presence of a pink Cadillac. It is not, in other words, a hippied-out place like the Utopia or the Cricket or a serious foodie palace like Simpatica.

And yet the Cadillac is pure Portland, in an older, richer, Irvington kind of way. But why should I bother to describe it, anyway? There's a 90 percent chance you've already been there and made up your own mind. And if you haven't, well, I suppose you should, at least once.

Wait: Legendary on weekends: up to 90 minutes in good weather. **Large groups:** With notice. **Coffee:** Kobos. **Other drinks:** Espresso, breakfast martinis, hot liquor drinks, Oregon Chai, freshly squeezed juice and lemonade, Tazo Tea, sparkling cider. **Feel-goods:** None that're touted. **Health options:** Substitute fresh fruit or tomatoes for potatoes or toast ($1); staff will make two-egg or whites-only omelets. **WiFi:** No.

Cafe du Berry

Classy

French café, with French prices and French staff.
6439 SW Macadam Ave. (SW/Inner) ~ 503-244-5551 ~
cafeduberry.ypguides.net
Breakfast weekdays 7 a.m. to 3 p.m., weekends 8 a.m. to 3 p.m.
$15–20 (all major cards, checks)

———————◆•◆———————

After the first edition of this book came out, folks often asked if I wrote anything negative about a place in my book. To this, I always said, "Kind of." About a couple places I said the food is not that great but I don't care (see Tosis). But more often I think of what I wrote about Cafe du Berry.

It's not that I trashed the place. I even said the food was good—in fact, I said their custard-recipe French toast was borderline orgasmic. It's just that my Snootiness Alarm went off, the prices seemed ridiculous, our server was rude, and I said at the time that only the French toast would bring me back.

Here's a sample:

> My omelet, which wasn't on the menu, was $14, which the server didn't mention. Sure, I could have asked, but a $14 omelet? The server didn't mention the sauce, either, which was tasty but doesn't generally appear on omelets. In fact, whenever he came to the table, we were left somewhat dazed by his rapid-fire, straight-to-the-point, not-even-looking-at-us delivery. He greeted us, described three specials, poured water, and was gone in about 5.2 seconds. So, is that efficient or rude?

> Jean rightly pointed out that for $7.95, the French Toast with Potatoes and Fruit was one piece of the toast, one smallish helping of potatoes, one strawberry, and half of a banana. That ain't much for $7.95.

I confess I did get rather snarky. In short, my whole thing with the cafe felt a little off, like nobody was getting along, and I didn't know why.

So I decided to go back. And I have to say, I now wonder what I was so worked up about.

Yes, it's a little expensive. It's a French bistro in Southwest Portland. You're warned.

Our server was fine, the food was fine (the hollandaise in particular), and this time the place came off a little more "creaky grandma's house" than "snooty French place." Hell, even the French toast wasn't as good as I recall. It was good, but I didn't want to run into the kitchen and make out with whoever created it, like I did the first time.

So here's my new take: Cafe du Berry is a popular, French-style bistro that's on the high end of the local scale, serves pretty good food in a casual, old-timey feel, has a unique and tasty French toast, and otherwise isn't really my kind of place.

Do with that as you will. And try the French toast sometime.

It's a French custard dessert recipe, made with Hawaiian egg bread thoroughly soaked, then grilled to just crisp on the outside, with a touch of lemon in the finish, dusted with powdered sugar, and served warm, syrup be damned. I could add details like the firmness of the bread and how it played perfectly with the bouncy delight of the custard, but I'm on my way to have some right now.

Wait: Not bad, mostly outside. **Large groups:** Upstairs with some notice. **Coffee:** Kobos. **Other drinks:** Espresso, tea, cocktails, champagne, fresh juice. **Feel-goods:** None that I noticed; it's French food! **Health options:** I think if you eat the custard-based French toast, or the béarnaise sauce, or the hollandaise sauce 10 times, you get a punch card for a free angioplasty. **WiFi:** No.

Cafe Magnolia

Mom & Pop

Portland casual, Southern flair.
1522 SE 32nd (SE/Hawthorne) ~ 503-206-6305
Sunday through Wednesday 8 a.m. to 4 p.m., Thursday through
Saturday 8 a.m. to 10 p.m.
$12–$14 (all major cards, no checks)

Josh Parker's career as a chef traces both the American Dream and the
classic Portland story.

He grew up in Nashville, raised by a Bostonian and a North
Carolinian who made regular, large breakfasts a part of his life. In 1995
he "decided to check out the West Coast" and drove to San Francisco,
only to find it too hectic. He drifted north to Eugene to see buddies
from the University of Tennessee and picked up his restaurant career,
then to Portland to go to cooking school. After an internship at the
legendary Paley's Place on Northwest 21st, he took a job with a friend
who owns the Cup and Saucer, and he cooked there and at Cafe Lena,
then at Jam on Hawthorne—breakfast classics, the lot of them.

But in the back of his mind, there were always two things: memories of Southern food and the desire to open his own restaurant.
When a place just off Hawthorne called the Chance of Rain Cafe
(how Portland!) closed, he bought the location, fixed it up with some
friends, and late in 2009 Cafe Magnolia was born. While he was originally thinking Southern bistro, he says he toned it down a little. But he
remembered one thing, which tells you a lot about his attitude towards
cooking:

Jimmy Dean Sausage.

That's the secret to Magnolia's tasty biscuits and gravy, and I share
it here because he shared it with me on my podcast. Jimmy Dean,
for you non-Southerners, was a country singer and actor (he played
Willard Whyte in *Diamonds Are Forever*) who started a sausage company in 1969. Although it's now owned by Sara Lee, the brand says
"old-fashioned" to us Tennesseans, and I love that it's used at Cafe

Magnolia—because "that's how my old man used to make it," Josh told me. By the time he told me about the cheese grits casserole, my drool and my drawl were both running high.

But Cafe Magnolia isn't just a showcase for southern fare; it also lets Parker show off what he learned in school and all those kitchens. The signature dish is the Hawthorne Scramble: rendered bacon, spinach, caramelized onions, and Rogue Creamery blue cheese. It's colorful, tasty, aromatic, and local. In fact, all his ingredients are local, and most are organic.

He also has some fun with hash browns, mixing purple potatoes, baby reds, and Yukons with a little garlic, salt and pepper, and chives. "I'm not trying to win any James Beard awards or get my own Food Network show," he said. "I'm just trying to give neighborhood people a good place to go, great food, and a comfortable atmosphere."

I have to say, as Jimmy Dean might, "That ol' boy's done real good."

Wait: None. **Large groups:** With notice. **Coffee:** Stumptown, free on Mondays. **Other drinks:** Espresso, juice, tea, house-infused liquors, and beer. **Feel-goods:** Local, organic ingredients, cage-free eggs. **Health options:** Garden sausage. **WiFi:** Yes.

Cafe Nell

Classy/Weekend

Casual . . . in a fancy kind of way.
1987 NW Kearney (NW) ~ 503-295-6487 ~ *cafenell.com*
$15–$17 (all major cards, no checks)
Weekdays 11 a.m. to 3 p.m., weekends 9 a.m. to 2 p.m.

In restaurant world, the word *casual* has to be taken in context. So Stanford's might seem casual to some folks and fancy to others. What's casual on Hawthorne might seem filthy to somebody in the Southwest hills.

I say all this because you should know that Cafe Nell is a particular kind of casual restaurant. You can hang out as long as you want (at least at breakfast, which is the only time I've been), it's in a quiet little nook of Northwest, and you can get fed for as little as $7 for a basic two-egg meal with home fries and toast.

But it's a fancy and sophisticated casual. Even if the prices (a spinach-feta omelet with home fries and toast is just $11) don't sepa-

rate Cafe Nell far from other places, the décor certainly does. Nell is sleek, with black and white dominating and a red fireplace giving accent, and the mere presence of wine cooler buckets holding bottles of Pellegrino telling you, "You're not at the Cricket Café."

So it won't surprise you to know that the owners of Cafe Nell moved from New York, where they had careers in restaurants and theater. They say Cafe Nell is meant to be an "American *brasserie.*" I say that simply using the word *brasserie* implies a certain sophistication on the part of the listener; did you know that a *brasserie*, in France, is a combo cafe/restaurant with a relaxed setting, serving the same menu all day? Well, I for one, had to look it up.

Cafe Nell isn't exactly that; it has a breakfast/lunch menu separate from the dinner menu, as well as an expanded menu for weekend brunch. But it is certainly relaxed, and the combination of tall windows, high ceilings, and several large mirrors makes it an open and attractive place.

Since opening in 2008, they've expanded the weekday fare quite a bit. Now you can get three different grains and four egg-based options. Prices peak out at $12 for omelets or the Cafe Nell Breakfast, which is scrambled egg whites, fresh fruit, mixed greens, quinoa, whole wheat toast, grapefruit juice, and coffee or tea. I should say the menu changes frequently, and this is what they had when I was there.

Things get even more interesting on weekends, when their full-on brunch menu adds things like several Benedicts, a NY Strip and eggs, Hangtown Fry, Lamb Hash, pan-fried trout, brioche French toast, and homemade éclairs. Prices tick up a bit then, as well.

If I were suggesting a breakfast place for out-of-town visitors whom I wanted to impress, and they just wanted a tasty little something in a casual setting, Cafe Nell would be perfect. And since my office is right down the street, I might join them for some casual hanging out—fancy Northwest style. Or éclairs.

Wait: Most likely on Sundays. **Large groups:** With notice. **Coffee:** Caffè Umbria. **Other drinks:** Espresso and a few cocktails. **Feelgoods:** Menu says they limit "the use of added fats, butter or dairy" and try to use fresh local ingredients. **Health options:** Vegetarians and vegans could do okay. **WiFi:** Yes.

Cameo Cafe East

Mom & Pop/Old School

Grandma's Kitschy Korean Roadhouse!
8111 NE Sandy Blvd. (NE/Outer) ~ 503-284-0401 ~ *cameocafe.com*
Daily 6:30 a.m. to 3 p.m.
$10–$16 (all major cards)

Argue all you want about the best or worst breakfast places in Portland, but the Cameo is definitely one of the strangest.

I used to drive by and think it was a roadhouse or greasy-spoon joint, with a cheap motel behind it and highways all around. But inside, the décor practically screams Grandma, with flowered wallpaper, tea sets on shelves, and clay figurines of chefs over the stove. The *Mercury* said it "looks a little like an insurance office," and my friend Jane said it looked like an ice cream parlor. Keep looking and you'll spot a bulletin board covered with signed photos of Miss America contestants who apparently ate there. There's also an accordion, a flashing carousel, a parasol, and more clay figurines of hillbillies, Cupid, and a naked lady.

When you sit down and check for the specials, there's another shock. Nothing can prepare you for the words *Kimchee Omelet*. When I told Jane that kimchee is a very spicy fermented cabbage dish popular in Korea, she asked, "And they make an omelet with it?" Well, apparently. I can't tell you what it's like because I've never convinced anyone to order it. But when I first saw it, I wondered, "What kind of place is this?"

Well, it's a, um, kitschy Korean roadhouse. I guess.

After you peel through the layers of oddness, you'll see that Cameo is in most ways a pretty straightforward breakfast joint—with big portions and high prices. It shares the famous "acres" of pancakes from the old and famous Cameo West on NW 23rd, but Cameo East's Full Acre is listed at market price (I forgot to ask why, but it's $10.95). The 'cakes come with apples, bananas, strawberries, raspberries, or peaches.

But there is a Korean thread running through the menu. There are tofu pancakes (made with mung beans and rice) with vegetables and cheese. And there is Sue Gee's FUSION Pancake (that's how it's written on the menu) with rice and vegetables in a "special prepared batter" with cheese. And then there's what I had, the *Pindaettok*, which is pro-nounced pin-day-tuck and is, according to the menu, "a Korean word meaning pancake."

I was on my way out of town for a hike, which might be the only time that a soy-based pancake with vegetables, beans, spices, and ground rice in a "flavored batter," cooked thin and crispy and with something called Duck Sauce on the side, sounds about right for breakfast. It also comes with two eggs, bacon, and two pieces of their yummy, multigrain, house-made STONG BREAD. (Again, that's how it appears on the menu.)

Cameo also has the usual assortment of waffles (plus a coconut option), French toast, and about a dozen combinations of egg, meat, and carb. But the Pindaettok defined the place for me. I had never heard of it, wasn't quite sure what it was, and was not at all used to spicy vegetables at breakfast.

But I also liked it, and there was more of it than I could eat. And walking out of a breakfast place, all filled up and ready to hike, was the first non-strange thing that happened to me that day.

Wait: None. **Large groups:** Not the best option. **Coffee:** Farmer Brothers. **Other drinks:** Tea, juice, hot chocolate, old-fashioned RC on tap. **Feel-goods:** The house bread is preservative free. **Health options:** Pretty good range for vegetarians. **WiFi:** No.

Chez Joly

Weekend

A French outpost on the edge of Le Pearl.
135 NW Broadway (Downtown) ~ 503-200-5544 ~ *chezjoly.com*
Brunch Sundays from 9 a.m. to 3 p.m.
$12–$20 (all major cards, no checks)

———————◆•◆———————

At first glance, Chez Joly seems in a lonely spot, both in its location and its niche. It's a French bistro with the usual associated charms: wrought-iron chandeliers, old-fashioned light fixtures, a freakishly large mirror, even a painting of Napoleon. It's not over-the-top fancy like Fenouil, nor quite as down-home as Cafe du Berry.

It's on Northwest Broadway, two blocks up from Burnside. Think about that stretch of road: What's there? Can you picture it? Well, there's a sushi place across the street, and down the street you have Outside In, the main post office, the Tiger Bar, that freaky Embers place, a Dollar Rent a Car . . . and now a French bistro.

Of course, they say on their website they are in the Pearl District, and I say we give it to them. I don't know anybody who'd say Northwest Broadway is in the Pearl, but hey, *c'est la mercatique!* Chez Joly is in the Pearl. Let's move on. But when one owner said in a YouTube video that the scene across the street looks like Rue Royale in Paris, I had to hope his nose is better than his eyes.

The owners, a couple named Joly, lived in Paris for years and fell in love with the bistro lifestyle there. While many Americans may think French food is automatically fancy, in fact, bistro cuisine is based on traditional French dishes, made with fresh, local ingredients, reasonably priced, and usually served with wine. On that, we can all agree, Chez Joly nails it.

The place looks nice, perhaps even better at night, but comfy with high-backed chairs and plenty of light. The menu—a true brunch with both breakfast and lunch items—is filled with French goodies . . . I assume. I haven't eaten much brunch in France, but this is certainly not a typical Portland brunch menu, since it has stuff like French

Canard Salade Tiede (a salad with duck breast, pine nuts, spinach, finished with something called *garlic scented pan jus*). There's also a Quiche Lorraine, Nicoise Salad, and crepes—both the menu version with berries and sugar, and a special with poached salmon and chanterelle mushrooms.

The food at Chez Joly seems a little less ambitious than the plan for the place, or the whole idea of opening a French Bistro in ~~Chinatown~~ the Pearl. We all agreed the food was good, but nobody thought it was great.

On the other hand, the service was nice, parking a snap, and the line nonexistent. All in all, it's like the *Oregonian* said in their not-too-flattering review: you want to like the place. Their reviewer is hoping for a better chef to come along. (*Willamette Week*, by the way, said in their similar review, "So far, the earnest, family-run business isn't a special destination.")

Je dit le meme, which I think means "I say the same." But I would add a *merci* for giving French bistro life a shot downtown.

Wait: Reservations recommended. **Large groups:** Yes. **Coffee:** Kobos. **Other drinks:** Juices, wine, and several cocktails. **Feelgoods:** All local ingredients, and French is spoken. **Health options:** Vegetarians would do okay. **WiFi:** *Oui*.

Country Cat Dinnerhouse

New

A new happening in a newly happening area.
7937 SE Stark St. (SE/Outer) ~ 503-408-1414 ~ *thecountrycat.net*
Brunch daily from 9 a.m. to 2 p.m.
$13–$17 (all major cards)

———————◆•◆———————

You could just about drive right past the Country Cat and never notice it. The same may be true for the Montavilla neighborhood. But Montavilla is becoming a happening place, and the Country Cat is part of it.

The Country Cat's generic exterior hides an exquisite interior made of wood, with shades of blue and brown, spacious booths, hanging lights, and an open kitchen. It's modern, yet comfy.

Likewise, the brunch menu at first seems rather down-home: pancakes, a Benedict, a basic breakfast, a scramble, biscuits and gravy, and lunch items like chicken wings, a ham sandwich, and fried chicken (more on that later). But the details tell you that you're dealing with something different: the pancakes come with things like syrup-glazed seasonal fruit or roasted apple maple syrup. The scramble might be of wild mushrooms and goat cheese; the ham sandwich might be the Blackstrap Molasses Ham Sandwich with pickled red onions, herbed cream cheese, and whole grain mustard. The Cast Iron Skillet Fried Chicken comes with mixed greens and toasted pecan spoonbread. The hash might be of duck confit with leeks and collard greens.

See where I'm going here? The Country Cat aspires to be both a cozy neighborhood place *and* a new-Portland-style cutting-edge restaurant.

At the Country Cat, a pig is butchered once a week; bacon, ham, and other meats are made on site. Almost all other ingredients are local. After it opened in 2007, the picky folks over at *portlandfood.org* went nuts over the place. Some were from the neighborhood and were excited about the Cat in conjunction with the Academy Theater, a wine bar, and a new farmers' market on Sundays. Others were just fired up about such serious cooking with fresh, local produce and an ever-revolving menu based on the season.

And then there is the fried chicken. Just about everybody mentions the fried chicken, for two reasons. One is the decent chance that it will be some of the finest fried chicken you've ever eaten, unless you're a purist and believe that fried chicken should still have the bones and skin. The Cat's is a brined, skinless piece of thigh meat with seasoned breading; at brunch (for $12) two pieces come with a mixed green salad and a slab of toasted pecan spoonbread, which is at the same time moist and cakey, firm and soft, and sweet and crispy. It and the chicken are drizzled with real maple syrup.

At dinner, apparently, three pieces of chicken is $18, and this is where some folks get a little sideways about the Country Cat. The theme here is, "What's a place, much less in this neighborhood, doing charging $18 for fried chicken?" Some folks even lobbed the nuclear bomb of these conversations: *gentrification.*

I don't wade into such chatter. If a guy can get $18 for fried chicken, I say more power to him. All I can tell you is that the chicken is darn good, as was everything else we had at the Cat, and who cares what neighborhood it's in? My friend Alice spent the whole meal saying, "Wow, this is good," and, "I need to come back here for dinner." I'll just agree with Alice.

Wait: Maybe a half hour on weekends. **Large groups:** Yes. **Coffee:** Stumptown. **Other drinks:** Espresso, Tao of Tea, Bloody Marys, mimosas, fresh juice. **Feel-goods:** Plenty of local ingredients, and much of the meat is prepared on-site. **Health options:** Some veggie options. **WiFi:** No.

Cricket Café

Hip/Veggie

Dude, dig the size of this menu!
3159 SE Belmont St. (SE/Belmont) ~ 503-235-9348 ~ *cricketcafepdx.com*
Breakfast daily from 7:30 a.m. to 3 p.m.
$10–$13 (Visa, MasterCard)

———◆•◆———

The Cricket Café has long been known for a few things: long waits, decent food, big menu and portions, and slow service. I have seen all these in action at various times. Try it sometime: ask your friends if they've been to the Cricket, and they'll probably say, "Yeah, the food is all right, but I waited forever and the service was comical."

The Cricket is nearly the perfect Southeast breakfast place: good ideas, good food, slow pace (for better or worse), good folks, a little rough around the edges. Colorful artwork of baked goods and outdoor scenes adorn the simple white walls. Bamboo blinds block the summer sun and Belmont Street traffic noise. The ceiling and concrete floor are crisscrossed with cracks.

The Cricket roasts its own coffee and buys from local growers and farmers, which suggests a commitment to health and community. It also serves a large list of "liquid breakfast" cocktails. The baked goods are made from scratch, and the Cricket is known for absurdly good cinnamon rolls, which are only available some weekends. The apple bread is served warm, soft in the middle, and crunchy outside—rather like the whole place, now that I think about it.

And the menu! It's a Denny's level of variety: about 20 omelets, scrambles, hashes, skillets, plates, and specialties, *plus* you can build your own omelet, scramble, or potato dish. And there are two other wonderful touches: $3.99 specials before 9 a.m. and $2.99–3.99 to-go orders. And you won't leave hungry. You can get the Big Farm Breakfast with potatoes, pancakes, *and* toast, if you want. The bacon is thick and crispy. The pancakes are thin but very flavorful and crisp around the edges, served with pure maple syrup. They have home fries (simple, lightly peppered, with the smaller pieces crunchy) as well as crispy shoestring hash browns. The granola is excellent—of course. The fruit bowl is large and the fruit fresh, but none is peeled; again, that just seems to fit the theme.

Still, what I am going to remember about the place are two things. One is the relaxed vibe that exists, whether it's crowded or calm. The other is an interaction we had with the ~~hipster punk~~ young man pouring water for us. There was some music playing, and we were discussing whether it would be called rap or hip-hop. (We're very white.) Pitcher Boy mumbled loud enough for us to hear, in a voice dripping with disdain, "Just call it *music*."

Then he walked off, and we all looked at each other for a moment, caught between shock and humor. Then we remembered where we were, shrugged it off, and dived back into our food.

Wait: Long on weekends after about 9:30 a.m.; some chairs and cover outside, very little room inside. **Large groups:** Easy. **Coffee:** Roast their own organic Madera. **Other drinks:** Numi Tea, Tao of Tea, DragonFly Chai, full bar. **Feel-goods:** Local fruits, veggies, cheeses, butter, and meats. **Health options:** Egg Beaters or tofu in any dish for $1.75; vegetarian gravy, vegan and vegetarian options. **WiFi:** No.

Cup and Saucer Cafe

Hip/Veggie

Like an old friend: dependable and nonthreatening.
3566 SE Hawthorne Blvd. (SE/Hawthorne) ~ 503-236-6001 ~ daily
7 a.m. to 9 p.m. ~ *cupandsaucercafe.com*
3000 NE Killingsworth (NE/Alberta) ~ 503-287-4427 ~ daily 8 a.m.
to 4 p.m.
8237 N Denver (N) ~ 503-247-6011 ~ daily 8 a.m. to 3 p.m.
3746 N Mississippi (N) ~ 503-548-4614 ~ daily 7 a.m. to 7 p.m.
$10–$13 (Visa, MasterCard, checks)

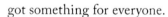

You wake up medium-late, like 10 in the morning. You want some breakfast, but you don't want to spend 15 bucks. You want something more than a coffee shop, something less than a fancy brunch. You don't want to go too far. You figure the lines are already huge at the local giants. You talk it over with your friends, you waver for a minute, and then somebody says, "Screw it, let's just go to the Cup and Saucer."

Now, you might think I just demeaned the Cup and Saucer. Not so. In fact, here's another way of saying the same thing: The Cup and Saucer is *The Princess Bride* of Portland breakfast places. Get some friends together to pick a movie sometime, let them hash it out for a while, and then say, "What about *The Princess Bride*?" Somebody will say, "Oh, I love that movie!" And everybody will agree it's all right. It's got something for everyone.

That seems to be how Portland feels about the Cup and Saucer. It's friendly and casual, and it's in three very happening neighborhoods. It's hippie, hipster, kid-friendly, and dependable. It serves breakfast at all hours, and the menu is bursting with options. Chances are, nothing you eat there will be the best you ever had, but chances are even better that whatever you want, they'll have it.

The 18 egg or tofu plates include just about every ingredient you can think of, and you can add the works (cheddar, salsa, and sour cream) to your side potatoes for $2.75. Split plates for the 18 come with a scone and a side of potatoes for $2.75, and you can substitute fruit for your potatoes for $1.75. Oh, and there are five house specialties (smoked salmon and Florentine Benedicts, biscuits and vegetarian gravy, huevos rancheros, and the Super Saucer, which is two eggs, a meat choice, and a pancake), challah French toast, granola, oatmeal, and four pancakes: buttermilk, blueberry, vegan cornmeal, and a daily special. There are more than a dozen side dishes, including brown rice, sautéed veggies, muffins, toast, and tortillas.

See what I mean? Just try to go into the Cup and Saucer and find nothing you want. Can't eat sugar or wheat? Dig into the Basil Pesto Scramble with spinach and sun-dried tomatoes. And, for the record, before I even read this review to one non-wheat-eating friend, she said, "That place is like a generic breakfast place, but it's pretty good!"

Other than the variety and dependability, the Cup and Saucer is known for scones and their spin on breakfast potatoes. The scones . . . well, they're called the Cup and Saucer Classic Buttery Vanilla Delight. Need to know more? A basket of three is $2, so don't skip them. The potatoes are a combination of russets and sweet potatoes, with cloves of roasted garlic thrown in. They come with most dishes and are $3.50 as a stand-alone.

Now I'm hungry and need a break and some food, so what the heck, I'll just walk over to the Cup and Saucer.

Wait: Medium on weekends, with some space inside and cover outside. **Large groups:** Good choice. **Coffee:** Portland Roasting Company. **Other drinks:** Espresso, DragonFly Chai, Italian sodas, cocktails at some locations. **Feel-goods:** Plenty of organic options. **Health options:** Egg substitute or tofu; vegan and vegetarian options abound. **WiFi:** Yes, in all.

Daily Cafe

New/Hip/Weekend

Possibly the perfect Pearl place.

902 NW 13th Ave. (Pearl) ~ 503-242-1916 ~ *dailycafeinthepearl.com*

Weekdays 7 a.m. to 11 a.m., Saturday 8 a.m. to 2 p.m., Sunday brunch 9 a.m. to 2 p.m.

Locations also at:

1100 SE Grand Ave. (SE/Inner) ~ 503-234-8189

Weekdays 7 a.m. to 3 p.m., Saturday 9 a.m. to 3 p.m.

3355 SW Bond Ave. (Downtown) ~ 503-224-9691

Weekdays 7 a.m. to 11 a.m., Saturday, 8 a.m. to 2 p.m.

$7–$12 Monday through Saturday, $17–20 on Sundays (Visa, MasterCard)

───────◆•◆───────

Consider the Pearl District. Is it modern, efficient, and Euro-style, or is it bland and sterile? Is it home to computer-slinging hipsters, fashionable posers, or a new generation of young families? Are its restaurants of the pass-through variety with no food of great interest or destinations all their own?

Well yes. And to my eyes Daily Cafe is all those things, which is why it may be the most perfectly Pearl place to eat breakfast. Workers gather there for quick meetings, stroller-pushing moms take breaks from shopping, and especially on weekends, diners come from all over the city.

During the week, breakfast at the Daily Cafe is a very casual, quick affair; you order at the counter from a menu on a chalkboard, grab a seat, and the ultra-friendly staff will bring it out. The choices are similar to the weekend brunch, only fewer. One day there were griddlecakes with granola and cranberries; two eggs with home fries, eight-grain toast, and marionberry jam; a breakfast panini with bacon and pepper jack cheese; granola; a daily-special quiche; and oatmeal.

Nothing much to that, right? One time I had a frittata with roasted red peppers, caramelized onions, spinach, cheddar, fries, and eight-grain toast, all for only $7.95. I was in and out in less than an hour. I've had better frittatas, but this is a place where you can eat in a flash for less than $10 or linger for two hours with your computer and free coffee refills.

On weekends, though, the Daily Cafe is a different animal entirely. The lines form early and stay long, and although the options and prices go up, it's still a value. The $13.95 fixed-price menu includes one appetizer, one entrée, and a basket of house-made pastries. There's even more staff and full table service, and it seems like the food gets better. One time, for example, I had a whipped mascarpone and dried black fruit compote with cherries, currants, and plums. I also had some laughs with the server about how to pronounce *mascarpone*. I wondered if the folks at Fenouil in the Pearl could have had that kind of fun.

Other appetizers that day were fresh papaya with a wedge of lime and some mint; granola with fruit and nuts; a fruit salad; Irish oatmeal; and the "best ever mug of hot chocolate," with "62% bittersweet chocolate bar, Madagascar vanilla and Natalie's house made marshmallows." Okay, so there *is* a little Pearl snootiness going on.

The options for the next course were a broccoli scramble, huevos rancheros, a basic omelet, a two-egg classic breakfast, and a smoked salmon plate with a grilled bagel, capers, cucumbers, red onions, tomatoes, and cream cheese. I had a stack of three buttermilk griddlecakes with orange marmalade and ricotta, and I was astonished how filling they were. My server told me that the only types of people who finish that stack are teenage boys and skinny women who run marathons.

I would have added stoned college students, but I'm not sure they go to the Pearl. Maybe they will after they grow up and get a little more sophisticated.

Wait: Long on Sunday after about 9 a.m. **Large groups:** Yes. **Coffee:** Stumptown. **Other drinks:** Soda, mineral water, juice, tea, milk. **Feel-goods:** Some organic, locally raised ingredients. **Health options:** Usually a vegan soup and some gluten-free options. **WiFi:** Yes.

Delta Cafe Bar

Weekend/Veggie/Hip

Sit ya'self down and le's eat!
4607 SE Woodstock (SE/Outer) ~ 503-771-3101 ~ *deltacafebar.com*
Weekends 9 a.m. to 2 p.m.
$12–$14 (cash and check only)

———————◆ • ◆———————

So there's this way we like to do things down South. It's part food, part booze, part folks, part music, part attitude. It's a little hungover, and it's a little drunk. It's slumped back in the chair too. It ain't light, but it's serious—like when a blues band hits its groove: nobody's smiling, exactly, but it's just right. It's gettin' down.

The Delta Cafe just about gets me to this place every time I go in. I say "just about" because I'm getting a little old for the hipster vibe, and no place does the hipster vibe like the Delta. Still, it's got some old-school funk in there, and I don't mean filth. I mean soul. Somebody's got a Southern groove goin' on there, more my kind of South than, say, the Screen Door.

The Screen Door, God bless 'em, is all foodie and stuff. Excellent stuff. But the Delta is Smoked Brisket Hash kind of Southern. Blackened Snapper over white cheddar grits with collard greens and a crayfish cream sauce. Po'Boys with snapper, oyster, shrimp, pork, or andouille sausage. Mmm!

Okay, so there's also a barbecued tofu Po'Boy—and a lot of other tofu available—but hey, this is Southeast Portland, not the French Quarter. I can get with that. Nothing wrong, either, with a Brioche French Toast served with berry compote, organic maple syrup, and whipped cream.

I went there with a big Breakfast Crew one time—foodies, friends, and assorted loonies—and I'm not sure it was the best meal we had, but it was one of the longest, and one of the loudest. In part that's because they're not afraid to crank up the tunes at the Delta, nor are they afraid of Johnny Cash, or some occasional hard rock. But it's also because there's booze going around and some folks are either hungover or still working on something from the night before. And there're some wacky decorations that I can't even describe, but I can tell you that the whole place is kind of a trip. And none of the chairs match. And you might get sweet tea in a mason jar. And their lunch- and dinnertime Creole Gumbo with shrimp, chicken, and sausage is just about my favorite plate in town.

So it's right at a cool intersection between the groovy Southeast Portland thing and that down-home, get yourself-a-cocktail Southern thing. Sit yourself down and fill yourself up. Take a little tour of the Southern food thing.

Wait: Maybe a little. **Large groups:** With notice. **Coffee:** Stumptown. **Other drinks:** Beer, cocktails, Bloody Mary bar, juice. **Feel-goods:** None in particular. **Health options:** Good veggie varieties. **WiFi:** Yes.

Detour Cafe

New/Veggie

A literally hidden gem.

3035 SE Division St. (SE/Division) ~ 503-234-7499 ~ *detourcafe.com*

Daily 8 a.m. to 4 p.m.

$9–$13 (Visa, MasterCard, no checks)

———————◆•◆———————

One of these days I'll be sitting around in who-knows-what kind of breakfast place, telling folks I was in Portland when the organic/local-grown/sustainable revolution happened—a time when so many good places opened all over town that a yummy, cool place like the Detour Cafe could exist right under my nose and I wouldn't even know about it.

I mean that literally: starting in 2001, this little place hid behind all the vegetation on its porch for six years before I knew of its existence. I guess the folks in the neighborhood didn't want the rest of us to know about it.

Detour represents everything the "new" Portland is all about. Its website says, "We use free range eggs, organic flour, and when possible, organic and/or locally farmed produce and meats. We also feature freshly baked pastries of all kinds, housemade vegan soups, and Stumptown coffee." It then goes on to offer a feel-good hodgepodge of links: Gathering Together Farm, the Oregon Humane Society, Planned Parenthood, art studios, bands, you name it.

Detour is cute and friendly, with yellow and green dominating the décor while plastic chairs and tables give it a semi-goofy feel, and on the shady porch the overhanging plants cut down on the noise from Division Street. Detour has house-baked goods, including one of the finest cheddar biscuits in town, spiced with scallions and sweetened with corn.

What really sets Detour apart, though, can be stated in four words: build your own frittata. As soon as I saw my smoked-salmon-and-goat-cheese three-egg frittata sitting on my plate with roasted potatoes and whole wheat toast (all for just $8.25), I thought, "Why doesn't everybody do this?" My frittata was the perfect combination of egg, cheese, and meat with just a little crust from the baking and plenty of fresh, creamy, cheesy goodness.

The basic option is any two of 24 frittata ingredients, so a vegetarian can do well. Extra ingredients are only $0.50, and you get roasted onions for free. You can get any three of the same ingredients from the same list with potatoes for only $7.50, so even the vegans can get their groove on (there's a daily vegan soup, as well). And for only $3.50 you can get toasted focaccia with cream cheese, tomatoes, and fresh basil.

The portions aren't overwhelming, but everything looks nice and colorful. My friend Chela's French toast was made with cardamom bread, which sort of grounded the sweetness from the custard dip; the topping of cherry compote, toasted almonds, and organic maple syrup brought it home wonderfully. A half-order for $4.25 was just what she wanted.

Tom even found his bacon-and-egg sandwich. But it was a BELT, with bacon, two eggs sunny side up, mixed greens, tomato, with house-made mayo and focaccia ($7). Other sandwich options included the Original, with baked eggs, cream cheese, roma tomatoes, fresh basil, and pepper bacon ($7); the All Fired Up, with spiced cream cheese and red peppers; and the Don ($8.50), with portobello mushrooms, onions, and feta mixed into the eggs and topped with Italian sausage, avocado, tomato, and basil.

Everything was fresh, tasty, and down-home in that "new Portland" way. That seemed to wrap up Detour perfectly.

Wait: Long on weekends, with self-serve coffee and some cover outside. **Large groups:** Yes. **Coffee:** Self-serve Stumptown. **Other drinks:** Espresso, Chai, Tao of Tea, Kombucha, soda, and juice. **Feel-goods:** Organic, local ingredients and cage-free eggs. **Health options:** Plenty here for vegetarians and vegans. **WiFi:** No.

Dockside Saloon & Restaurant

Mom & Pop/Old School

Where there's still some "Port" in Portland.
2047 NW Front Ave. (NW) ~ (503) 241-6433 ~ *docksidesaloon.com*
Weekdays 5 a.m. to 11 a.m., Saturday 6 a.m. to 3 p.m., Sunday 8 a.m. to 3 p.m.
$8–$12 (all major cards, no checks)

———————◆•◆———————

I used to cook on fishing boats up in Alaska, and no place in Portland reminds me of those days more than the Dockside.

First, there's the location: down along the river, surrounded by railroads and industry, almost underneath a massive bridge. Then there's the exterior of the place: it looks like it may have been slapped together with planks from old boats. An owner told the *NW Examiner* that a long-time server "circled the place three times before venturing inside for a job interview."

The interior makes it seem even more down by the docks, with lifesavers hanging from the ceilings, old photos on the walls, and folks drinking at all hours. But the Dockside is not a rough place at all—quite the opposite. There's a decent chance you'll meet one of the husband-and-wife owners while you're there, and the same *NW Examiner* reviewer said it met her Grandmother Vera's three requirements: "A good Bloody Mary, family ownership, and video poker."

To that, you may add large, filling breakfasts at reasonable prices, made with what all reviewers agree is a complete lack of pretension. In fact, since I moved back to Northwest, the Dockside has become my favorite place to meet people for a casual, private breakfast—in part because of their reaction when they walk in. They usually say either, "I've always wondered about this place!" or, "I used to come in here years ago, and it hasn't changed a bit."

I also love the combination of simplicity and thoroughness in the menu. You'll find 17 combinations (all named for bridges) of meat, eggs, cheese, potatoes, and various other carbs. Almost as an afterthought, down at the bottom of the menu is Cream of Wheat, oatmeal, and fresh fruit with toast. The most expensive item in this section is the 7-ounce rib eye with two eggs, hash browns, and toast for $10.50.

Another section has three-egg omelets, all with meat, topping out with the Dockside Super Omelet of ham, bacon and sausage, onion, green pepper, mushroom and tomato—for $11.75. There are also 24 breakfast sides, including the aforementioned steak for $4.50, so basically, whatever you want for breakfast, you can get it quick, cheap, and with a smile at the Dockside.

One story about the Dockside has to be repeated: One day back in 1994, one of the owners found somebody's home garbage in the dumpster and went through it. Somehow they made a connection, and some of it became evidence that connected Tonya Harding to the clubbing of Nancy Kerrigan. They like to joke, "We're best known for our garbage, but we think our food is pretty darned good."

I do too.

Wait: None. **Large groups:** With notice. **Coffee:** Bridgetown. **Other drinks:** Espresso, beer, cocktails. **Feel-goods:** None in particular. **Health options:** Not so much. **WiFi:** Yes.

Doug Fir Lounge

Hip/Old School

Live music and good food, at the same place.
830 E Burnside (E Burnside) ~ 503-231-9663 ~ *dougfirlounge.com*
Breakfast daily 7 a.m. to 3 p.m.
$10–$14 (all major cards)

◆━━━●━━━◆

Perhaps you've heard that the Doug Fir Lounge, that "music place" on East Burnside, serves breakfast. And perhaps when you heard it, you thought, "Bar, club, breakfast . . . no thanks." Well, the Doug Fir is trying to be more than a music place, and its food is definitely beyond bar chow.

First and foremost, the Doug Fir is a music place featuring bands that this 40-something has absolutely never heard of. Maximo Park's bus was parked outside when I ate at the Doug, and had the entire band been sitting at a table next to me singing its #1 song, I wouldn't have known them.

Like any music place, the Doug is trying to be young and hip— trying too hard, if you ask its detractors, who also bemoan its stylishly casual approach to service. Supporters generally chime back with, "Chill out, it's a rock-and-roll place." Even among rock-and-roll places, though, it's going for a particular niche. The shows start on time downstairs in the smoke-free room and are finished around midnight—both attempts to draw a wider range of audiences. Its owners told *Willamette Week* that their goal was to make the club itself a destination "like Disneyland."

You might think you've walked into LoggerLand when you come into the ground-floor restaurant. Or maybe RetroLoungeLand. The walls and ceiling are a fancy-looking version of a log cabin, bulbous chrome fixtures drop amber light on Formica tables and round booths, and the colors are various shades of brown, from the two-tone padded chairs to the etchings on the ubiquitous mirrors. In the lounge area you'll find couches, padded ottomans, and a fireplace. It's Retro Maximo.

The menu is as classics-oriented as the décor. There's a Logger Breakfast of eggs, roasted rosemary potatoes, and various options for meats and breads. There are buttermilk and banana/hazelnut pancakes as well as French toast made with croissants and a touch of orange zest; all come with a choice of maple or blueberry syrup. Three Benedicts (ham, spinach, or smoked salmon) are served with a lime-chili hollandaise that has a nice little bite to it. Four scrambles are named for defunct local clubs. I had the smoked salmon hash and found it a little long on the new potatoes but still flavorful, with the salmon mashed up and creamy, mildly spiced with capers and red onions.

As for the feel of the place, I found the defining moment to be when the heavily tattooed (and entirely pleasant) bartender shut off the start of Lynyrd Skynyrd's "Freebird," put on some '70s funk instead, started flirting with a two-year-old boy to try to get him to eat, and served a (reputedly strong and expensive) Bloody Mary to a scruffy-looking, twitching dude in a flannel shirt sitting at the bar with a very attractive young woman. Somehow, everything about the Doug Fir was right there: the family eating a hearty breakfast, the pre-9 a.m. booze, the guy who may well have been with the band, the staff dancing on the line between rockin' and professional, and the whole place moving to a funky '70s groove.

Wait: Maybe a little on weekends. **Large groups:** More than six might be tough, but they do host events. **Coffee:** Stumptown. **Other drinks:** Cocktails, Stash Tea, Red Bull. **Feel-goods:** Many of the ingredients are local. **Health options:** Slim pickings here for vegetarians. **WiFi:** Yes.

EaT: An Oyster Bar

Weekend

New Portleans!

3808 N Williams (N/Inner) ~ 503-281-1222 ~ *eatoysterbar.com*

Sunday 9 a.m. to 2 p.m.

$14–$17 (Visa, MasterCard, no checks)

Loud, friendly, loose, and boozy—that's what a New Orleans brunch ought to be. So when I put out the EaT invite to the Crew and only three people said yes, I was worried. Had we, and Portland, lost the NOLA magic when Roux closed and when Acadia quit doing brunch?

I could feel the vibe forming when I realized they were all women whose names started with J: Juliet, Jean, and Jeanette. That has to mean something. Then we got to walk past the immense line at Tasty n Sons and sit right down in the big, spacious EaT. There was a jazz trio playing, just loud enough that you had to raise your voice a little, but you could still hear. Yep, startin' to feel it.

Our server came dancing over to say howdy and take drink orders, and we dug into the menu. It's about one-third food and two-thirds booze. Even their signature oysters, at brunch time, are bathed in lemon and alcohol: vodka with spicy red sauce; chili-infused bourbon; chili-infused tequila; beer with Tabasco. When ocean brine meets citrus, spice, and liquor, something good is bound to happen.

In fact, most of the vast media praise for EaT (the name is a compilation of the owners' names) has to do with the oysters, which come in throughout the week from local farms. Most of the complaints have to do with slow service. At brunch, the Crew's opinion was that oysters were beside the point, and slow service—even though we didn't have that problem—would have fit just fine. Remember: loud, friendly, loose, and boozy.

We were all about the eggs and protein, New Orleans style. Juliet got the Eggs Sardou, which is a poached egg on top of an artichoke heart filled with creamed spinach, all covered in hollandaise sauce. I went Shrimp and Grits with a spicy buttery Cajun sauce, and even had fun teasing the ladies with the heads of the shrimp; the server, still spinning, told me to play nice with the girls. Jean had the Hangtown Fry, which is actually a San Francisco dish, but who cares? It's an omelet with bacon and oysters, and at EaT the latter are fried in cornmeal and sitting on top. Jeanette, meanwhile, wanted a Po'Boy, which on our visit was done open-faced with soft-shell crab. If you don't know, the magic of a soft-shell crab is that you eat the whole thing, shell and all. Sadly, she couldn't bring herself to chomp down on the big bug on her sandwich, perhaps because she was lacking in the boozy part of the brunch equation.

Now, you want some Portland flavor? Apparently some of the band, Reggie Houston's Box of Chocolates, works at New Seasons! Can't get any more PDX than that. Sitting there watching all my friends meet each other, watching the NOLA-transplant server boogie around (and insist she's a shy mom during the week), listening to the jazz blow, with my belly full of shrimp and grits, I felt myself start driftin' down South for a spell.

Wait: Not much. **Large groups:** With notice. **Coffee:** Rotates. **Other drinks:** Sweet tea, cocktails galore. **Feel-goods:** Local oysters. **Health options:** Not much for vegetarians. **WiFi:** Yes.

Equinox

Weekend/New

More like a paradox: good place, short wait.
830 N Shaver (N/Inner) ~ 503-460-3333 ~ *equinoxrestaurantpdx.com*
Breakfast Friday through Sunday 9 a.m. to 2 p.m.
$12–$14 (all major cards, no checks)

Folks often ask me, "Why isn't so-n-so place in the book?"

Well, when I wrote the first edition of this book, I knew there was a place called Equinox, but somehow I had it in my head it was a coffee shop. Or it was so hippie-granola that I didn't want to go there. And therefore, Equinox just slipped through the cracks. Bottom line: I'm kind of an idiot sometimes.

So now I have a question: Why the hell is everybody waiting in line at Gravy when Equinox is less than a block away?

For one thing, Equinox has a fine patio, removed from the chaos of Mississippi Street and set off by brick walls and an iron gate. It also doesn't seem to have much of a wait. And it has the Breakfast Nook. Or Cave. Or Lair. The Crew and I called it all of these. It's a little . . . closet . . . off the main dining room where you can just barely pack seven people, and you can even close the curtains. This led to quite a few strikingly crude jokes.

Equinox was also, should you care about such things, built with recycled building materials, and they are a member of PGE's 100 percent renewable energy program. So says the website, which adds, "Equinox offers fresh, hand made seasonal cuisine. . . . Pacific Northwest ingredients inspire new dishes and amplify classic combinations. Ambitious, affordable menus bring the urbane and the rustic together on plates, in glasses, and on chairs."

I quote all that to emphasize the classy and serious part of Equinox, but it's also a young, family-friendly place with some pretty classic breakfast fare, often served with a little twist—and by a particularly young and attractive staff, I must say. (For the record, sweetie, it wasn't just me saying it!)

I had the Mississippi, which is grilled orange French toast with potatoes and bacon. See what I mean? It's French toast, but it's made with grilled orange bread. Elsewhere on the menu, you'll find the Breakfast Pillow, a puff pastry stuffed with roasted bell peppers, mushrooms and caramelized onions, topped with two poached eggs and guajillo-cheese sauce. There's also steak and eggs, smoked salmon hash, a Roasted Portobello Benedict, two egg sandwiches, and six scrambles and omelets.

I didn't get the impression any of us was blown away, and one person said she's had dinner there and often found the food to have too much going on, like they need to focus a little. That might be taken care of, because early in 2010, the owners closed their other place, the much-missed Belly Timber, and sent the staff over to Equinox to work there. That can only help.

I would share more details, but really, these Breakfast Crew gatherings are too damn much fun for "research." I'd recommend you try to lock yourself in a Breakfast Lair with my friends Shari and Jerry and the rest of the Crew and see what you remember of the food. I'd also recommend you not do what I did originally, which is fail to eat at Equinox.

Wait: Maybe a little. **Large groups:** Notice helps. **Coffee:** Stumptown. **Other drinks:** Espresso, fresh juice, Bloody Marys, and seasonal mimosas. **Feel-goods:** Local ingredients. **Health options:** Good veggie options. **WiFi:** No.

Everett Street Bistro

New/Classy

A casual hangout, Pearl style.
1140 NW Everett Street (Pearl) ~ 503-467-4990 ~ *everettstreetbistro.com*
Breakfast daily 8 a.m. to 3 p.m.
$12–$16 (Visa, MasterCard, no checks)

———————◆—•—◆———————

The four ladies were having quiche and enjoying the toddler who kept trying to get into the kitchen. The woman in the corner, in her matching workout suit, was groovin' to the Motown. A gray-haired gent was working on a crossword. The server was telling a woman about his pet rabbit and how much they both (he and the rabbit) like spinach.

I felt a little out of place in my flannel shirt, baseball cap, and jeans, but it sure was nice to be stylin' it up in the heart of the Pearl. And if the Pearl, that "upscale" development with the semiprecious name, has its own casual hangout, it's the Everett Street Bistro. It also fits that such a place would call itself, as the Bistro does, a "European style charcuterie." (I had to look that word up, and it means, very roughly, "a place that serves a lot of meat.")

I had always taken the place for a glorified coffee shop—then I got a menu with two dozen cocktails on it. So it's all about leisure at the Bistro.

The menu is full of options hovering around $10. There's Grand Marnier French Toast and a Dutch Baby, and you can also choose from two quiches (you *knew* this place would serve quiche, right?) with bacon-mascarpone or a daily special. Ten egg-based dishes assure your protein needs will be met, whether you're feeling light (a seasonal Caprese Scramble with tomatoes, mozzarella, and basil) or heavy (corned beef hash or a benedict with Nueske bacon and spinach on grilled baguette).

There's an amazing dessert case when you walk in, the place is lovely, and the crowd runs upward in both age and apparent income. From there, reviewers' opinions vary on the food, but none are very strong one way or another, though a lot of folks think the lunch and dinner menus are a little too pricy for what is served. In their defense, I can only imagine what the rent must be at the corner of Northwest 11th Avenue and Everett.

I chose the Crabcake Benedict with Spinach and Creole Hollandaise (a special), and took some satisfaction from it being served on *pain au levain*—even though I had no idea what *pain au levain* is. I was just happy to relax in my wicker chair in the bright, airy room, surrounded by the sophisticated black-and-white decor with chandelier-style lanterns on the walls, enjoying the company of my fellow Pearlites. I felt like I should go shopping afterward, or hit a gallery or something.

I've had better Benedicts, and paid less for them too. And I wouldn't always want to be the youngest and worst-dressed person in a place. But the food was just fine, and I did get to see the gray-haired gent flirt with the four ladies on his way out, and I laughed with the ladies at one of the server's jokes, and for a few moments I got to feel like a stylish Pearl District denizen, just passing a drizzly Wednesday morning with my Crabcake Benedict, wondering what the working folk are up to.

Wait: Maybe a little on weekends. **Large groups:** Not a great place for it. **Coffee:** Stumptown. **Other drinks:** Espresso, juice, and a huge variety of cocktails. **Feel-goods:** None that they brag about. **Health options:** Vegetarians could do okay here. **WiFi:** No.

Fat Albert's Breakfast Cafe

Old School

No nonsense, from them or you.
6668 SE Milwaukie (SE/Sellwood) ~ 503-872-9822
Weekdays 7 a.m. to 2 p.m., weekends 7 a.m. to 3 p.m.
$8–$12 (cash and checks only)

Nobody is going to kiss your ass at Fat Albert's. The staff will seat you, feed you, and move you out, professionally and efficiently. And you'll get only a single page of options to choose from; that's one way to keep both the kitchen and you moving right along. So sit down, eat, and then go do whatever it is you're supposed to be doing.

Another thing, as a sign will inform you as soon as you walk in: cash and checks only, and incomplete parties will *not* be seated.

So as you might sense, there can be an edge to the place, and sometimes there seems to be an "in" crowd that's treated better. Marginally. I think the signature dish is the egg-and-ham breakfast sandwich, which my friend Jeff once told me, while wiping off the excess moisture with a napkin, that it "went over the butter line." I loved it, but I'll probably die of a heart attack when I'm 50.

You could also be thinking, "Finally, a breakfast place that doesn't  try to be what it isn't, doesn't encourage people to surf on their laptops all day, doesn't try to break new ground in cuisine." Well, that's Fat Albert's, too.

Eggs, meat, potatoes, bread, and something sweet. That's the menu. Six omelets, pancakes, the sandwich, bottomless oatmeal, and biscuits and gravy. The omelets are straight to the point: one has good ol' ham and cheese; the Yuppie has sun-dried tomatoes, artichoke hearts, and feta;

Kim's Fave has avocado, cheddar, and bacon; the Salad Eater, with its spinach, tomatoes, onions, and mushrooms, is a nod to the veggie crowd.

I'm not much of a biscuits and gravy guy, but I can tell you that most reviews I've read don't consider them the café's strong point. The pancakes, however, are quite popular: big, fluffy, and a little crisp around the edges (of course). The maple syrup is nice and light; that's because, as the menu says, Fat Albert's uses "<u>real</u> maple syrup" and "<u>real</u> butter."

In fact, the menu also explains that it's policy to ask you to leave after you're done eating. You'll appreciate this when you're waiting in line for a table, but one online review recounted having fresh silverware placed in front of the reviewer along with the check! Every time I've been there, the food has arrived so quickly I'm always astonished.

Jeff and I had a quick work lunch there, and as we were leaving, I wasn't sure who was paying. We stood at the register, each with a $20 bill at the ready, and after we hesitated for about one breath, the server dinged open the register and said, "I know! Why don't you pay separately!" Then she rolled her eyes, took our money without another word, and went back to serving food and coffee.

We were briefly stunned, then remembered where we were, admitted she had a point, and hauled our full bellies back to our day.

Wait: Fairly long on weekends. **Large groups:** No. **Coffee:** House blend. **Other drinks:** Tea and juice. **Feel-goods:** None in particular. **Health options:** None in particular. **WiFi:** No.

Fat City Cafe

Mom & Pop/Old School

In a small town, a long, long time ago . . .
7820 SW Capitol Highway (SW/Outer) ~ 503-245-5457 ~ *fatcitycafe.net*
Daily 6:30 a.m. to 3 p.m.
$8–$11 (all major cards)

———————◆•◆———————

Here's how you do a breakfast with the fellas. You meet too damn early on a weekday, 'cause fellas have to work. On weekends, fellas have to sleep. You show up on time so you can give a load of crap to the guy who shows up late. You say something about not being awake until you've had your coffee. You order the same thing you always get. Any mention of an attempt at weight loss is completely understood and thoroughly ridiculed.

Most important, you don't go someplace that has candles on the tables, or *bistro* in the name, or Asiago cheese. You go to a place like Fat City Cafe.

Ponder the name for a moment: Fat City. Every time I've been there, the special on the chalkboard was some kind of sausage: Italian, Cajun, spicy, smoked. The spicy sausage is precisely that, and a guy can earn points for eating it without complaint. The menu includes omelets, scrambles, and sizzles, and the only difference is consistency

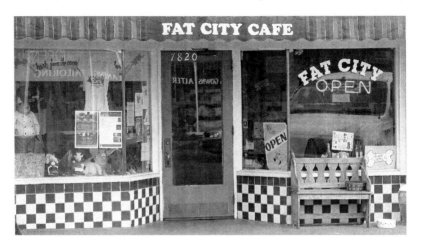

and egg-to-potato ratio. The bacon is crisp, the coffee never stops coming, and the servers work hard, do a great job, and take no slack.

I eat there with Bob, Phil, Al, and Mick, and one time I told the server that we don't hang out with guys who have two syllables in their names. I always get the Fat City Sizzle—a pile of hashbrowns, ham, green peppers, onions, and cheddar with two eggs on top that's so big it looks like it may have been served with a shovel.

The décor of the place is kind of a road theme, with old signs and license plates stuck up on the wall, plus seasonal decorations and Fat City T-shirts. The bathroom is pure American goofy: a super-narrow door between the counter (which is always filled with fellas) and the kitchen (don't look!), and once you're in you can't even take a step forward before you have to turn right for the barely-bigger-than-the-toilet room.

If the place looks like it's old and in a small town, it is. Multnomah Village dates to the 1910s, when a community sprang up around an Oregon Electric Railroad station. Today, the Village itself is much more of a natural lady habitat, with shops and bookstores and whatnot; it's often called quaint.

On your way back to your table, you might notice an *Oregonian* article on the wall: the account of the 1987 Fat City Firing, perhaps the ultimate breakfast with the fellas gone wrong. In this very booth, the mayor of Portland, Bud Clark, fired his police chief, Jim Davis.

I mean, where *else* would two fellas who needed to talk some stuff out go for breakfast? It wasn't the Alameda Ass-Kicking, was it? Or the Bread and Ink Bashing? Tin Shed Tanking?

Nope. It was the Fat City Firing. Mmmmmm.

Wait: Long on weekends, mostly outside. **Large groups:** Not at the same table. **Coffee:** Organic Cafeto Coffee. **Other drinks:** Tea, milkshakes, hot chocolate. **Feel-goods:** You don't have to eat the whole thing. **Health options:** Ditto. **WiFi:** Check back in 30 years.

Fenouil in the Pearl

Classy/Weekend/New

Gosh, look *at this place!*

900 NW 11th Ave. (Pearl) ~ 503-525-2225 ~ *fenouilinthepearl.com*

Brunch Sunday 9 a.m. to 2 p.m.

$15–$20 (all major cards)

————————•————————

First of all, if you're wondering, it's "fen-yu-wee." That's French for "fennel." And it's in the Pearl.

If you forget either of those critical elements, you will be reminded, often and not subtly. The space—that's what the foodies call it, a "space"—is massive, glamorous, and completely over the top. The impressiveness stretches from the overhead dining area and view of Jamison Square all the way to the saucer with a Fenouil logo on which your coffee cup rests, and the little silver dish with small serving spoon in which the salt and pepper reside.

Four of the Breakfast Crew showed up and felt like we needed to sit up straight and not say anything stupid. Jenny hoped we could keep the little jars of preserves, and when we wondered if the staff gives the leftovers to the Pearl District homeless, somebody made the "Let 'em eat preserves" joke.

Our tea bags were in little paper pyramids with a leaf sticking out the top of each! Jenny called them "little pieces of art," and we all marveled that they cost more than the coffee. We also didn't realize at first that the dish of "little rock things," as David put it, was the sugar. Seemed about right for a French place in the Pearl. (Did I mention Fenouil is French and in the Pearl?)

The food was outstanding, and we were all on our (mostly) best behavior. Each egg dish comes with a croissant (with or without chocolate) or weekly-special pastry (I had a marionberry-lemon-cream-cheese roll). All were tasty and fit perfectly on our little saucers, next to the logo. We also had fun watching David pick out just the right size rock thing to sweeten his coffee.

Elsewhere on the menu, you might get a wild mushroom omelet with Pierre Robert cheese, a smoked salmon hash, a black truffle egg scramble with sage, a duck confit hash with caramelized shallots and Taleggio cheese, seafood quiche, steak and eggs, and more than half a dozen lunch items. The steak was the priciest thing, at $15. We particularly enjoyed a $5 fruit plate with pineapple and melon pieces, even though we had to ask what "the stuff on it" was (turned

out to be *crème fraîche*). Just as this book was going to press, the kitchen saw some serious turnover, but these things should give you a general idea of what they're up to.

We felt all grown up, sampling the confit and the compote and Pierre Robert and not really knowing what any of it was. Duck and jam and cheese, we figured. I couldn't contain my sarcastic side, though, and busted out my best Jethro Bodine accent to announce that "this here *jambon grille* is good; tastes jes' lak grilled ham!"

The conversation inevitably led to the subject of gross displays of wealth, unnecessary fanciness, and what we'd do if we won the lottery. "Eat lots of jambon grille at this here French place" is what I said.

Wait: Reservations recommended. **Large groups:** Up to 12 with a reservation. **Coffee:** Stumptown. **Other drinks:** Steve Smith tea, cocktails. **Feel-goods:** All local vendors; Cascade Natural Beef, Carlton Farms bacon. **Health options:** None in particular. **WiFi:** *Oui!*

Fuller's Coffee Shop

Old School/Mom & Pop

Some call it old-fashioned.
136 NW 9th Ave. (Pearl) ~ 503-222-5608
Weekdays 6 a.m. to 3 p.m., Saturday 7 a.m. to 2 p.m., Sunday 8 a.m. to 2 p.m.
$9–11 (cash and checks only, but there's an ATM on-site)

———————————◆—•—◆———————————

A common misconception about Fuller's Coffee Shop is that it's in a place called the Pearl District. The folks at *pearldistrict.com* say Fuller's is "a reminder of when the Pearl District was into lifting heavy loads off the docks." But the Pearl District never did an ounce of heavy lifting; the name was created as a marketing tool in the 1990s when a warehouse-brewery district was being turned into a land of condos, art galleries, and boutique shopping.

Although Fuller's is geographically in the Pearl, it's really in the 1940s. And although there's nothing wrong with yoga and doggie day care, it sure is nice to have an old-style coffee shop around.

Perhaps I sound snide. I will miss the old warehouse district when it's totally gone, but I don't think of Fuller's as a reminder of times gone by. I think of it as a place where people eat breakfast, read the paper, sit close to one another, and have conversations. Somehow that has become quaint, which seems a shame. I'm just glad I can still do it.

Fuller's has all your old favorites: pigs-in-a-blanket, strawberry waffles (in season), great hashbrowns, crispy bacon, chicken-fried steak smothered in gravy, huevos rancheros, and that homemade bread sliced by a machine you can spot from the counter. Actually, you can spot the whole kitchen from the counter.

The prices, many of them written by hand on the menu, top out around $9. Newspapers are generally strewn on the counter, and on the walls are photos of the same place in 1955, back when it was at Union (now MLK) and Pine. It moved to 9th and Davis in 1960.

Michael Stern, of *roadfood.com* and *Eat Your Way Across the USA*, had Fuller's in his first book. Then he came back 10 years later and found that it hadn't changed at all! He even found a man at the counter who ate there 30 years ago and said it hasn't changed since then, either—other than the prices.

It's funny that people expect a place like Fuller's to change. Why should it? It's pretty simple, really: cook basic, good food; charge reasonable prices; treat people nicely; otherwise, stay out of the way and let folks be.

My friend Craig used to work with the homeless population downtown, and he loves Fuller's. I think it's because he sees the Pearl as a land of posers and Fuller's as a place where nobody's full of it and a guy living on the street can be welcomed. I don't see the Pearl so harshly, but to see Fuller's getting some notoriety for being old-timey is somewhat humorous.

After shaking hands with Craig on the sidewalk at 9th and Davis, with another condo tower rising behind the car repair place across the street and a stream of thirty-somethings walking their dogs by us, I can only rub my bacon-filled belly and hope the old way lives long into the future.

Wait: Medium-long on weekends. **Large groups:** If there's room at the counter. **Coffee:** Boyd's. **Other drinks:** Stash Tea, espresso. **Feel-goods:** Getting to know folks at the counter. **Health options:** Egg whites available. **WiFi:** Hardly.

Gateway Breakfast House

Mom & Pop

Family, regulars, piles of food, and a touch of goofy.
11411 NE Halsey St. (NE/Outer) ~ 503-256-6280
Monday through Saturday 6:30 a.m. to 3 p.m., Sunday 7 a.m. to 3 p.m.
$7–$10 (all major cards)

The defining moment of our trip to the Gateway Breakfast House was when Tom's pancakes arrived. Our table of friends let out a collective *wow* that was part awe, part humor, and part fear. Tom looked like he had walked into a pickup basketball game and found out he was guarding Shaquille O'Neal.

Diana said they were "pancakes you could sleep on," and when Tom cut somebody a portion, he said, "White meat or dark?" The server said that two or three times a year, one person eats the whole pancake order.

So, you get the idea. Very. Large. Portions. Seven of us each ordered something, we could have easily fed a dozen people, and the pre-tip bill was only $53. Gateway does breakfast the way James Michener writes books.

Gateway is cozy, crowded on weekends, and has a vibe that's part

homey-family and part, well, mildly odd. For example, the nice young women hustling food, the large wreath, and the painted skillets and washboards hanging on the wall all say down-home. Despite the long lines, the Gateway doesn't keep a seating list; it just sort of . . . works out.

You sit down to a cup of coffee in those truck-stop brown mugs and water in plastic cups. You read the menu and notice both hamburger steaks *and* hamburger patties (at which point you know you're not in for an exotic meal). The ribeye-and-three-egg platter is described as seasoned.

The building used to be a Chinese place and a doughnut shop (presumably not at the same time), so the architecture isn't much of a turn-on. The first description I heard, from my dedicated breakfast spotter, Linda, was "strange-looking place with a huge line." Hanging from the ceiling are about two dozen large, white orbs of different sizes, some of them lights, in a pattern that suggests a bizarro solar system or, as Leslie put it, "the molecular structure of fat." Her thought seemed reasonable when my pork-chop-and-eggs special arrived: two large pork chops, three eggs, a half-plate of hashbrowns, and two pieces of toast.

The size of these portions, I mean . . . consider the country breakfast. You get a pancake or French toast or a waffle or toast or biscuits and gravy. *And* you get two eggs, hashbrowns, and bacon or links. *And* you get a choice of one pork chop or ham or sausage or pastrami or chicken-fried steak. For, like, eight bucks.

Though we could hardly walk out, we had a good time; good friends, big portions, and cheap prices will do that. The world o' pancakes (my term), for example, was only $3.75 (single big pancake) and the two big pancakes are $4.75. The staff was friendly and attentive, and they volunteered to let us pay separately at the register. (Even our check was about four pages.) We saw kids and old folks and families and loners and regulars and everything, and now I know why they always have a line outside this place: they're nice folks, and they feed the hell out of you!

Wait: Maybe 30 minutes on weekends. **Large groups:** Sure, but send somebody early on weekends. **Coffee:** Boyd's. **Other drinks:** The usual. **Feel-goods:** Do the by-the-pound price comparison! **Health options:** Can't imagine. **WiFi:** No

Genies Cafe

New/Hip/Veggie

Look at what these kids are up to!

1101 SE Division St. (SE/Inner) ~ 503-445-9777

Daily 8 a.m. to 3 p.m.

$9–$14 (all major cards)

Years ago, when Genies opened, the *Oregonian* raved about how Genies uses all local ingredients, serves fancy cocktails, has a chef (a chef!), and a menu with smoked tomatoes, cremini and oyster mushrooms, artichoke hearts, and an Italian sausage frittata with nettles and fiddleheads. Genies also got a lot of press for the cocktails, including an Emergen-C Elixir (orange vodka, Emergen-C, muddled lemon, and a splash of cranberry juice) and a Bloody Mary made with jalapeño-infused vodka.

And I thought, "Really? At 11th and Division? What's going on in Southeast?" So I went to check it out—and was immediately turned away by a Tin Shed-level weekend line. Fortunately, Genies expanded soon after opening, adding a small espresso bar and an indoor waiting area, an idea I always thought somebody should act upon.

Then there's the space itself: large, open, and airy, but divided to somehow still feel private, and the choice of sitting in the sun or in a shady corner. The décor is clean and open, yet colorful with slight art nouveau touches. The staff and the vast majority of patrons are quite young; I was there once for a crowded Monday lunch and, at 40, was among the four oldest people in the building.

The menu is massive: five omelets, seven scrambles, five Benedicts, five "specialty egg dishes," three kinds of pancakes (buttermilk, huckleberry, white chocolate chip hazelnut), French toast made with house-baked brioche, more than a dozen sides, and rotating seasonal specials like a morel scramble with asparagus tips, or huckleberry pancakes. Goodness!

Here's a typical weekday visit: I take a table in the corner and immediately have a cup of strong coffee. I admire both the number and youthful energy of the staff and the other customers. After fighting through the menu, I force myself to rule out things like an omelet with locally grown button, cremini, and oyster mushrooms topped with shallots and chives. I settle on the Tasso Benedict featuring Cajun-style ham. For a $2 sweet treat, I toss in a single white-chocolate-chip-and-hazelnut pancake.

I see that on the table we are simultaneously old school (Heinz ketchup), local quirky (Secret Aardvark sauce), and artisan (house-made raspberry jam and orange marmalade). My big plate comes with two large portions of the Benedict and a heaping side of tender, flaky red potatoes seasoned with rosemary, thyme, and parsley. The ham had fat and just a little toughness and spice to it, the closest thing to Southern-style country ham I've found in Portland. Playing that against the thick, creamy hollandaise, clearing the palette with the occasional potato, I occasionally visit the massive pancake sitting nearby. It's just a little crunchy on the underside, giving it a nice snap to go with the chewy hazelnuts, fluffy cake, and fine sweetness of white chocolate.

By the end I realize, again, that I need to do two things immediately: get over my silly notions about Southeast Portland and get back to Genies more often.

Wait: Long on weekends, with uncovered benches outside but an espresso bar inside. **Large groups:** Absolutely. **Coffee:** Stumptown. **Other drinks:** Tao of Tea, espresso, beer, and a world of cocktails. **Feel-goods:** Everything is local, and much of it is organic. **Health options:** Plenty of vegetarian options, and both tofu (free) and egg whites. **WiFi:** Yes.

Golden Touch Family Restaurant

Old School

"It's just a family restaurant."
8124 SW Barbur Blvd. (SW/Inner) ~ 503-245-2007
Monday 6 a.m. to 3 p.m., Tuesday through Saturday 6 a.m. to 9 p.m.,
Sunday 6 a.m. to 7 p.m.
$8–$13 (Visa, MasterCard, no checks)

———————————◆•◆———————————

Let's say you have a favorite hike. It doesn't change from trip to trip, doesn't have great views, doesn't even give a great workout. You just . . . like it. So you keep doing it.

My friend Corky and his friend Sam have a favorite hike. It's in the Columbia River Gorge, the loop from Wahkeena Falls to Multnomah Falls. And almost every Sunday for about 30 years Corky and Sam have hiked that loop—after they've eaten at Golden Touch.

I eat breakfast with Corky often, and 90 percent of the time it's at what we affectionately call the Touch. This is largely because Corky lives nearby and is stubborn, but the Touch is one of my favorite places to eat. It's not about the food, though it is good. In fact, when I told the server that I was writing a book about breakfast places and was including the Golden Touch, she actually looked at me funny and said, "Really? *This* place?"

Yes, the Touch. And here's why: It's about the least pretentious place in the world, most of the staff has worked there forever and call it a "family restaurant," it has a million options on the menu, and you can get in and out in half an hour. Or you can sit there and shoot the breeze for hours.

Put it this way. A negative review on *citysearch.com*, while noting the quick and friendly service, said, "The decor suggests a scene from the mid '70s and the bacon flavor is cooked right into the paint and fixtures." To which I say, "Exactly!"

It's the kind of place where you can just tell the server what you want, and she'll say, "Sure, that's the [fill in the blank] with a couple changes, no problem." I like the honey wheat cakes special, which comes with a couple of eggs and four pieces of thick bacon (buttermilk, blueberry, and Swedish cakes are also available). Corky always gets a veggie omelet and fruit, and he likes to put Heinz 57 sauce on the omelet. After all these years he hardly needs to order; one time he was still cracking jokes and didn't even realize the server had written down his whole order and was looking at me, the two of us sharing an "Isn't Corky funny?" glance.

Sometimes we sit in one of the fancy round booths in the back room, which is straight out of a 1970s cafeteria. Nora, another fan of the Touch who I worked with at FedEx, said she always wanted to sit back there but thought you had to be special. I told her, "Shoot, next time just say you want to sit in the back," and that night at work she was glowing: "I sat in one of the fancy booths!" We talked for a while about how much we liked the Touch and how we felt special to sit in back, and it occurs to me now that I didn't even ask what she ate.

Who cares? It'd be like asking Corky how that loop to Multnomah Falls was. I know how it was. And next time, I want to go.

Wait: None. **Large groups:** Anything over 15 needs a reservation. **Coffee:** Farmer Brothers. **Other drinks:** Farmer Brothers tea. **Feelgoods:** "It's just a family restaurant." **Health options:** Egg substitute available. **WiFi:** No.

Gravy

New/Hip/Veggie

Once new-cool, now establishment-cool.
3957 N Mississippi Ave. (N/Inner) ~ 503-287-8800
Daily 7:30 a.m. to 3 p.m.
$10–$14 (all major cards)

———◆—•—◆———

I'm not sure when Gravy stopped being a place that was new and exciting just because of what and where it is.

It isn't that the place changed so much. It's still got that sort of relaxed vibe about it, which some folks call funky and others call slow. The menu still offers a wide variety of down-home style choices, often with locally raised, organic ingredients. It's still so miserably crowded on weekends that waiting outside for up to 45 minutes is an accepted part of the experience.

Gravy set up shop back in March 2004, when North Mississippi Street was just accelerating its fairly quick, and utterly inevitable, transformation from a neighborhood worried about abandoned homes and drug raids to one fighting over high-density housing and saving some diversity. You might say Gravy was to Mississippi sort of what Tin Shed was to Alberta. Suddenly on Mississippi there was a place with local organic ingredients, live piano music on weekends, modern art on the walls, a few tattoos on the staff, and food that is a kind of homage to old-school diners.

In fact, the main gripe about Gravy is that the food is just that: basic breakfast food, not too exciting but in ridiculous portions. Honestly, if you can knock back a full order of the Challah French Toast, I'd have you immediately tested for marijuana. When I do go to Gravy, it's often to get a hash or pork chops and eggs as a kind of long-term investment: eat breakfast and walk out with dinner!

Still, there is a lot to be said for variety, and Gravy certainly delivers: numerous scrambles, hashes, omelets, meat-and-egg combinations, and griddle specialties. And if that isn't enough, there's a large build-your-own omelet section with vegetarian and vegan options. Also, the meals don't come with just potatoes; you can add bacon, sausage, ham, fruit, hashbrowns, or pancakes.

In a sense it's almost too much, and one can feel a little overwhelmed. Certainly, the weekend crowds are insane, but even during the week you may feel like the tables are pushed awfully close together. It's not a place to visit if you're looking for peace, quiet, and personal space. Or if you're impatient; complaints about slow and spotty service have been around since Gravy opened. My take has always been that the staff is just as overwhelmed as we diners sometimes are.

The décor might make you think the place is still evolving, with its bare ceilings, exposed pipes, mismatched light fixtures, a facade in front of the kitchen, a side of wood panel with a tile section implanted acting as a podium, and an old sideboard near the kitchen.

But why should Gravy change? Even though you rarely hear it mentioned as one of the best places to eat breakfast in Portland, it's easily one of the most popular. I think it just quit being novel to people, sort of like Mississippi Street itself.

Wait: Legendary on weekends. Very small area for waiting inside, with self-serve coffee. **Large groups:** Maybe during the week, with some notice. **Coffee:** Cellar Door. **Other drinks:** Fresh orange juice, vegan Bloody Marys, full bar. **Feel-goods:** Many ingredients are local and organic. **Health options:** Egg substitutes or tofu available, and build-your-own omelets give plenty of options. Vegan cheese and sausage. **WiFi:** Yes.

Hands On Cafe

New/Classy/Mom & Pop

This is no student cafeteria!
8245 SW Barnes Road (SW/Inner) ~ 503-297-1480
Brunch on Sunday only, 9:30 a.m. to 1:30 p.m.
$13–$15 (cash and checks only)

Here's what I once thought I knew about the Hands On Cafe: it's the student cafeteria at the Oregon College of Art & Craft, and it's really nice up there. I admit that didn't overwhelm me, but at the time I was dating an artist, so I said, "Honey, let's go check out that place at the art school!" I had her at *art*.

We parked in a shaded lot and wandered down a path to a building in which we found an art gallery, a gift shop, and just the kind of "student cafeteria" you'd expect at an art school in the West Hills: a little fireplace, some art on the walls, jazz playing softly, flowers on the tables, and a room full of affluent-looking folks chatting amiably. It wasn't, in other words, the Mustang Cafe, which I used to haunt for chicken strips and pizza back at SMU.

The place must not be all that well-known, because we arrived at 10:15 on a Sunday morning and there was exactly one couple waiting for a table—who promptly informed us about the community table in the back corner near the wide-open kitchen. A moment later we were at that table, where we were instantly presented with a free plate of baked goodies, half a red grapefruit, and candied ginger. The other couple there told us the wait is never more than 15 minutes, and the server said that in the summer, when tables are set up under the trees, rhododendrons, and azaleas, "there's hardly ever a wait."

The staff, made up of students and the owner's family, was friendly, sweet, and efficient. While they got Jenny at *art*, they got me with grilled salmon cakes on corn, basil, and red peppers topped with poached eggs and hollandaise sauce. It was served with tomato, arugula, and avocado relish and roasted potatoes.

There are always four items on the menu—when you see the size of the kitchen, you'll know why—and one item is usually a pancake. When we visited, it was buttermilk cakes topped with winter fruit compote, crème anglaise, sweetened whipped cream, and toasted almonds. It came with scrambled eggs and a choice of sausage or bacon for $10.50. So you'll spend about $14 to eat at Hands On Cafe, but considering what all you get, it's a bargain. I'm told there's always a meat dish as well (often lamb or pork), and the one I had was out of this world: sautéed tenderloin on a roasted red pepper and tomato topped with pork demi-glaze sauce and served with two poached eggs, creamy polenta, shaved Parmesan, and greens with pancetta and mushrooms.

I ate every bit of it, then shamelessly swooped in on the rest of Jenny's pancakes. We made a joke about telling the server this should be the Hands Off Cafe, because I would have hurt anybody who tried to get those pancakes from me.

Wait: Maybe in winter, with a whole gift shop and gallery to explore. **Large groups:** Sure. **Coffee:** San Francisco Bay. **Other drinks:** Tea, juice, lemonade, iced coffee. **Feel-goods:** None that they tout. Supporting students, maybe? **Health options:** Ditto. **WiFi:** Yes.

Hash

New/Hip

Clean, simple, humble, and fresh.

8728 SE 17th Ave. (SE/Sellwood) ~ 503-239-3966 ~ *hashrestaurant.com*

Tuesday through Sunday 8 a.m. to 3 p.m.

$13–$15 (all major cards, no checks)

———————————————•————————————————

Okay, bear with me on this one.

Whenever somebody builds a new golf course, they first have to clear a huge swath of land. That means that, even with the added hills, sand traps, lakes, trees, and shrubs, a new golf course looks a little bland at first. An old golf expression is that new courses need to "grow in."

They mean the trees need to fill out, the grass needs to get lush, and the course needs to develop its own charms. Plus, you need to play it on windy days, sunny days, different times of year . . . build a relationship with it, as it were.

Well, Hash looks and feels like a place that needs to grow in a little. Even the positive press it has received makes it clear it's not a blow-your-mind place. Words like *simple* and *fresh* and *value* and *basic* are often used—as in, the small menu is filled with basic dishes done well, using local sustainable ingredients.

There are always four hashes, which change with the seasons. A typical set is mushroom, root veggie, corned beef, and chicken fried steak. Next are four house specialties: brioche French toast, braised bacon Benedict, biscuits and gravy, and *aebleskivers* (aka Danish pancakes). Three two-egg omelets—including a build-your-own option—round things out. See? Nice and simple.

I have had two different hashes (duck and artichoke) and liked them both. I might say I "only liked" them, but (a) they were very well cooked and fair portions for what I paid, and (b) the long lines at Hash tell me a lot of folks more than "like" it. Also, for the record, I personally like places that are either more down home, like a diner, or more . . . well, grown in. So you might read this, check the place out, have

a great meal, and tell me I'm full of crap. And I wouldn't argue with you on any of that.

My friends and I decided Hash looks like a big room in an art gallery, into which somebody has installed a restaurant. It has very tall ceilings—which look to be unfinished—lots of light, and plain walls with a smattering of modern art. A few plants thrown in here and there really *do* need to grow in a little. Hash feels airy and spacious, and while they do get credit for a low volume level, it also doesn't quite feel like a place you want to linger in. A small lending library of books is meant to take the edge off long weekend waits.

When folks ask what I think of Hash, I like to say, "Not much"—as in, I can't find much to get worked up about. It's a nice-looking place in a nice neighborhood, and I think they know how to run a restaurant. When it grows in a little, it'll be a Portland classic.

Wait: Varies. **Large groups:** Not great. **Coffee:** Courier. **Other drinks:** Jasmine Pearl tea, juice, hot chocolate. **Feel-goods:** Fresh, local, cage- and hormone-free ingredients, meat cured in house, and bread made in house. **Health options:** Not much for vegans. **WiFi:** No.

Hawthorne Street Cafe

New/Hip/Veggie

We can all agree: it's a happy place!
3354 SE Hawthorne Blvd. (SE/Hawthorne) ~ 503-235-8286
Daily 7:30 a.m. to 2:30 p.m.
$8–$12 (cash, checks, all major cards)

———————————◆•◆———————————

The Hawthorne Cafe has a happy vibe that's a pure dose of Hawthorne's much-stereotyped hippie scene. There's even a place above it called Moonshadow, "serving the Portland Pagan community since 1995" and the home of a local Druidic group.

The Hawthorne is in a creaky old house with sloped floors, a glass-enclosed porch, wood blinds on the numerous windows, homey red-and-white tablecloths, hanging plants, flower boxes, even paintings of flowers on the cheery yellow walls. So it's a happy place. And it's kind of a hippie place.

I'll tell you what it's like: it's like the Grateful Dead of the local breakfast scene. Even folks who like it would never describe it as particularly efficient. I was a huge fan of the Dead, too, and whenever people get going about the Dead, it's always the same conversation. One

group says, "Oh, I *loved* those guys!" Another group says, "God, they were hardly even proficient musicians!" And the majority of people just wonder, "What's the big deal about them, anyway?"

I always thought that the Dead was, at worst, a party band that didn't always succeed in knocking your socks off. If you were into what they were putting down, and if they got it right, there was magic in the air. And sometimes they weren't so good.

Sometimes they forgot their own lyrics. And occasionally the staff at the Hawthorne might forget your order.

So back to breakfast. Here's a typical batch of notes from a trip to the Hawthorne: "pear crepe super-tasty, warm, and sweet . . . smoked-sturgeon Benedict interesting but not great . . . turkey wrap has a little spice to it, nice . . . sign near bathroom for a class called Wicca 101 . . . staff friendly and cute, not too efficient . . . homemade marionberry coffee cake like a big ol' slab of goodness . . ."

See? Even somebody who's eaten breakfast in more than 100 places in town couldn't tell you if the Hawthorne is consistently good. For the record, I never made the argument that the Dead was a particularly good band, either—just that it was, and is, my all-time favorite. And a lot of folks feel that way about the Hawthorne Cafe, which explains why it's been open and popular for so long.

So the Hawthorne Cafe isn't a restaurant that gets consistently high marks—or consistently low ones, for that matter. But it is a relaxed, happy place where you can get lots of veggie options (but not many vegan ones), wheat or buttermilk or daily-special pancakes, French toast, seven omelets, and a couple of Benedicts. You can also get some classic hippie-type fare like a bowl of granola with yogurt and fruit; a high-protein breakfast with oatmeal, 2% milk, peanut butter, yogurt, and fruit; and the Country Pancakes: walnut wheat cakes layered with peanut butter and topped with bananas, raisins, and hot syrup.

Looking for an amazing, life-changing performance every time? Skip the Hawthorne. And the Dead. Looking for a relaxed, friendly scene that does the basics pretty well, has fun, and doesn't take itself seriously? I recommend both.

Wait: Fairly long on weekends. **Large groups:** Yes. **Coffee:** Kobos. **Other drinks:** Espresso, fresh OJ, Stash Tea, plus house blend of fine quality tea. **Feel-goods:** A certain Pagan vibe, if you're into that. **Health options:** Egg substitute available and several vegetarian options. **WiFi:** No.

Helser's

Hip/New
Open, spacious, simple, casually elegant.
1538 NE Alberta (NE/Alberta) ~ 503-281-1477 ~ *helsersonalberta.com*
Daily 7 a.m. to 3 p.m.
$10–$15 with $4.95 portions available before 9 a.m. on weekdays (Visa, MasterCard)

I went to Helser's once when I had been driving around Oregon for days, hosting a friend from Switzerland, staying in fancy hotels, and eating rich food. I was ready to settle back into my Portland routine and calm down, eat something simple and tasty. Manuela was still looking for a place to eat breakfast in America where she could get only what she wanted—pancakes and fruit—and not leave a meal's worth of food behind. She said it made her feel guilty.

So we walked into Helser's, and I got the Yukon gold potato hash, lightly seasoned, with poached eggs. Manuela asked about the pancakes, was told there were four to an order, asked if she could have only two, the server said absolutely, and she got a side of yogurt and fruit. Ate the whole thing. We spent $10 each. Perfect.

Another time I went to Helser's when I was heading out for a hike, and I wanted something filling but not too much so. I was there before 9 a.m. and got the single portion of ham Benedict—the fish moist and the sauce creamy. I paid $4.95 for it and didn't eat a thing during the hike. Perfect.

Another time I just wanted to feed my sweet tooth, so I walked over and got the full portion of the brioche French toast, sliced thick and soaked in vanilla cinnamon batter. I walked out with a little buzz working. Perfect.

The feel at Helser's is very simple, in a good way. It's borderline Zen. Wood tables, comfortably spaced from one another. Wood chairs that are wide and comfortable. Tall ceilings. Plenty of windows and light. A few flowers on the table. Some bamboo. Beige walls. Servers wearing black. Simple light fixtures. Soft jazz playing.

The menu hits many classic breakfast themes: Dutch Baby, Scotch Eggs, three kinds of sausage, Russet potato pancakes, *and* Yukon gold hash, mushroom hash, pepper bacon hash, three Benedicts, and New York steak and eggs. (Any of these may rotate off the menu, by the way.)

I'm biased, because I used to live about five blocks away and had a crush on pretty much the entire wait staff. Consider that your disclaimer. All I know is that every time I go to Helser's, I'm in the mood for something in particular, and they always have it.

Here's perhaps the ultimate feedback: In 2010 I was approached by a guy named Rick Sebak, who was working on a PBS documentary called *Breakfast Special*. He had found this book online and wanted to know a couple places in Portland he should visit to see what our scene was all about. I said go up to Alberta Street and check out the Tin Shed and Helser's.

He fell in love with the Scotch Egg and Dutch Baby, blogged about how passionate Portland is about breakfast, and when it came time for his crew to follow me down to tape my breakfast radio show, they decided instead to stay at Helser's.

Can't say I blame 'em. It's perfect.

Wait: Up to 30 minutes on weekends. **Large groups:** Yes, but might be a while. **Coffee:** Kobos, with French press available. **Other drinks:** Kobos loose-leaf teas, espresso, mimosas. **Feel-goods:** Local meats; pure maple syrup for $1.25 extra. **Health options:** Egg whites and meatless options for no charge. **Wi-Fi:** No.

Hollywood Burger Bar

Mom & Pop/Old School

Just grabbin' a bite before I head into town.
4211 NE Sandy Blvd. (NE/Hollywood) ~ 503-288-8965 ~
hollywoodburgerbar.com
Breakfast weekdays 7 to 11 a.m., weekends 8 a.m. to noon
$6–12 (all major cards, checks)

I sat on the little spin-around counter seat at the Hollywood Burger Bar—there's a counter and about three tables, total—and my knees hit the wall underneath. But since I was about to eat breakfast for around six bucks, I didn't complain. What I thought was, "I bet this place has been here a long time." Folks used to be shorter, you see.

So I asked the guy behind the counter, who was already pouring a big mug of strong coffee, and he said, "We've been here since the early '90s." Then he added, "It's been the Burger Bar since 1954. The place was built in the '20s, been serving food since the '30s. Before that it was a dry cleaner. Before that it was a trolley stop."

A trolley stop! It all came together for me. The small seats. The tiny kitchen. The church bells I heard as I walked in. The pure simplicity of the menu. This used to be the hub of a little community.

Turns out two trolley lines ended here: the one that came out Sandy and the one that came up 39th. Back then, when Sandy was Highway 30 heading out toward the Columbia Gorge, what we now call the Hollywood District (named for the theater, which was built in the '20s) was a little village on the edge of civilization, and folks would come in here to get a cup of coffee and a paper before hopping on the trolley to go into Portland.

Look around the neighborhood: Sam's Hollywood Billiards has been there since 1962, Pal's Shanty since 1937, the Pagoda and the Mandarin since the '40s, Sylvia's since 1957, St. Michael's church since 1910, Paulsen's Pharmacy since 1918 (and they have an old-style soda fountain, too)!

That morning at the Burger Bar's counter, there was a woman keeping a journal, a young guy waking up and stretching, an elderly couple being taken out by their daughter, and a man and woman talking religion and politics. Three bus lines run by the door, and I wondered how much had really changed.

But perhaps you're wondering about the food. Well, I can tell you this: for me, it's all about the bacon. I don't put a lot of energy into being a food critic, since I'm no good at it, and besides, I have never noticed any correspondence between my tastes and a place's popularity. But I do like bacon. And I like it just so: crispy, but not so much that it snaps in my hand, lean, tasty, with some spice, but not chunks of black pepper—all this, and it should be shamelessly greasy.

In my world, the Burger Bar's bacon is perfect, and it has a nice story behind it.

See, the owner got his meats from a company that got bought out by Sysco, and the whole thing went south. So he started shopping around. "Turns out," he told me, "one of the guys we were looking at lives five blocks away from us, and that was pretty much it."

Perfect bacon, from the guy down the street, in an old trolley stop surrounded by longtime friends and neighbors. I love the Burger Bar.

Wait: Maybe on weekends. **Large groups:** No chance. **Coffee:** Boyd's. **Other drinks:** Juice, tea, and there're RC Cola signs all over the place; need I say more? **Feel-goods:** You can see how clean the dishes are, because you're basically sitting on the dishwasher. **Health options:** Veggie burgers at lunchtime—and is RC healthy? **WiFi:** Hardly.

Original Hotcake & Steak House

Old School

Family by day, circus by night.
1002 SE Powell (SE/Inner) ~ 503-236-7402
Breakfast served 24 hours
$7–$12 (Visa, MasterCard)

Saturday, 1:15 a.m. I haven't seen 1:15 a.m. since I quit drinking. I stumble out of the Crystal Ballroom, dazed. It's finally time to go to the Hotcake House. Some things have to be seen in the middle of the night.

I pull into the lot, see a few bikers, and watch as a drunk couple staggers to a car . . . and doesn't drive off. Well.

My God, there's a line! I get in line and look around: prom kids. Another drunk couple; she's draped over him, asking if he remembers their first date. Zombie-looking dudes are coming out of the kitchen with steak and eggs, massive stacks of hotcakes, and piles of hashbrowns . . . at 1:30? Black-clad teen boys in a booth. A guy at a table telling two women about somebody screwin' him over. Every now and then he gets a little loud and profane, and the place goes quiet.

Are those three girls at the head of the line *still* ordering? I've been here 10 minutes already. My ears hurt.

There's a woman next to me in line, and an old guy ahead of us waves at me, points at me, then points at her, then *licks his lips*. She and I exchange a nervous glance.

The cashier is giving the three chicks a dumbfounded look. She isn't getting one word of whatever they're saying. I just realized one of the guys in a tux with a horrible red tie is not a guy.

It's now 1:35. I do some math: At 2:15 I'm either gonna be here, waiting for my food . . . or in bed after taking a shower. I bail. On the car radio, Tom Petty is singing "Breakdown," and I realize I shouldn't be awake at this hour.

■ ■ ■

Thursday, 9:30 a.m. I walk in and go right up to the counter, where the specials, on sticky notes, are cinnamon rolls, Polish sausage, biscuits and gravy, and smoked pork chops. The menu, on a board under "Peter and Cheree Welcome You to the Hotcake House," is a tour of Americana: steaks, eggs, ham, bacon, sausage, beef patties, country-fried steak, waffles, hotcakes, mined ham and eggs, corned beef

hash. Pretty much everything is under $10. For $9, you can get three eggs with your choice of meat or corned beef hash *and* two cakes or hashbrowns or toast!

I order the blueberry waffle ($6.75), get some coffee, and grab a seat in a booth next to a guy who's singing along with Jimi Hendrix on the jukebox while playing Here Comes the Airplane to get his little daughter to eat. I see folks involved in friendly, multi-table conversations and pictures of the Little League teams the place sponsors, and it occurs to me that this is one of the few Portland places where I've seen blacks and whites eating breakfast together. The cashier is wearing a gray ponytail and tie-dyed bellbottoms.

I decide that I prefer the Hotcake House's friendly daytime persona a lot better than the crazy evenings, and I dig in.

Wait: Up to half an hour from about 10 p.m. to 3 a.m. on weekends. **Large groups:** During the day, sure. **Coffee:** Self-serve Farmer Brothers. **Other drinks:** Juice, milk, soda. **Feel-goods:** Does the security guard count? **Health options:** Eat here during the day. **WiFi:** No.

Hungry Tiger Too

Hip/Veggie

It's vegan and *greasy spoon!*
207 SE 12th Ave. (SE/Inner) ~ 503-238-4321 ~ *myspace.com/hungrytigertoo*
Weekdays 11 a.m. to 2 a.m., Saturday 9 a.m. to 2 a.m., Sunday 9 a.m.
to 10 p.m.
$9–$12 (all major cards, no checks)

———————◆·◆———————

Generally, when I venture into the foreign (to me, anyway) world of vegan dining, I defer to the local experts. So when I started up my podcast, I invited Jess and Webly from *stumptownvegans.com* to come on and tell me about vegan breakfast. And the first place they mentioned was Hungry Tiger Too.

First, the name. There was a dive bar called Hungry Tiger at East Burnside and 28th, but then it closed and this one opened. By all accounts it's a cleaner establishment. I can't comment on the *Too* spelling. The new location is in the vegan hub of Portland, right up the street from the little vegan strip mall of Sweetpea Baking Company (see page 244), Herbivore Clothing, and Food Fight Grocery.

But that scene down there seems all clean and healthy. When I walked into Hungry Tiger Too, I figured I was in the wrong place. The entrance is through a bar. I confess to a certain stereotyping about vegans, and when I came to Hungry Tiger Too, I remembered they *drink* too. And they eat greasy-spoon food at all hours (breakfast is served at the bar until 2 a.m. Monday through Saturday). And, in this case anyway, they're super-hip and down-home. It's a casual, comfortable place, with funky art all over the walls, and in the rare case that there's a long line, there is a bar to wait in—which was showing animated porn when I was there, by the way. Just sayin'.

To be clear: it's not all vegan here. There are two menus, so get the one that appeals to you. The classic menu has something for everybody. All breakfasts come with either "1 giant pancake" or hash browns and toast—or you can sub in a house-made biscuit with country sausage gravy. Or veggie gravy. See? Options abound. A Classic Breakfast is all of these options with two or three eggs for around $5, and for another $2 you can add meat or veggie sausage or bacon. And for $8.75 you can get the Tiger's Feast: three eggs, bacon, *and* sausage.

Omelets and scrambles are made with three to six eggs, and come as Veggie, Tiger (lots of meat) and Spanish—all for less than $10. Or you can just build your own.

Now, go through all of that and turn all the eggs into tofu, make the gravy vegan, make to bacon out of tempeh, throw in some nutritional yeast, and you've got the vegan menu.

A big part of HT2's appeal is the vegan corn dogs, which are $1.25 each on Wednesday evenings. Many, many of these are washed down with $1 Pabst Blue Ribbon in what can only be called a Portland Orgy. They get high marks for cocktails, as well, particularly the Bloody Mary.

I guess the bottom line is that for a lot of folks, and in particular vegetarians and vegans, Hungry Tiger Too is just a relaxed, friendly, semi-hungover place with cheap, down-home food. It's as far from fancy as you can get, and that seems to be exactly how folks like it.

Wait: Maybe a little, but inside. **Large groups:** With notice. **Coffee:** Boyd's. **Other drinks:** Tea, juice, soda, and a whole bar. **Feel-goods:** None they brag about. **Health options:** It's vegan heaven. **WiFi:** Only in the dining room.

Industrial Cafe and Saloon

Weekend/Old School

A quiet place with loud fans.
2572 NW Vaughn St. (NW) ~ 503-227-7002
Weekends 8 a.m. to 3 p.m.
$12–$14 (Visa, MasterCard, no checks)

————————◆•◆————————

There seems to be a small number of people who absolutely adore this place, and a whole mess of us who've never heard of it.

I say "us" for the latter, because I've lived in Northwest Portland for years and I only ate at Industrial when a friend thoroughly berated me for not having it in the book. Truth is, I didn't know it was there for a while, and then the name turned me off. Then I kept reading newspaper and magazine stories saying it had some of the best biscuits and gravy in town, and if you want my attention, saying "gravy" is generally a good start.

It sure doesn't look industrial from the outside, but it's right on the edge of the part of town called Northwest Industrial District. Across the street you'll find Schmeer Sheet Metal Works and Reed Electric. Not far away are sprawling rail yards. And the outside of the cafe fits the name a little, with its tin walls and metal outdoor tables.

But the real "industrial" theme is on the inside. There's a big tangle of pipes and valves, an eagle painted on a saw, various pieces of metal all over the place, even some of those metal hand puzzles sitting on the counter. The real fun is in the men's room, where the pipes for the urinal are exposed, so when you flush you can see the pressure drop and then build back up. They even added a red light and green light to show when water is flowing or not.

The food, even according to its biggest fans, is straight-ahead, American diner chow—and lots of it. The best known breakfast dishes seem to be the biscuits and gravy—the super-firm biscuits are called "gears" and shaped like that—and the chipped beef on sourdough toast, which a glowing *Oregonian* review called "pristine, tender slices of organic beef doused in rich cream sauce, with paprika giving a dash of spice." Since the biscuits also come slathered in cream gravy, I think we can detect a pattern.

The rest of the menu is as down-home as their two signature dishes: steak and eggs, spicy Italian sausage scramble, hash, ham and cheese omelet, veggie omelet, breakfast burrito, etc. And other than the steak and eggs ($15), everything is $9.50 or less. On the sweets menu, there are a couple of things that seem a little out of the ordinary: the Industrial Toast is French toast with candied hazelnuts and orange honey butter, and Gingerbread Pancakes are topped with house-made lemon curd.

I've never seen it more than three-fourths full, so I think the Industrial fits a very welcome niche in the Northwest Portland food scene. It's got outdoor seating like Meriwether's, without the prices—and down-home food like the Stepping Stone, without the lines. And if the food happens to turn you on, you can be on the short list of this place's ardent fans.

Wait: Hardly ever. **Large groups:** Decent option, and they take reservations for six or more. **Coffee:** Kobos. **Other drinks:** Juice, beer, wine, and cocktails. **Feel-goods:** None they tout. **Health options:** A few things for vegetarians. **WiFi:** No.

Isabel

New

Sleek, healthy, and a little out of place?
330 NW 10th Ave. (Pearl) ~ 503-222-4333 ~
isabelscantina.com/isabel-pearl.php
Breakfast daily 8 a.m. to 3 p.m.
$9–15 (all major cards)

————————◆•◆————————

The first person who told me about Isabel was my friend Wendy. She's very attractive, extremely fit and healthy, ambitious, upbeat, and all-around striking.

She is also, it seems, always about to leave Portland. It's not her kind of town. She is a big-city gal, and I'll be amazed if she's not living in Seattle soon, dating a rich, good-looking corporate guy who can take her on fabulous trips all over the world and generally keep up with her.

Well, as I so often say, what the hell does this have to do with breakfast in Portland? Not much, except the fact that Wendy told me about Isabel should tell you something about the place. It is not quite like other breakfast places in town, and I'm not sure exactly how it fits here.

Isabel is a chain, with locations in Ashland and southern California. And according to their website, "Chef and cookbook author Isabel Cruz (has a) trademark blend of Puerto Rican, Cuban, Mexican, Japanese, and Thai cooking." So that's ambitious.

When I walked into the "stunning" location (so says the website), I thought maybe they were still working on it. There's a lot of exposed concrete, virtually no art hanging, big vents visible along the ceiling, and huge metal wheels along the walls. But those turned out to be for opening the massive, floor-to-ceiling windows, which I bet makes it nice in the summer. Wendy said she really liked the décor because it had a modern, Euro feel to it. It felt a little cold to me at first, but it's improved since opening.

I ordered the artichoke scramble and a blackberry pancake. Wendy, just in from 24 Hour Fitness, ordered something from the Power Menu, which is half a dozen things like egg-white scrambles and various combinations of grilled chicken, black beans, and brown rice.

Since I have become accustomed to heavier, probably less healthy breakfasts, I was initially underwhelmed, though the food was clearly cooked right and with fresh ingredients. I thought the scramble was too long on artichokes and otherwise short on seasoning, but the rosemary potatoes were good: mashed up, then grilled so there were little crispy bits throughout. The blackberry pancake was tasty, but not among the top 10 pancakes in town. I did enjoy some *chilaquiles* there on a subsequent visit.

Among the 23 breakfast dishes, there's a wide variety: coconut French toast with "a palette of raspberry puree," various pancakes (blackberry, banana-blackberry, peanut butter-banana-chocolate chip), roast beef hash, burrito, quesadilla, coconut granola, oatmeal, fruit cup, etc.

There's another advantage, if you will, to Isabel: hardly anybody seems to go there. I've been twice and ridden the streetcar past it many times, and I've never seen it even half full.

In fact, Wendy and I were talking about the Pearl District and might as well have been talking about Isabel. We agreed that we liked the idea, and also that parts of the Pearl still look like they were built in anticipation of something happening . . . which hasn't happened yet. As she put it, "I look around and see the buildings and the shops and the restaurants . . . but where *is* everybody?" Like I said, Wendy is, no doubt, leaving soon for someplace more happening.

I hope that Isabel doesn't follow her out of town.

Wait: Little to none. **Large groups:** With some notice. **Coffee:** Stumptown. **Other drinks:** Juice, espresso, cocktails, iced juice-teas, Mexican mocha and hot chocolate, Thai coffee. **Feel-goods:** Organic ingredients. **Health Options:** Tofu and egg whites available **WiFi:** Yes.

J&M Cafe

New/Classy/Veggie

A place where you can take your parents—and pay!

537 SE Ash St. (SE/Inner) ~ 503-230-0463

Weekdays 7:30 a.m. to 2 p.m., full breakfast until 11:30 plus some limited breakfast offerings until close; weekends 8 a.m. to 2 p.m., breakfast all day

$8–$12 (Cash and checks only, but there's an ATM in the lobby)

———————————————◆•◆———————————————

When my parents travel, they pick their restaurants from *Gourmet* and the *New York Times*. But my freelance-writer income is a bit more Beaterville than Morton's. Hence, I keep the List of Places I Want My Parents to Take Me to When They Visit.

There are two other lists. One is the Places My Parents Wouldn't Go to in a Million Years: Fuller's Coffee Shop, Tosis, Johnny B's, and so on. And then there's the list J&M Cafe is on: Places I Would Take My Parents To. To get on this list, a restaurant has to be clean, comfortable, serve good and interesting food, not cost too much, exhibit some class, and yet include a touch of what makes Portland the great, goofy city it is.

Here's the case for the J&M: It's in an industrial neighborhood, within eyeshot of empty buildings, a rehab center, and busy, grimy Grand Avenue. But as soon as you walk in, you see high ceilings, wood floors, big windows, brick walls . . . and a restaurant design that could easily offer the most stylish of foods. Nonthreatening modern art

(just my parents' style) hangs on the wall, there's plenty of space between tables, and the clientele includes lots of families and young people.

And then there are the small-town Portland touches: self-serve coffee (Stumptown, of course) from an oddball collection of mugs hanging on a metal vine, water served in Mason jars, an old-world wood-fronted refrigerator, the restroom keys on a burger and a lizard, butcher paper and crayons on the tables.

J&M's food is a step above your basic breakfast place. One time my special was a scramble with black forest ham, shallots, zucchini, cherry tomatoes, fontina, and spinach pesto. The texture was perfect, and the pesto had just the right amount of zing. Another special had roasted eggplant, pine nuts, green onions, fontina, and fresh artichoke salsa. A regular item is a tofu, garlic, spinach, and feta scramble.

Even J&M's take on the basics has a classy twist. The J&M Plate has natural bacon with basted eggs, fontina, cheddar, and Parmesan on a toasted English muffin. The Belgian Cornmeal Waffle is made with cornmeal and is delightfully light.

The wait staff shows up, treats you well, takes your order, comes back with food, and otherwise pretty much leaves you alone. I've seen some online reviews that consider such service unfriendly, but I think of it as, "You have your food, coffee and water are self-serve, and if you need anything, we're right here."

Somehow, the basted egg captured the whole thing for me. The J&M could have just poached it or fried it, but instead they did something that was simultaneously unique, effective, and healthy. Sipping my excellent, local coffee and looking around at all my nice fellow citizens enjoying a relaxed, tasty meal in pleasant surroundings, I kind of felt proud of Portland.

Wait: Up to 20 minutes on weekends; there are a few padded benches to wait on inside, no shelter outside. **Large groups:** Yes. **Coffee:** Stumptown. **Other drinks:** Foxfire Tea. **Feel-goods:** Local, natural meats; wild-caught Pacific salmon; homemade granola. **Health options:** Some veggie options, and tofu can be subbed for eggs. **WiFi:** No.

Jam on Hawthorne

New/Hip/Veggie

Clean, simple, basic, and sweet.

2239 SE Hawthorne Blvd. (SE/Hawthorne) ~ 503-234-4790

Daily 7:30 a.m. to 3 p.m.

$8–$12 (all major cards)

For the first edition of this book, I wrote a rather tortured comparison of Jam to Billy Joel, concluding that their lemon ricotta pancakes are, metaphorically, their "Piano Man." I'll spare you the rest.

The little corner of Southeast Hawthorne and 23rd Avenue has been a breakfast destination for years; Cafe Lena was the previous inhabitant, and Jam fits in the same groove. It's a place that locals walk to, even if folks from other parts of town might not know exactly where it is. To them it may be "the little place across from Grand Central Bakery and that produce place (Uncle Paul's)." This means the lines aren't too bad. Jam's colors are bright, the staff is young and cheerful, and it's a relaxed place and cozy, with just six booths and eight tables.

Jam leads with its signature namesake spreads, which are on the table before you order. Even disparaging reviews of the place say things like, "Don't go unless you just really like homemade jams." The *Portland Mercury* called them "spectacular," and the seasonal flavors I've seen include blueberry, strawberry-mango, and pear chai.

The other sweet signature dish is the lemon ricotta pancake, which the *Oregonian* showcased in a pancake special feature: "With a drizzle of warm blueberry sauce, these 'cakes sound more like a haute dessert than a flapjack breakfast. But the citrus hit is subtle, the mild ricotta lends body to the batter and the house-made topping is vibrant with fruit. A sweet way to start your day."

For me, the rest of Jam's food doesn't live up—which isn't saying much. The pancakes are among my favorite things in town. The biscuits, though freshly baked, weren't too exciting; the salmon scramble and the hash seemed a little dry; and my chair was a little goofy. But the coffee was good, the service nice, the atmosphere relaxed, and the prices downright reasonable, so the Crew and I weren't upset. We walked away saying things like, "Well, it wasn't the greatest breakfast ever, but I liked it." Besides, I'm a sucker for sweets, although I wasn't quite up to the Cinnamon Sugar French Toast or the wheat-free Vegan Oatmeal Blueberry Chai Pancake.

Jam also gets a stamp of approval from the veggie crowd. An Internet blog called Stumptown Vegans said Jam "know(s) what vegan is" and gave them credit for stocking Odwalla juices (plus a full bar with breakfast cocktails), local produce from Uncle Paul's, and soy margarine (I wasn't aware it existed). Indeed, the veggie options do seem more interesting than most, including the much-appreciated build-your-own option. I also give credit for hashbrowns that are crispier and less greasy than many and how the Stumptown coffee is brewed: strong and smooth.

Jam has a lot of options and doesn't try to do too much. Being friendly and healthy, getting produce from the stand across the street, and having two or three items that really stand out are enough to make it a nice little place for breakfast.

Wait: Can be bad on weekends. **Large groups:** Up to six not a problem if it's not busy. **Coffee:** Stumptown. **Other drinks:** Tea, Odwalla, cocktails. **Feel-goods:** Produce from the place across the street. **Health options:** Good variety for vegans and vegetarians. **WiFi:** Yes.

Joe's Cellar

Old School

Victim-to-be of Pearl expansion?

1332 NW 21st. Ave. (NW) ~ 503-223-2851 ~ *joescellarcafe.com*
Monday through Saturday 7 a.m. to 7 p.m., Sunday 8 a.m. to 7 p.m.
Breakfast served until 2 p.m. in the café and until 7 p.m. in the bar.
$8–$11 (Visa, MasterCard)

———————◆—●—◆———————

Sitting in front of me was a pile of bright yellow, eggy French toast and two pieces of limp, thick bacon on a sturdy, white oval plate; butter in a paper cup; and coffee in a white mug. Across the room the server was working on a crossword puzzle. It was 8:15 a.m. on a rainy Wednesday, and we were the only two people in the place.

I looked across the empty street and saw an abandoned building. There was a single shoe on the sidewalk. "What was that place?" I asked.

"An old truck company," the server said. "It's been closed a long time. Now they say it's gonna be part of the Pearl District."

Now, Joe's Cellar is at the corner of Northwest 21st Avenue and Overton Street—quite a few blocks from the Pearl. But she wasn't confused on geography.

"Condos, huh?"

"Yep."

"Well, won't that be good for this place?"

She shrugged. "For a while. We'll get some of the construction workers."

At that moment I realized I was eating an $8 full breakfast on the edge of a cultural divide. Or maybe at the end of an era. Either way, Joe's may be the last of its breed in Northwest Portland.

Funny thing is, it wasn't even always here. Joe's is actually three buildings that were down by Union Station and were moved back in the '30s or so, then crammed together into the semi-landmark it is today. It's been a restaurant since 1941, and the upstairs (which the server says used to be, of course, a brothel) is now condemned.

Here's a funny note about the place: a goofy crowd that uses instruments to look for ghosts came to Joe's, found several "conscious entities," and arrived at a common conclusion: "The biscuits and gravy are to die for."

My server took me on a tour. We left the quiet café for a smaller back room with video poker, then went through another door—and into a completely different world. A whole *bar* was back there, with AC/DC cranking, conversation rolling, and about 25 people scattered around—at 8:30 in the morning! Apparently there's a happy hour from 7 to 11 a.m. for (one would hope) folks getting off the graveyard shift, and the reputation is that it's a friendly place with stiff drinks.

The prices in the café are decidedly not stiff. The special is likely to be an egg, a piece of sausage or bacon, and a pancake for $3.50, or a sausage and cheese omelet with potatoes and toast for $5.95. There's not much of that left in Northwest Portland.

While I was finishing breakfast, a nice car pulled up and a stylish lady wearing a leather jacket got out. The server and I both watched quietly as she went across 21st Avenue. I went back to my bacon and wondered if she knows about the ghosts at Joe's.

Wait: None. **Large groups:** No. **Coffee:** Farmer Brothers. **Other drinks:** Hot cocoa, sodas, Bigelow tea, and one of those Sunshine milk dispensers. **Feel-goods:** They'll probably remember your name. **Health options:** Low-carb items on the menu, cottage cheese and fruit substitutes for starches, vegetarian specials. **WiFi:** No chance.

John Street Café

Mom & Pop/Old School

Come out and eat in our backyard!
8338 N Lombard (N/Outer) ~ 503-247-1066
Breakfast Wednesday through Friday, 7 to 11 a.m., Saturday 7:30 a.m.
to noon, and Sunday 7:30 a.m. to 2:30 p.m.
$8–$12 (Visa, MasterCard, checks)

I was wrong a couple times about the John Street Café. First I thought it was just the tiny, unadorned place you can see from the street; I didn't know about the garden patio out back. Another time I walked by on my way to Pattie's Home Plate across the street and saw young couples waiting in line reading the *New York Times*, so I thought maybe it was a snooty hipster joint.

Wrong and wrong. It's the old, very popular Tabor Hill Cafe from Hawthorne, reborn in downtown St. Johns. The owners sold the old place and moved north in 1997, and behind that sterile-looking front is one of the warmest, most colorful outdoor seating areas in town. And there isn't a whiff of snootiness about the place.

Walking through the front room to the patio is like going through an art museum and emerging in somebody's backyard. Before I knew it, the owner was pouring coffee while greeting by name two regulars among us, and we were looking at a one-page menu with a major focus on omelets. A quick glance at the ingredients showed a whole lot more cheddar, Swiss, and Monterey than Brie. The staff also calls hazelnuts filberts, like good Oregonians, and will give your kids Gumby dolls to play with.

Before we get to the food, here's a picture of the patio: a seating area with 10 or so picnic tables is ringed by beds of fuchsia, bleeding heart, columbine, geranium, creeping phlox, Japanese maple, and bamboo. Dogs, welcome on the patio, sit curled up beside picnic tables filled with families. An enormous fig tree looms overhead, providing shade—and fruit in September.

The homey, simple feeling kept right on coming with the food. All the omelets come with oven-roasted red potatoes and wheat toast. The day's special was huckleberry-blueberry coffeecake, which had just the right balance of fluffy, moist, and crunchy. The bacon was sweet without being too mapley. The corned beef in a special hash had a little more zing to it than usual, and the leftovers were a meal in themselves. A spinach and bacon omelet had a hearty portion of greens as well as avocado, sour cream, and salsa. My friend Toni summarized her generous Shrimp Scramble: "Usually these things are egg-egg-egg-shrimp-egg-egg, but this one is more like egg-and-shrimp, egg-and-shrimp, egg-and-shrimp."

At first the prices seemed high—$6.75 for two eggs, potatoes, and toast; $6 for just one black currant and filbert pancake. But that pancake was a telling example of what the café is up to: yes, it was just one, but it was dinner-plate size, thick, and perfectly cooked, with an almost-burned crust outside giving way to a light, fluffy inside made a little chunky by the nuts and sweet-chewy by the fruit. It was served with warm maple syrup, and we fought over it.

John Street's signature dish—oatmeal—is another example of its homey friendliness. It comes with milk and brown sugar plus your choice of dried raisins, currants, apricots, or cranberries, and chopped filberts or walnuts. If eating a nice bowl of cereal at a picnic table in a sunny garden sounds like, well, your bowl of oatmeal, then head to John Street Café and gather your own first impressions.

Wait: Long on weekends after about 9:30, no cover outside. **Large groups:** More than six can be a hassle. **Coffee:** Kobos. **Other drinks:** Espresso, fresh orange juice, Kobos tea, hot chocolate, milk, beer. **Feel-goods:** Homemade cookies and truffles, banana bread, cheesecake, and mimosas. **Health options:** Omelets can be made with egg whites only for $1. **WiFi:** No.

Johnny B's

Mom & Pop

Dad's cookin' and Mom's servin'!
1212 SE Hawthorne Blvd. (SE/Inner) ~ 503-233-1848
Weekdays 6 a.m. to 2 p.m., weekends 7 a.m. to 2 p.m.
$7–$10 (all major cards)

———————◆•◆———————

It doesn't get any more mom-and-pop than Johnny B's. Dad cooks it and Mom brings it out. On Saturdays their kids work. The family photo is on the menu. One time I showed up and a sign on the door said it was closed because they were feeling under the weather.

It doesn't get much more down home than Johnny B's, either. The motto is "We're hooked on cookin'," and it's apparent they don't put much energy into anything else, other than making the place enjoyable. The decorations consist of red-and-white checkered curtains, white lights strung up over the windows, an aerial photo of the neighborhood . . . and that's about it. Tennis balls are on the bottoms of the chair legs so they don't scrape the checkered floor, and the high chair has socks on it.

You might think Johnny B's has been there awhile, but it opened in 2000. Before that, it was a Winchell's Donuts, and I doubt the clientele has changed all that much. Johnny B's gets city workers on breaks,

 students in for slacker breakfasts, old guys commenting on somebody's new haircut, a postal worker who trades barbs with the cook.

At this point you may have an idea of what the food is like, and you're probably right. The hefty, oval-shaped plates brim with eggs, meat, golden hashbrowns, and French toast made with that big Texas toast and a dash of cinnamon. Plenty of meat options.

Sweet yellow peppers in the Denver omelet. Water in red plastic cups. Farmer Brothers coffee, which my friend Julia, who normally likes two or three creams in her coffee, said needed only one. And, when you're done, there's candy and breath mints at the register.

Though it's fairly new, Johnny B's is probably the closest thing to a neighborhood hangout that Ladd's Addition has. And if there's a neighborhood that needs a breakfast hangout place, it's Ladd's Addition, a quiet cul-de-sac between two bustling neighborhoods. Johnny B's is like a quiet outpost on the fringes of Ladd's, out on the nutso border at the intersection of 12th Avenue and Hawthorne. Back behind the restaurant lie community rose gardens, a central traffic circle filled with rhododendrons, narrow streets lined with American elms, and a diagonal street pattern that dates back to 1891, when William S. Ladd, a Portland mayor, broke up his 126-acre farm into residential lots.

Johnny B's isn't the only breakfast place within walking distance of Ladd's. Junior's is over on Southeast 12th, and Genies is down at Division. They both have more interesting (and expensive) food, but a classy old neighborhood like Ladd's seems best served by a place where the folks all know each other, the staff is family, and Special #7 is "Don't move my tables."

Wait: None. **Large groups:** "Don't move my tables." **Coffee:** Folgers, "Just like at home." **Other drinks:** Stash Tea. **Feel-goods:** Um, the atmosphere? Says everything he does is fresh on the spot. **Health options:** Limited vegetarian. **WiFi:** Yes.

Junior's Cafe

Hip/Veggie

Kitschy, cozy, comfy, cramped, and cool.
1742 SE 12th Ave. (SE/Inner) ~ 503-467-4971
Weekdays 8 a.m. to 2:30 p.m., weekends 8 a.m. to 3 p.m.
$7–$13 (cash, checks; credit cards)

———◆•◆———

To look at Audra Carmine, you might not think she owns a restaurant. She seems so nice and sweet and young, not haggard and nutty like many restaurant folks are. Yet since 2005 she has owned Junior's Cafe on Southeast 12th Avenue, for years one of Portland's favorite little breakfast joints.

Although there have been some subtle changes to the menu and crowd, Junior's is still a friendly, popular place that will fill you up, not empty your wallet, and not rush you along at all.

Carmine worked for years at Dot's, the Clinton Street institution that spawned Junior's a decade ago. Still, she admits she had a lot to learn.

For example, there was the dedication of some customers. "People would call me over and be like, 'Why did you change the way you chop the zucchini?'" she says. "People have a huge emotional attachment to this restaurant."

And what were these radical changes? She tweaked some of the classic dishes like the Country Scramble (now with mushrooms, sausage, flat leaf parsley, jack cheese, and black pepper), the 12th Avenue (zucchini, corn, green onions, tomatoes, and Parmesan), and the Migas (green chiles, jalapeño, sausage, and tortilla chips topped with salsa, cilantro, and salty goat cheese). Several kinds of French toast replaced the waffles and pancakes, and she brought in fresh herbs for the first time. Crazy, huh?

The biggest change has been a greater emphasis on vegetarian and vegan options. *Stumptownvegans.com* gave the place high marks, especially the Superhero (sautéed tofu, tomatoes, garden sausage, green onions, and spinach).

"We don't use any partially hydrogenated oils or corn syrup," Carmine says. "We use real ingredients, and we make everything by hand. We try to use local providers and fresh eggs, and I handpick all the fruit, which is all organic."

I must admit, I was one of those old-time customers concerned about the changes at Junior's. I miss the waffles, and I'm a dedicated meat eater, but I loved the heaping Vegan Potatoes, topped with mushrooms, corn, zucchini, and spicy tofu sauce for $7.50. I also got two meals out of it. And being a sucker for French toast, I liked that there were options: a regular version, one topped with organic fruit, and another with yogurt, a whole chopped banana, and toasted almonds covered in honey. Of course there was also vegan French toast soaked in bananas, applesauce, and soy milk.

There's still a relaxed, slightly goofy vibe to the place. About a dozen gilded mirrors adorn the walls, the booths are still a glittery gold, and the tiny bathroom is still a hallucinatory sea of graffiti.

For me, Junior's used to be a place I'd stumble to from an apartment down the street when I was hung over or still working on a buzz. I remember being impressed that staff applied butter to the toast with a paintbrush and often seemed to be as stoned as I was. Those days may be gone, in more ways than one, but Junior's is rolling right along with the times.

Wait: Long on weekends, with very little room inside or cover outside. **Large groups:** One booth could handle five or six. **Coffee:** Stumptown. **Other drinks:** Tao of Tea, juice, and lemonade. **Feelgoods:** Most ingredients are locally grown or made and organic. **Health options:** Plenty for vegetarians and vegans. **WiFi:** No.

Kenny and Zuke's

Hip/Old School

A big ol' slab of New York in Downtown Portland.

1038 SW Stark Street (Downtown) ~ 503-222-3354 ~ *kennyandzukes.com*
Monday through Thursday 7 a.m. to 8 p.m., Friday 7 a.m. to 9 p.m.,
Saturday 8 a.m. to 9 p.m., Sunday 8 a.m. to 8 p.m. Some breakfast
options available all day. Full breakfast menu served weekdays until
11 a.m., weekends until 2 p.m.
$11–$18 (all major cards, checks)

———————————◆———————————

I was amazed by Kenny and Zuke's even before I ate there. I heard
there was a good New York–style deli downtown, so I went to check
it out. Now, I was thinking about delis I had gone to in New York;
I recall they were about the size of my college apartment, somewhat
grimy, and filled with unpleasant people but good food.

When I saw Kenny and Zuke's, I said to myself, "Holy smoked
whitefish! *That's* the deli?" It's enormous, bright, clean, and well-
ordered, and the people seem nice. It's like a palace compared to my
deli memories. And then I saw the menu, a whopping four pages of
options. The breakfast page alone made my head spin. Pastrami and
eggs; salami and eggs; lox, eggs, and onions; four omelets (including, of
course, pastrami, as well as the lox, cream cheese, and chives omelet);
pastrami hash; corned beef hash; salmon hash; a few Benedicts on
weekends; latkes; challah French toast;
and maple granola.

But I've seen big breakfast menus.
Kenny and Zuke's had me at the sodas.
Any place that has 10 root beers, four
ginger ales, five cream sodas, four colas
(including Mexican Coke and Pepsi,
with real sugar), six diet sodas, 17 fruit
sodas, two "Others" (including Yoo-
Hoo!) and seven "Premium and Rare
Sodas" from places like Germany and

Jackson Hole, Wyoming . . . well, like I said, think palace more than deli. What I think is, "I better go hiking on Saturday 'cause I'm getting some pastrami and a premium soda on Friday!"

Ah, you ask, but is it all good? Well, yes. How good depends on whom you ask—and it seems like everybody in town has an opinion. Kenny and Zuke's exists at the rare intersection of deli culture, big-time restaurant culture, and foodie culture. This means some folks get really worked up about the place, generally in a positive way.

Just about every blog in town has heaped praise on the place, usually along the lines of, "This is the closest thing to real New York pastrami and bagels you'll ever find in Portland." The *Oregonian* said of the Reuben (lunch service starts at 11 a.m., by the way), "You'll name your firstborn after it." *Willamette Week* hailed it as marking downtown coming full circle after an old Jewish neighborhood was destroyed to make way for the Portland State campus and called it "downtown PDX's first truly egalitarian new restaurant in decades," whatever that means. A writer for *Seattle Magazine* ate there three times in 24 hours. Even Matt Groening, Portland native and creator of *The Simpsons*, dropped off a sketch of Homer saying "Mmmm, Kenny and Zuke's!"

Sure, it seems a little exorbitant. I mean, it's a *deli*, right? The prices, surprisingly, are not really high. The Smoked Salmon Benedict is $12.75, and for $8.75 you get more challah French toast than a single person should be able to eat. I usually go for the pastrami hash with two eggs ($10.75), and I eat the leftovers with a couple of eggs for breakfast the next day.

Whether Kenny and Zuke's is authentic is entirely up to you. It's sure as heck impressive, and I recommend you check it out for yourself.

Wait: A bit on weekends, with little room inside. **Large groups:** Yes. **Coffee:** Stumptown. **Other drinks:** Numi Tea, milk, fresh orange juice, and a wide world of sodas. **Feel-goods:** They buy local beef and make their bagels. **Health options:** Come on, it's a deli! **WiFi:** Yes.

Kornblatt's

Old School

"Would do just fine in New York."
628 NW 23rd Ave. (NW) ~ 503-242-0055
Weekdays 7 a.m. to 8 p.m., weekends 7:30 a.m. to 9 p.m.
$10–$15 (all major cards)

———————————◆———•———◆———————————

Whenever a place has a location for its theme—like Kornblatt's calling itself a New York–style delicatessen—I have a system to test that assertion. I call it the Memphis Barbecue Test, and it goes like this: Since I am from Memphis and love barbecue, I ask myself how a particular barbecue place would do if it were in Memphis. So to apply this test to Kornblatt's, which humbly asserts it has the finest deli food west of the Hudson River, I invited David, a Jew who grew up in New Jersey, and Rich, who grew up on Long Island, to have breakfast with me.

I had always thought the décor might be a bit too New York: the autographs from Derek Jeter and Alex Rodriguez, the poster of the 1955 Dodgers, the picture of the guys eating their lunches on the beam high over the city.

On the plus side, I once had a wonderfully spastic server who kept calling me "my friend," sang loudly along with Frank Sinatra on "Chicago," and stepped outside for a smoke while saying he was "going out to lower my life expectancy." I also appreciate that the place has a glossary of deli items, including egg cream, phosphates, blintz, kasha vanishes, knish, nosh, kishka, kugel, lox, matzo balls, matzo brei, rugelach, pastrami, and latkes.

Rich immediately said that on appearance alone, Kornblatt's would easily fit in Great Neck, where apparently there's a large Jewish population. And David said he'd been coming here for years. So it was looking like a pass on my test already. David got the Eggs Bageldict, and the server repeated the line from the menu: "If you say it, we'll make it."

The Bageldict is a Benedict with salami (or pastrami or smoked salmon) and hollandaise on a bagel of your choice. David thought the sauce was a little light, but he also cleaned his plate, and since there was a female among us, nobody made any off-color jokes.

I got a full order of blintzes (four for $11.75), and they were light and delicious, served with sour cream and blueberry and strawberry preserves. It's best to get them if you're splitting your friend's savory dish; I was trading them for chunks of a mushroom-onion omelet, a massive but mildly flavored corned beef hash, and David's (ahem) dish.

The menu has nine omelets, ranging from basic options to, I assume, New York staples: sautéed chicken livers and onions, lox and onions, lox and cream cheese, and the Famous Mixed Deli, which is made with salami, corned beef, and pastrami and served pancake style. (Take my word: plan on taking a nap after that one!)

If that's not New York or Jewish enough for you, you can also get Matzo Brei (scrambled eggs with matzo balls) or French toast with homemade challah—and practice your pronunciation of *challah*. And for dessert, some kugel, a jumbo éclair, or some New York cheesecake. Might make you want to go home and sing along with Sinatra, too.

Wait: A little on weekends at lunchtime. **Large groups:** More than eight might be tough. **Coffee:** Allann Brothers. **Other drinks:** Espresso, Dr. Brown's soda, egg cream, hot chocolate, phosphates, seltzer, mimosas, and Bloody Marys. **Feel-goods:** You don't have to deal with too many real New Yorkers. **Health options:** Wrong place. **WiFi:** No.

Le Bistro Montage

Weekend

Still crazy, after all these years.
301 SE Morrison St. (SE/Inner) ~ 503-234-1324 ~ *montageportland.com*
Weekends 10 a.m. to 1:30 p.m.
$10–$12 (Visa, MasterCard, no checks)

I have to admit, Montage cracks me up.

I can't think of a place that's more Portland—or a place that brings out such heated opinions from people. The main objections boil down to the staff being rude, the noise level outrageous, the communal seating a pain, the food mediocre, and the clientele too drunk to care. And near as I can tell, it's been that way since they opened in 1992. It's kind of like hearing people complain that Bob Dylan has a bad voice and his lyrics don't make sense—except there's no reason to think Montage rises to Dylan's talent or importance.

Montage's bread and butter, as it were, is serving variations on mac and cheese to the late-night crowd. It's an enormous, loud, crowded scene around two in the morning, and its placement under the Morrison Bridge has always added a certain dingy flair. To me, it really has kind of a New Orleans feel to it, and I quit going years ago when I first gave up late nights and then gave up drinking and getting high. Maybe Montage is a phase that all us Portlanders go through in our 20s.

Now they do brunch on weekends, and it still has a New Orleans feel to it—not a classy, Brennan's, Benedict feel, but an out-too-late, slept-in, need-some-sustenance-for-another-day-of-drinking feel. I tried to go there once around New Year's Day and they were closed, with a sign on the door basically explaining they'd gotten a little carried away and needed some time off.

It's also funny to be in there when it's lit. Or maybe it's disconcerting, as you can clearly make out the funny tin cans pounded into the floor, as well as all the bumps and smudges usually blurred by darkness and booze. But the white tablecloths still suggest a certain (faded) elegance, and they'll still put your leftovers in wacky animal-shaped foil statues. I don't know which server you'll get, but ours was as far from rude as could be—in fact, cute and charming in the extreme. And I've seen other online reviewers say the same.

As for the food, it's amazingly cheap! The priciest thing on the menu is a steak and eggs—five-ounce Flat Iron with onions and bourbon demi glaze—for $9. Otherwise, there are Southern favorites like chicken fried steak with Cajun potatoes and toast ($6!) and a biscuit sandwich with bacon, a fried egg, country gravy, and cheddar cheese ($5 with onion rings). There are decadent New Orleans touches like a Banana Rum French Toast with fruit compote and *crème anglaise* ($5). And, for you Montage regulars, happy news: one of the six omelets is a Green Eggs and Spam (pesto, parmesan, and tomatoes) for $6.66.

They got kudos from my friend Maria for their oatmeal, which she said didn't need sugar. That's because it's Apple Date Oatmeal and comes with French vanilla crème sauce and pecans. Brown sugar and syrup come on the side, just in case. And they got kudos from this Tennessean for their white cheddar grits, which come with eggs and toast for $4.50.

For our little group, consisting of mainly folks too old or restrained for the late-night scene, it was nice to go visit the place when it was safe and relatively sane. To get thoroughly stuffed for about $10 total and be able to hear each other speak was quite a bonus.

Wait: None. **Large groups:** Absolutely. **Coffee:** K&F. **Other drinks:** Tazo tea, several beer, wine, and cocktails. **Feel-goods:** None in particular. **Health options:** A few things for vegetarians. **WiFi:** Yes.

Lili Patisserie

Classy/Veggie

Breakfast's answer to the chick flick.
8337 SE 17th Ave. (SE/Sellwood) ~ 503-233-8844 ~ *lilipatisserie.com*
Friday through Sunday 8 a.m. to 3 p.m.
$13–$17 (all major cards)

———————————◆•◆———————————

I was a little embarrassed that Lili Patisserie wasn't in my first edition. When I walked into the sunny little cafe in Sellwood for the first time, I felt like it really ought to be in there. I asked how long they'd been open, hoping I'd hear, "Just a few weeks," and instead got, "A few years."

By the end of the meal, though, it was entirely clear why I didn't know about Lili: 10 percent because I live elsewhere, and 90 percent because I'm a dude. Lili actually caused me to create a new word: chickified. It's the most chickified breakfast place I've ever been to. Only Mother's gives it a run for its purse.

It isn't just that there were, counting me and my friend Beth, two males and 20 something females in the place. Or that there's only one meat dish. The décor—Beth called it "country French cafe"—included drawings on the floor of pastries, mixing bowls, and loaves of bread. There's also a ceramic cookie jar in the shape of a smiling French chef, a cake box covered with flowers, and a coffee menu with a gilded border in which I made out various fruits, vegetables, and a butterfly. I'm sure there was a kitten in there somewhere.

There are flowers all over the place, everybody is really friendly, and in this estrogenized atmosphere I felt a little brutish for ogling my very pretty server. And yes, I just made up another word: estrogenized.

I thought the food was tasty, and at the same time a little light—both in impact and portions. The potatoes (big, boiled, and lightly seasoned chunks) seemed lacking, and my wild mushroom and Brie omelet (please don't tell my guy friends!) was quite good but was also small and didn't pack much punch. Meanwhile, Beth—who weighs about 105 pounds and thinks she's overweight—said it was nice that they didn't load us up on all those carb-filled potatoes and also mentioned how filling her spinach scramble was. In fact, she ate three bites of it and took the rest to go.

So, again, I am a dude, and I usually eat in Dude World places like the Stepping Stone, home of the ManCake.

The bathroom was the kicker. There's a wicker chest, etched birds in the window, and a lace lampshade. On my way back to the table, I saw a painting of a Paris neighborhood, in which I'm pretty sure somebody was wearing a beret. Part of me was screaming, "Get out now!"

When I got back from the bathroom and Beth pointed out that the logo pens (*logo pens!*) matched the blue on the walls, I kind of shut down for a minute. Back in my car, with sports radio blaring, I filed Lili Patisserie away under "future date breakfast" and headed back to Dude World.

Wait: Maybe a little, but they'll make sure you have coffee. **Large groups:** Maybe, with notice. **Coffee:** Mudd Works. **Other drinks:** Organic espresso, fresh juice, mimosas, Bellinis. **Feel-goods:** Organic, local, cage-free stuff. **Health options:** Everything's vegetarian; gluten-free and vegan options available too. **WiFi:** *Non.*

Limo

Weekend/Classy

These Peruvians eat well!

2340 NW Westover Rd. (NW) ~ 503-477-8348 ~ *limorestaurant.com*

Sunday 10 a.m. to 3 p.m.

$12–$14 (all major cards, no checks)

When I invited the Crew out to a Peruvian brunch, I told them honestly, "I don't know what Peruvians eat for brunch, and I don't care." And after 10 of us had a fantastic meal there, I still didn't care if what we had was a traditional Peruvian brunch.

When I had the manager of Limo on my podcast, I asked him what Peruvian food was, and he said that with all the immigration to that country over the years, the food had Japanese, Cantonese, French, British, and Italian influences with lots of seafood. When you also consider that peppers were invented in South America thousands of years ago, and in fact Limo is named for the spiciest of those peppers, you know that this isn't your ordinary Portland brunch.

On the other hand, a funny thing about local brunches is that whatever your theme is, folks want their standard dishes. So when I asked the manager what the best-selling item was, he said French toast! But this French toast is a baguette soaked all day in three kinds of milk and Grand Marnier. It's served with fruit and real maple syrup, though I can't imagine folks needing to add much syrup to it.

Limo's owner/chef was born and raised in Lima, Peru, and trained in classical French cooking. He came to Portland in 2009 and took over part of the old Cameo's Cafe just off Northwest 23rd, and the upgrade couldn't be more stark. The space has gone from $11 (and mediocre) waffles with eggs to sub-$10 entrees like wonton-wrapped mozzarella served with black mint sauce.

The space is much cleaner and more intimate, as well. They've preserved the sense of openness from all the windows and the patio, the soft pastel colors give it a warm vibe, and there's still the nook-and-cranny feel—with only about 25 seats inside, it feels like a classy hideout in a fairly crazy neighborhood. We were a group of 10, easily handled with advance notice.

As to what else Peruvians eat, they are apparently crazy about seviche, or raw fish "cooked" by marinating in citrus juices. A great way to find it here is in the Bloody Mary Ceviche, a big goblet with a colorful mix of tomato-based sauce, peppers and other spices, lemons, limes, prawns, and fish, made just spoon-able by a splash of buttermilk.

Another way to tour around via the menu is by getting some of the smaller, tapas-sized dishes. For example, there's a potato stuffed with cheese, rib eye steak, and veggies. Also try the yucca, a root vegetable that resembles big French fries and is served with a traditional cheese-based sauce with crackers and yellow peppers. It's creamy with just a little kick. There's also a quiche with feta cheese, greens, eggs, and Peruvian spices, and a Chimosa, which is a mimosa made with a boiled-together combination of purple Peruvian corn, cloves, cinnamon, lime, apples, and butter.

It's that kind of combination that makes Limo stand out in the brunch scene. The food, like the place, has light, color, and taste while also feeling very traditional and comfortable. I'm still not really clear on what they're having for brunch in Lima these days, but if it's anything like what Limo serves, they must be happy folks.

Wait: Not too bad, plenty of indoor space. **Large groups:** With notice. **Coffee:** Illy. **Other drinks:** Espresso, mimosas. **Feel-goods:** None they tout. **Health options:** Decent for vegetarians. **WiFi:** No.

Lorn and Dottie's Luncheonette

Old School

Wait, how long has this place been here?
322 SW 2nd Ave. (Downtown) ~ 503-221-2473
Weekdays 6 a.m. to 2 p.m.
$10–$12 (Visa, MasterCard, no checks)

———◆——•——◆———

Funny place, Lorn and Dottie's. Start with the name: doesn't it sound like a 60-something woman with horn-rimmed glasses and a giant, bad wig is going to greet you at the door? At any rate, you'd expect to meet Lorn and/or Dottie. And you figure it's in an old, run-down corner of some brick building downtown. And it's got a few years on it, including quite a few meals since the last deep cleaning.

Then there's the word *luncheonette*, which is defined as "a small place serving light lunches," but which is historically associated with counters at stores like Woolworth's, where working-class people would grab quick, cheap meals on their lunch break.

Almost none of that is true of Lorn and Dottie's. Well, there is a counter. It's in a fairly new federal government building, and it's spit-shine clean, bordering on sterile. In fact, they got a 100 on their spring 2010 health department inspection. The only decorations are old-timey black-and-white shots of Portland, hanging on white walls—although tall wood booths and vintage light fixtures add a dash of class. The staff, when I've been there, was quite young—if slow. And as for being a luncheonette, they are tied to the working schedule—among their oddities is the fact that they're closed on weekends!—but they do seem a little pricier than, say, Fuller's Coffee Shop (see page 118).

Somehow, with at least eight years under their belt, they've also slipped under the radar for most Portland breakfast-goers. They have four reviews on Yelp, one on Urban Spoon, and six on Citysearch. (Compare that, for example, to 150+ for Mother's Bistro [page 180] on Citysearch alone.) The few reviews you can find break pretty evenly into three categories: "This place is a hidden gem," "This place sucks and/or is overpriced for what it is," and "This place is all right if you're downtown and not in too big a hurry."

For what it's worth, I fall into the latter category. It's kind of an all-things-to-all-people type of place, with one noteworthy exception, also another goofy point about the place: no potatoes. Seriously, they don't serve potatoes, except in a German potato pancake. No hash browns, no home fries. The eight egg dishes come with a choice of breads: banana nut, jalapeño cornbread, white, wheat, or rye with jam.

There are a lot of hotcake options, including blueberry, banana pecan, and Big Fluffy. There's also a "famous" Dutch Baby, and one with apples, a yeasted waffle, and cinnamon roll French toast. For the health conscious, there's a whole section of chilled fruits and juices, but some of these prices are questionable to many: $2.95 for sliced bananas in cream? $2.75 for orange slices? Oh, and under the cereal section you can pay $4.95 for a bowl of Kellogg's Corn Flakes. And they used to serve a hot cereal called Zoom, but only on Fridays.

Like I said, strange place. But not a bad one—if you're downtown, not in too big a hurry, and don't feel like waiting to get into some other place.

Wait: None. **Large groups:** No. **Coffee:** Starbucks. **Other drinks:** Espresso, Lipton tea, Italian sodas, plenty of fruit juices. **Feel-goods:** None. **Health options:** Not much. **WiFi:** No.

Lucca

Weekend/Classy

Good looks and taste, just like Italy.
3449 NE 24th Ave. (NE/Fremont) ~ 503-287-7372 ~ *luccapdx.com*
Brunch served Sunday 10 a.m. to 2 p.m.
$14–$16 (Visa, MasterCard, American Express, no checks)

———————◆•◆———————

After eating, oh, 250 breakfasts in the last two and a half years, at something like 130 different places, it is pretty rare that a place makes me lean back in my chair and say, "Damn." But that's what happened at Lucca.

The Crew and I hit the place at 10:30. There were six of us, so I gave a heads-up call at 10, when they opened. Was appreciated, wasn't necessary. In fact, only three other tables were occupied, two of them with groups bigger than ours. *That* doesn't happen too often, either.

Lucca is in one of *those* locations, the corner of Northeast 24th and Fremont. Seems like nothing has worked there since the original Nature's pulled out a decade ago. Anybody remember Aja? Or the Dining Room? Me, neither. But Lucca might make it, going on my highly scientific sense that several people I know who are serious about food have told me they like it. Meanwhile, there are no lines at Sunday brunch, and I'd say the food is in the top 15 in town, based on one visit. Plus, the Italian flair really puts it in a class shared only with Accanto. (And now, a moment of silence in memory of brunch at Basta's.)

Speaking of class, Lucca is a beautiful place! The ceiling is adorned with a basket-style woven pattern, the art is subtle, the colors warm, there's plenty of light, and a side room (available for private parties) is just the right amount of set-off. The staff, too, is lovely; in fact, we agreed our server looked a little like Sophia Loren. And no, we weren't drinking.

The menu is a true brunch, with pizza and salads in addition to breakfast faves like French toast, hash, frittata, and a polenta–fried eggs–eggplant combo that was a highlight. They even had a bacon and egg pizza, which we didn't order. It sounded odd at first, but really, it's bacon, egg, cheese, some sauce, bread . . . what's so odd? They are cooked in a (partially) wood-fired oven in plain view of the tables, and they are lovely, with a fried egg in the middle.

A couple of us got there early and shared a blueberry-lime scone that was just as buttery and flaky as could be. Then I had the frittata, with goat cheese, zucchini, potatoes, apple, fennel and arugula), and while it was among the better frittatas I've had in town, it wasn't the best meal on our table. Chela's baked French toast (really more of a strawberry soufflé with fresh cream) was amazing, and Jerry's mushroom hash had just the right mix of flavors. The coffee was strong, good, and never ran out.

Everybody agreed the place was top notch, and the word *romantic* even got tossed around. I bet in the evenings the place is even warmer and more inviting. I think I spent $15 or $16 with tip.

I think from now on, when somebody complains about lines at brunch, I will send them to Lucca—assuming what they are looking for is excellent food in a beautiful place served by Sophia Loren look-alikes.

Wait: None. **Large groups:** Definitely; notice is nice. **Coffee:** Caffè Umbria. **Other drinks:** Espresso, juice, cocktails. **Feel-goods:** They list a dozen local farms on their site. **Health options:** Some veggie options. **WiFi:** Yes.

Marco's Cafe

Classy

Because a village needs its own restaurant.

7910 SW 35th Ave. (SW/Inner) ~ 503-245-0199 ~ *marcoscafe.com*

Weekdays 7 a.m. to 9 p.m., Saturday 8 a.m. to 9 p.m., Sunday 8 a.m. to 2 p.m.

$12–$16 (all major cards, local checks)

───────────────◆ • ◆───────────────

Multnomah Village really does have a small-town feel to it, and I've always thought that, like any small town, it has subtle class divisions. I don't mean animosities—the Village is hardly a place with class tension—but in the breakfast scene. The working-class Villagers have the Fat City Cafe, where old guys sit at the counter talking city politics and there's an item on the menu called the Fat City Sizzle.

Now consider Marco's, where the last time I visited, the specials (written on etched glass just inside the door) were a tomato-basil eggs Benedict and an asparagus, bacon, tomato, and spinach scramble in fennel butter topped with Asiago. Well. And on their website you'll see a picture of chef Maurice in a tuxedo and you can read about his work experience in Laguna Beach and Switzerland; he's also fluent in both French and Spanish!

Marco's has been a wildly popular restaurant since 1983, and there are some reasons for it. The food is always good, the folks are friendly,

the place is clean, and the prices aren't bad for some pretty classy food.

But it is very much a Southwest Portland place: a while back they tried to open a location on Northeast Fremont Street, and it flopped. And although I like to make some fun, I also agree with the *Oregonian*: "Marco's manages to be both nouveau and down-home at the same time."

I dragged my usual Fat City gang of fellas over there one time, and after all the jokes about whether they'd let us in and "I sure hope I don't drool on these nice tablecloths," etc., we chose among six omelets, eight egg dishes, and 16 specialties ranging from blintzes to roast beef hash to bagels and lox. Everything had a legitimate, expert touch to it, ike the light but sturdy hollandaise on three Benedicts.

We were impressed and satisfied, as I always have been at Marco's. And whenever the food or feel starts to get just a bit snooty, I see the Franz bread, the packets of freezer jam, the regulars, and all the accommodations for kids, and I feel a little more at home. I do still giggle at some of the goofier touches, like the collection of umbrellas hanging from the ceiling and the quotes painted on the wall: "One cannot think well, love well, sleep well, if one has not dined well," said Virginia Woolf, whom I'm almost certain no one has actually ever read. And "All happiness depends upon a leisurely breakfast," said John Gunther, whom I'm certain no one has ever heard of.

I can make up a breakfast quote too: "Since today is all we have, what better way to start our life than with a fine breakfast with good friends?" Maybe they'll put *that* up on a wall someday!

Wait: Pretty long on weekends, with a small space inside and some cover outside. **Large groups:** Yes, but no separate checks or reservations. **Coffee:** Equal Exchange (organic, fair trade). **Other drinks:** Espresso, Mighty Leaf teas, fresh juice, specialty coffee drinks, cardamom tea. **Feel-goods:** Solar hot water, local naturally grazed beef, local organic herbs and mushrooms, hormone-free milk, cage-free eggs, only Monterey Bay Aquarium–approved seafood, recycle 95% of waste, donate food to charities. **Health options:** Good options for vegetarians, egg substitutes available, trans-fat–free menu. **WiFi:** Yes.

Meriwether's

Weekend/Classy

Aiming for greatness.
2601 NW Vaughn (NW) ~ 503-228-1250 ~ *meriwethersnw.com*
Brunch weekends 8 a.m. to 2:30 p.m.
$12–$20 (all major cards)

———◆—•—◆———

Meriwether's looks great, it's in a great spot, the menu is amazing, and the patio out back is as nice a place as you can find to eat breakfast in Portland. It clearly aims to be a real restaurant; sometimes that comes off as attitude, sometimes as aspiration, sometimes as a business plan. But it certainly doesn't lack ambition.

The location has hosted a few restaurants over the years, and everybody seems to be pulling for the current one. The Breakfast Crew was suitably impressed by the exterior—a charming old house near Forest Park—and wowed by the amount of money obviously invested.

In the online world of restaurant reviews, the Meriwether's story went like this: It opened, had promise, but suffered from terrible service and inconsistent food. Then came its presumed hero, Tommy Habetz.

Ever heard of him? From Gotham Building Tavern fame? Well, join me and the 99 percent of Portlanders who haven't. But among the serious restaurant people, this was news. As the *Oregonian* put it in 2007, "Meriwether's was never on the radar of Portland's serious eaters, but with the coming of talented chef Tommy Habetz the restaurant is beginning to ride high again . . . knowing and dedicated diners are gradually coming back." That mostly positive review went on to say that Habetz "leans to classics . . . but he can riff on convention, as when he substitutes watercress and roasted pork belly for a traditional salad of frisée and lardons."

Habetz left Meriwether's after about a year, and soon after everybody on *portlandfood.org* stopped reviewing the place. But my point is the same: I have no clue what frisée and lardons might be. In fact, there are other things on Meriwether's menu (confit, frizzled onions,

basil *pistou*) that I can't identify. And
this is precisely what fascinates me:
it's a place where serious dining and
Portland breakfast intersect.

My crew was certainly impressed,
and we had a fine time. Jerry, a musician, loved the musical selection. We
all loved the patio, which is adorned
with wrought iron, heat lamps, cop-
per piping to hang canvas in cooler
weather, bamboo fencing, fuchsias,
hydrangias, hostas, and a fountain. And it's a *big* patio, with three
separate areas to it, one covered.

We had eggs Benedict with country ham and red-eye gravy ($14),
which I suppose constituted "riffing on convention" since it didn't
have hollandaise; Fried Chicken and Waffles with sage butter, apple-
wood smoked bacon, and pure maple syrup ($14), which was good. The
Rustic French Toast with mascarpone and rhubarb compote was also
impressive, even though I don't care for rhubarb.

I think the same food served in a lesser location would somehow
seem more impressive (and probably cost less). Regular food in this
setting would drive the place out of business, pronto. Instead, it's a
beautiful and impressive place with great outdoor seating and, well,
pretty darn good food.

Wait: Not bad, but reservations are recommended for Sundays. **Large
groups:** With notice. **Coffee:** Kobos. **Other drinks:** Espresso, cocktails, champagne, juice, hot chocolate. **Feel-goods:** It even has its
own farm. And it has a full parking lot west of the building. **Health
options:** Egg whites for omelets, substitute fresh fruit for potatoes
($2), salads on the brunch menu. **WiFi:** No.

Milo's City Cafe

New/Hip/Old School

If New York was down-home...
1325 NE Broadway Ave. (NE/Broadway) ~ 503-288-6456 ~
miloscitycafe.com
Breakfast weekdays 6:30 to 11:00 a.m., then a fair portion of the breakfast menu during lunch until 2:30 p.m.; weekends 7:30 a.m. to 2:30 p.m.
$10–$15 (all major cards, no checks)

My friend Bob and I love getting together for breakfast early on weekdays. Sometimes we meet with the fellas down at Fat City Cafe for a boisterous round of shit-talking, and sometimes it's just the two of us, talking writing and politics and perhaps a few personal things before he goes to the insurance company and I go home to chase pennies as a freelance writer. We're professionals, slackers, creative folks, and old buddies.

For these occasions, Milo's is our default choice. It's kind of like Bob and me: professional in that it's clean and has excellent food, slackerly in that it's not a problem hanging out for a while, and friendly in that we always have the same server and often see somebody we know.

To dig where Milo's stands in the Portland breakfast pantheon, you'd first have to get a handle on Northeast Broadway itself. What *is* the character of that street? Hawthorne is hippie, 23rd Avenue is shopping, Alberta is a little wacky, Broadway is . . . what? You've got your Elmer's Flag and Banner, Dollar Store, and tanning booths *and* your Peet's-Grand Central-McMenamins corner at 15th, a dozen kinds of food, both discount and high-end shopping, old-time places like Helen Bernhard Bakery a few blocks away from a sushi chain. It's like a neighborhood place and a mini-downtown. And in breakfast terms, you've got your blue-collar Village Inn, your happy-wicker-gay Cadillac Cafe, and good ol' Milo's.

Milo's is not a down-home place, mind you. The décor is sort of a sleek, stylish New York kind of thing, but the feel is both efficient like a serious restaurant and relaxed like a neighborhood place. Six omelets and six Benedicts feature veggies, pepper bacon, Italian and chorizo sausage, ham, and smoked salmon, and the Benedicts also offer petite tenderloin and crab cake options. Four hashes include pepper bacon, smoked salmon, and corned beef. Vegetarians need not run away, however. In addition to a veggie option on all of the above, there's granola, oatmeal, waffles, and Monte Cristo.

But Milo's makes its name on the meat dishes. The overall theory is simple. One of the owners, Loren Skogland, told the *Portland Business Journal* in 2002, "I buy really good ingredients and I don't screw them up." The article also said that the Skoglands, longtime restaurant folk, "opened Milo's in part so they could control their own hours and schedules, and chose the location, within a few minutes of their Alameda home and the grade school, in order to better juggle all the demands on their time."

All the kids have menu items named for them, and the vibe continues with Jeremy's Peanut Butter and Chocolate Waffle and the Peanut Butter and Jelly Stuffed French Toast, which is basically a big, gooey PB&J sandwich on sourdough French toast.

And such is Milo's: unpretentious and impressive at the same time, with a subtle dash of family and friendly. The same *Journal* article quoted Caprial Pence, co-owner of Caprial's Bistro in Southeast Portland and veteran host of TV cooking shows, "They do really nice food—nothing earth-shattering in terms of being innovative, but sometimes really nice food is earth-shattering by itself."

Indeed.

Wait: Can be long on weekends, covered benches outside. **Large groups:** With notice. **Coffee:** Boyd's. **Other drinks:** Tea, sparkling water, hot chocolate, juice, beer, wine, and full bar for cocktails. **Feel-goods:** Nothing in particular. **Health options:** Some veggie options; no-cholesterol eggs or egg whites $1 extra. **WiFi:** No.

Morning Star Café

Old School

A working place downtown.

500 SW 3rd Ave. (Downtown) ~ 503-241-2401 ~ *morningstarcafe.com*
Weekdays 8 a.m. to 3 p.m., weekends 8 a.m. to 2 p.m.
$12–$14 (all major cards, no checks)

———————◆•◆———————

You're coming off the Morrison Bridge into downtown, taking the first left you can, onto Southwest 3rd Avenue. As you wrap around the corner, you see a big, bright restaurant filled with people, and you ask yourself, "Wait, what's *that?*" It's the Morning Star Café, a downtown staple since 1994, but only recently a place for breakfast.

It's funny that most Portlanders don't seem to know about the place, even thought it's been serving breakfast since 2009. I have a theory: the Morning Star isn't an old-line place like Bijou or Mother's, and it isn't fancy or cutting-edge like Fenouil, and it isn't hipsterlicious like Byways. It's just a friendly, basic restaurant in the middle of town.

And when I say "the middle of town," I mean the historic core of Portland. Five blocks of 3rd Avenue contain seven buildings on the National Register of Historic Places. Morning Star is in the lobby of the 1902 Postal Building, which was put on the Register in 1978. From a table facing 3rd Avenue, you can see across the street to the 1891 Dekum Building, named for a German immigrant who opened Portland's first candy store in 1853. In the 1890s, that building (built entirely of Oregon materials) was Portland's City Hall, and more recently it housed Wieden and Kennedy, creators of Nike's "Just Do It" campaign. Next to it is the Hamilton Building, built in 1893 and named for Hamilton Corbett, son of a very famous Portland family. It was the first building in Portland designed in the Classical Revival style. (Thanks to Wikipedia, by the way.)

I tell you all this because I want you to remember that Portland is a historic town, though at times it feels like the crowded, bustling metropolis that it is. And such places need solid restaurants like the Morning Star. At breakfast and lunch, they serve a combination of tourists, office workers, and folks coming downtown for some weekend event. The décor is even built on gears to continue the working theme. It's a big, open space with huge windows looking out onto the busy street, and the food is classic breakfast fare: three sandwiches, nearly a dozen egg-based options, sourdough flapjacks, French toast, and oatmeal. During the week, you order at the counter and get a number; on the weekends they have table service.

I like the fact that the most expensive thing on the menu is $10, and that's quite a feat: the Biker Breakfast is two eggs, two bacon strips, one boar sausage patty, hash browns, and toast. For another $1.50 you can upgrade to French toast. And speaking of French toast, a full order of three slices with either fruit compote or maple syrup is just $6. The flapjacks are $5.75. And this is downtown!

It was about my third visit when I "got" the Morning Star. I had been hung up on the location, thinking that everything downtown is trying to be fancy or impressive. It finally dawned on me that I was sitting in the middle of town having a nice, reasonably priced meal with a great view of my happening city. I'm glad I gave in to my curiosity.

Wait: Some on weekends, mostly outside. **Large groups:** With notice, and they'll take reservations for six or more. **Coffee:** Illy. **Other drinks:** Espresso, tea, milk, soda, beer, wine, mimosas, Bloody Marys. **Feel-goods:** None they tout. **Health options:** Good options for vegetarians. **WiFi:** Yes.

Mother's Bistro

Classy

Somehow both dressy and faded.
212 SW Stark St. (Downtown) ~ 503-464-1122 ~ *mothersbistro.com*
Breakfast Tuesday through Friday 7 a.m. to 2:30 p.m., weekends 9 a.m.
to 2:30 p.m.
$12–$15 (all major cards)

If this place was called anything *other* than Mother's, I'd say the name was wrong. As soon as you walk in, you feel that combination of dress-up, old-faded comfort and class we associate with Mom. At least I do, but I was raised by a Mississippi native descended from French and Irish stock.

I ate at Mother's once with my friend Alice, who spent 10 years in Mississippi, and she said the same thing: kind of an Old South-French feel. It's by no means modern, and in places it seems like it could use a little dusting. But so can my mom's house.

We were seated by a white-clad hostess who indicated our table with that upturned hand I associate with people who've been trained in politeness, and when I looked around, I got another dose of that grown-up feel: there were women in heels and men in suits! I'd always wondered where the downtown business and tourist crowds eat breakfast, and here they were, bathed in the light of tall windows while Billie Holiday crooned through the speakers.

By now you may be thinking that the food is expensive and fancy. It is a little higher than in some places, but not all. On one visit I managed to spend $20 with tip, but most entrées range from $8 to $11. Alice and I shared a French press coffee for $4.50 and got three cups out of it. The low cost end is organic oatmeal for $5.50 (add raisins, bananas, pecans, or walnuts for $1) and the high is the House-Cured Lox Platter for $12.95.

What lies between is some down-home stuff. At lunch and dinner, Mother's is known for comfort food like meatloaf, macaroni and cheese, and chicken and dumplings. But there's also an international flavor as well; a message on the menu from the owner explains that she's after an international sense of Mom (pierogi, ravioli, green curry), and every month there's a Mother of the Month (M.O.M.) featured in the menu with her story and some of her dishes.

Breakfast doesn't veer too far from this, with a mushroom omelet, a prosciutto-garlic-basil-provolone scramble called Mike's Special, sausage and biscuits, and all your favorite Northwest must-haves: wild salmon hash, tofu scramble, and challah French toast. I had the French toast as a side instead of the potatoes (the substitute was no worries and I think they charged me $1), and I thought it was great: a little crunch on the outside, nice and soft on the inside. Alice had a portobello-spinach-Asiago scramble that was perfectly done. And yes, we cleaned our plates.

I've always found the food at Mother's to be basic, tasty, and well-done. It's never innovative or eye-popping, and I suspect we're paying another dollar or two per entrée for all that ambience and the seeming abundance of staff. Young folks think it's stuffy, foodies think it's dull, and many of the latter were shocked beyond words when owner Lisa Schroeder won Chef/Restaurateur of the Year from the International Association of Culinary Professionals during its 2010 Conference in Portland.

But Mother's seems to be full all the time, and it can't be just tourists and the suit crowd. I suppose there's always going to be interest in what Mom is cooking, even if it isn't fancy or cutting edge.

Wait: Quite long on weekends, with some indoor seating available. **Large groups:** Yes, but they request you make a reservation. **Coffee:** Stumptown drip and rotating blend for the French press. **Other drinks:** Harney & Sons tea, Oregon Chai lattes, mimosas and other cocktails, house-infused vodkas with seasonal fruits. **Feel-goods:** The menu says Mother's is "committed to making your meal a warm, fuzzy experience." **Health options:** Egg whites or tofu available (for $1), and vegetarians have several options. **WiFi:** Yes.

Navarre

Weekend/New
Love it, hate it, what is going on?
10 NE 28th Ave. (E/Burnside) ~ 503-232-3555 ~
navarreportland.blogspot.com
Weekends 9:30 a.m. to 4:30 p.m.
$12–$15 (all major cards, no checks)

Navarre blows my mind. Just trying to describe it is hard. It's definitely not what I call a breakfast place, or even a weekend brunch place. According to its website, it serves 50+ wines by the glass, offers small and large plates of food "based in Italian, French and Spanish origin," and "works with a CSA (47th Avenue Farms) . . . the specials are based on what is delivered that week along with the whims and interests of the staff."

It was also, according to the *Oregonian*, the Restaurant of the Year in 2009. And that's where the fun starts. For one thing, the article announcing such has disappeared from the paper's website, so good luck reading it. And the paper has since laid off both of its main restaurant reviewers—unrelated, but adding to the chaos. The award set off a frenzy of discussion on foodie websites, where Navarre had been universally written off years before, panned for inconsistent, mediocre food and poor service. A new book called *Fearless Critic: Portland Restaurant Guide* also trashed it.

To all this, Navarre's fans say things like "I love how the menu changes all the time," and "Sure, some things don't work out, but that happens if you're tied to the produce calendar, and at least they're honest. It's like having dinner at a friend's house." As a long-time admirer of the Grateful Dead, who were capable of awful nights, I recognize the outlines of this argument: it's love or hate depending entirely on taste. The *Oregonian* seemed to be rewarding Navarre for sticking to its principles and keeping things affordable in a recession. A lot of folks think there is better, more consistent food elsewhere. It's an argument with no solution.

So, what is brunch like there? For one thing, uncrowded—perhaps because many folks assume it's fancy and expensive, and many others hate it. The décor is pretty casual, with cookbooks all over the place and jars of pickled ingredients lining shelves. You get your own coffee, and the kitchen is right there for you to watch. Again, it's like eating at a friend's house.

They bring out a menu of small and large plates, and you check off what you want. Our group took a family-style attitude, going with a large plate of six Benedicts and a host of small plates. I don't recall what we had, but I've seen reference to things like braised greens, lentils, sautéed mushrooms, hash browns, steak and eggs, beet-and-basil salad, and a veggie scramble. Some of the stuff we didn't know about, like a leek and potato terrine, which is like a layered, compressed pie baked in a pot. *Pain d'épices* is kind of a hardy French gingerbread.

I can tell you that we all enjoyed ourselves and liked the food. I can also tell you that we might be bumpkins. And, finally, I can say that the Breakfast Crew has never said to me, "Hey, we should go back to Navarre!" But it sure is an interesting place.

Wait: None. **Large groups:** With notice. **Coffee:** Courier. **Other drinks:** Fresh juice, mimosas. **Feel-goods:** They work with a local CSA farm. **Health options:** Tons of vegetarian and vegan options. **WiFi:** No.

Nel Centro

New/Weekend/Classy

Turning the old into the new and fine.

1408 SW 6th Ave. (Downtown) ~ 503-484-1099 ~ *nelcentro.com*

Breakfast weekdays 6:30 to 10:30 a.m., Saturday 7:30 to 11:30 a.m., brunch Sunday 8 a.m. to 2 p.m.

$14–$16 (all major cards, no checks)

———————◆•◆———————

I'm not going to lie to you.

1. I was invited by the publicist for Nel Centro to have a Sunday brunch in exchange for me writing about them on my blog and having the owner on my radio show. I was going to do both, anyway, but I do enjoy free stuff.

2. As soon as I sat down in the place, I loved it, no matter who was paying. It's beautiful, had no line when I was there, and is a perfect example of what makes Portland cool: it used to be the diner of a Days Inn, which is now the super-cool Hotel Modera, with a bioswale, a "living wall," and an outdoor gas fire pit.

The first thing on that Sunday's brunch menu was Potato, Fennel, and Leek Puree. Right below that was Warm Hazelnut Crusted Goat Cheese with Peppers. And while I was deciding, I got a fantastic cappuccino (with Caffè Umbria) from an actual Italian, who was actually named Giovanni. When I asked about a muffin or pastry while I waited, he said he'd check with the "sweet girl" to see what she had. It turned out to be a still-warm brioche bun and a moist cherry-walnut scone. At that point, I was done for.

According to my host, among the place's virtues are that the tables are made from an old Willamette Valley barn, and a countertop is made with EcoTop, defined on its website as "a 50/50 blend of FSC certified post consumer recycled paper and rapidly renewable bamboo fiber, bound with a new 100% water-based system."

Nel Centro serves "the cuisine of the Riviera," and apparently, the people of the Riviera like to have Pugliese French Toast with Strawberries and Crème Fraîche, Poached Eggs on Grilled Polenta with Cured Pork Loin and Sage Hollandaise, an Individual Quiche Lorraine, and a Lamb Burger with Peppers and Feta Cheese.

In fact, I take David Machado's word on pretty much everything related to cooking and restaurants. He's won all sorts of awards, was the opening chef at Pazzo Ristorante and Southpark, is the owner/chef at the Mediterranean restaurant Lauro Kitchen, does the same at the Indian place Vindalho, and as of 2009 runs Nel Centro. He seems to be what you'd call a culinary rock star.

Another confession: I was too wrapped up in the food to take any notes—first the potato-fennel-leek soup, then the Florentine Omelet with Spinach, Mushrooms, and fontina. For my fellow *ignorami*, I looked up Mornay sauce on Wikipedia: it's a Béchamel (scalded milk and roux) sauce with white cheeses added. I can say with some authority that, when poured over a perfectly-cooked omelet of fresh spinach and mushrooms, and paired with chip-sliced potatoes sautéed with peppers and onions, it's damn good. And at Nel Centro, it's only $12.

So there I was, with a lot of other happy people, in a very cool restaurant with great food and no lines, right in the middle of my hometown, with the new MAX line going by the door, an Italian guy making great drinks and a sweet girl in the kitchen working magic. So free or not, I love that place!

Wait: Small on weekends, with a bar and plenty of room inside. **Large groups:** With notice. **Coffee:** Caffè Umbria. **Other drinks:** Cocktails, extensive wine list (local and imported), and espresso. **Feelgoods:** Locally sourced ingredients. **Health options:** Plenty for vegetarians. **WiFi:** Yes.

New Deal Café

New/Kid-Friendly

The paper, the kids, the dog, not much going on.

5250 NE Halsey Blvd. (NE/Hollywood) ~ 503-546-1833 ~
thenewdealcafe.com

Breakfast weekdays 7 a.m. to 4 p.m., weekends 8 a.m. to 4 p.m.

$7–$10 (all major cards)

———————◆•◆———————

Close your eyes and try to locate Northeast 52nd and Halsey. What's around there? What's that neighborhood called?

When the New Deal Café opened in the spring of 2006, the *Portland Tribune* said it "will be a fine addition to this rather barren (except for houses) stretch of Halsey." Barren, they said—except for houses. As if houses don't count. I mean, nothing there but . . . people . . . just . . . living there.

I asked the staff what the neighborhood was called, and several of us had a little conference. We knew we were east of Lloyd District, south of Hollywood, south of Alameda, north of . . . whatever is south of there.

"It's Rose City," somebody said.

"But all of Portland is Rose City, right?"

And that's when it hit me. The New Deal Café is the local café in a perfectly generic, maybe a generically perfect, Portland neighborhood.

As my friend Jane and I worked through our meal, chatting with table neighbors and watching kids in the play area, this perfect-Portland thing became a theme. The décor is light and airy, a combination of wood tables (cozy!) and plastic chairs (modern!) splashed in happy, cheerful oranges and yellows and greens that make the place feel like a chip off the New Seasons block.

The place is welcoming and cheerful, with high ceilings, plenty of light, fresh pastries under the glass, folks sipping self-serve coffee and surfing the WiFi, and a high percentage of customers who seem to know the staff.

The seasonal menu is written on a chalkboard above the counter. Keeping things grounded are a few classic scrambles—$7.50 with potatoes and toast or biscuit—and this being Portland, they use Naturally Nested eggs (egg whites and tofu are also available). The Farm has mushrooms, peppers, onions, cheddar cheese, and meat/veggie sausage or tofu. The Veggie Garden comes with broccoli, corn salsa, garlic, mushrooms, and roasted pepper sauce; the Mediterranean has basil, feta, tomatoes, garlic, and kalamata olives. French toast. Pancakes. Biscuits and Veggie Gravy. A Breakfast Sammich and a Burrito.

Then there are the progressive-good idea side dishes, all about $2.50: a single pancake, some sausage, coconut oatmeal, a biscuit, some potatoes, a piece of French toast . . . a peanut butter and jelly sandwich! You have to love a place where folks can get a PB&J for three bucks. We liked the food a lot, and it showed up quickly. The French toast was made with rustic white bread (wholesome!) and done old-school: crisp on the outside and eggy throughout (Mom!).

Speaking of good ideas, at New Deal, if you're eating with Poochie, you're close to Normandale Park, which has the ever-popular leash-free zone. So of course New Deal has a daily dog treat special.

What would you expect from a neighborhood café, especially when it's in a neighborhood that's named for a city known for good ideas and is a great place to live?

Wait: Little to none. **Large groups:** If you can get several tables at once. **Coffee:** Stumptown. **Other drinks:** Espresso, juice, Tao of Tea. **Feel-goods:** Organic ingredients, cage-free eggs, preference for local and organic. **Health options:** Tofu, egg whites available. **Wi-Fi:** Yes.

Niki's

Old School/Mom & Pop

Stop in, on your way through.
736 SE Grand (SE/Inner) ~ 503-232-7777
Breakfast daily 6:30 to 11:30 a.m.
$7–$11 (all major cards, no checks)

Somehow, Niki's always has the feel of folks just passing through, even though it's been in the same place since 1972. It's almost certain, if you've been in Portland a while, that you've seen the place; when you're sitting at the light on Southeast Morrison waiting to get onto the Morrison Bridge going downtown, it's there on your right, with gold bricks and a spiffy new awning. The #15 bus stops right in front of it too.

Niki's is surrounded by places to store your stuff, used office furniture stores, a few folks on the street, and of course, lots of traffic. And in the big-picture view of Portland planning, the whole area is considered the next big thing. One day they'll probably find the needed billions to bury I-5, and what is now known as the Central Eastside Industrial District will get a much catchier name.

But inside Niki's, change happens slowly. You're likely to hear diners at the counter talking on a first-name basis with the staff and older folks speaking Greek in corner booths; the place is owned by a Greek family, and the server once told me, "Dad used to work here." It's hard to imagine Niki's has changed a lot since it opened, from the food (fundamental American diner breakfast) to the mountain mural, ceramic figurines, beer steins, and faux roof over the kitchen.

I took my friend Jan there once, and after she slid into the brown booth and sipped from the white mug with the black rim, she closed her eyes in restrained ecstasy and purred, "Mmmm, coffee shop coffee." She ordered the French toast—big and thick, made the old-school way on Texas toast—and I had the Fresh Spinach Omelet with scallions and a heap of feta cheese that gave it a creamy texture. (There's also a Greek omelet, but most of the Greek influence shows up at lunch.)

Jan decided the food was "institutional, but good," and we both agreed a city needs places like this: honest, working-class restaurants with consistent cooking and expert, friendly staff. As trucks rumbled and a pack of brightly clothed bikers whizzed by, I spread Kraft grape jam on my sourdough toast, Jan smothered her abundant French toast with maple syrup from a glass pitcher with one of those pull-back metal tops, and we enjoyed casual breakfast conversation. My hash browns were the big-slice variety with no seasoning, and my toast was sourdough wedges on a side plate.

I recognized a sales guy from my old insurance job, but I didn't say hi because he looked like he'd chosen the place for some peace and quiet. I heard a server ask somebody, "How's the knee?" I saw a sign offering iced coffee, and Jan and I both wondered how long it'd been since iced coffee was new and exciting enough to hang a sign about it.

When I got home and looked for Niki's on the Internet, all I found were a few travel sites calling it a "comfy commuter's stop." I guess the rest of us are usually too rushed to stop in.

Wait: None. **Large groups:** Yes, and the side room can be rented for seriously large groups. **Coffee:** Boyd's. **Other drinks:** Espresso, orange juice, hot chocolate. **Feel-goods:** The staff will probably remember you. **Health options:** Nothing in particular. **WiFi:** No.

Old Wives' Tales

New/Veggie/Kiddie

Veggie-family-wholesome goes mainstream.
1300 E Burnside (E Burnside) ~ 503-238-0470 ~
oldwivestalesrestaurant.com
Sunday through Thursday 8 a.m. to 8 p.m., Friday and Saturday 8 a.m.
to 9 p.m.
$8–$15 (all major cards, checks)

———————◆ • ◆———————

When it comes to rating what the public thinks of a restaurant, it's best
to approach it the way figure skating is judged: throw out the highest
and lowest scores, then average what's left.

In the case of Old Wives' Tales, that venerable veggie-friendly,
family-friendly mainstay at the goofy (and being rebuilt) intersection
of Burnside and Sandy, what you have left is this: a place with lots of
room, a kids' play area, a quiet room in the back, a soup and salad bar
that's host to a very famous Hungarian mushroom soup, a massive
menu filled with wholesome cooking, dozens of vegetarian and vegan
options, and food that is not real exciting.

Even folks who like Old Wives' Tales, and there are plenty of them,
use words like *predictable* and *old-fashioned*. Folks who don't like it
say it lacks flavor, is overpriced, and has all the charm of a Denny's.
Vegetarians and vegans seem to appreciate the diversity of choices but
think the food is often better elsewhere. Do with all of that what you
will.

I dined there once with the Play Group, five moms and six kids
who go out once a week. When I arrived early and told the host what
was coming, he said, "Great!" He actually seemed excited, then put us
in a big room next to the kids' playroom, all the while telling me how
wonderful it is to get the kids out for a wholesome meal. With quilts
on the wall, wood tables and chairs all around, and several kids already
playing in the playroom, the place did feel homey.

It is also big. If you're looking for something cozy and charming,
this isn't it. If, on the other hand, there's a dozen of you or you're

dining with kids, Old Wives' Tales was made for you. Also, if you like peace and quiet, make your way to the Classical Music Dining Room in back, past the restrooms.

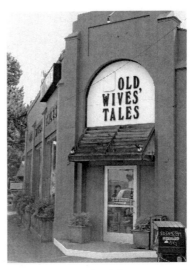

My take on the food is the same as the place: it's just the kind of stuff a bunch of old wives would come up with. They'd want the kids to have space and the grown-ups to have peace, they'd want to use healthy ingredients but not necessarily get it straight from local farmers (too pricey), and they'd try to cater to everybody's tastes and dietary restrictions.

The Play Group gave points on the kiddie stuff: a large menu in the $1–$4 range for standards like mac and cheese, applesauce, and a PB&J sandwich. "Someone gets it," one mom said.

When we were done, there was some sticker shock (I spent $14.50 with tip) as well as agreement there had been no real wow dish, except maybe the pancake with a mountain of whipped cream and fresh strawberries. So although I don't give ratings to restaurants, it's safe to say that if it were in the Olympics, Old Wives' Tales would finish and get polite applause, but probably not a medal.

Wait: Not bad; they also take reservations. **Large groups:** Absolutely. **Coffee:** Portland Roasting (organic). **Other drinks:** Tazo and Stash teas, espresso, beer, and Oregon wines, soy and rice milk. **Feel-goods:** Natural chicken and wild seafood. **Health options:** They handle (and label) any allergy or dietary restriction you can imagine. **WiFi:** No.

The Original

Weekend/Classy

So much fuss about a fancy diner.
300 SW 6th Ave. (Downtown) ~ 503-546-2666 ~
www.originaldinerant.com
Weekdays 6:30 a.m. to 11 a.m., weekends 7:30 a.m. to 2 p.m.
$13–$15 (all major cards, no checks)

Back in the Red Scare days, Senator Joseph R. McCarthy called the media a "jackal pack." Now, that might seem a heavy historical reference for a breakfast book, but you should have seen what happened when The Original opened downtown and the local jackal pack set after it.

The *New York Times* called it "a super-designy restaurant that wants you to think it's just a hipster diner." The *Mercury* followed up with "gimmicky, showy, and plagued with problems." With the blood now in the water, nobody would be outdone. *Willamette Week*'s review headline was "The diner is ironic. The pain is real." And the *Oregonian* wondered, "When you make a fried bologna sandwich with shallot mayonnaise, are you actually making it something more nuanced and sophisticated than a fried bologna sandwich?"

My take at the time was that everybody resented a place for aiming high and off the usual restaurant path. They call themselves a dinerant serving "evolved Americana cuisine." At one point they had a burger on a buttered and grilled Voodoo Doughnut. There was also a lobster corn dog. The collected response from the Portland media, and many diners, was "Hey, not in our town!"

It's definitely a themed place, the theme being "a diner somewhere on the road in the 1950s." I, too, was at first put off by the super-designy nature of the place, but since opening they've dialed down the goofy dishes quite a bit. It was obviously an expensive place to put in, and one suspects maybe they're aiming for tourists and businesspeople staying at the Marriott upstairs. But that would be if you think "normal"

Portlanders don't eat at themed places like this. Evidence throughout this book (see Broder and Screen Door) suggests otherwise.

While still a classied-up version of a diner, it's a pretty basic menu, and not terribly expensive: the griddle section has two kinds of pancakes and a decadent crème brulee French toast, all around $8. Specialties include an Eggs Benedict, a breakfast burrito with braised pork and guacamole, chicken fried flat iron steak, and a basic egg sandwich; all those are around $10 to $11, as are four basic omelets and a tofu scramble.

On the weekends their brunch menu spreads its wings a little, and some of the goofiness comes back in. Ever had Fruit Loop Pancakes or Mac 'n' Cheese Pancakes? If that seems odd, they also bring in waffles (classic and bacon) as well as a fish sandwich and three burgers, including turkey and House-Made Chickpea and Quinoa. There are also, on weekends, five shakes, four floats, and three house-made sodas: Bark Beer, Ginger Mint, and Five Flower. And you can get a bowl of Frosted Flakes, Fruit Loops, Cheerios, or Corn Flakes.

Maybe you're wondering, what's the big deal with all that? To which I say: Exactly. Ignore the jackals and go find out for yourself.

Wait: Maybe on weekends. **Large groups:** With notice. **Coffee:** Stumptown. **Other drinks:** Espresso, juice, shakes, and malts. **Feel-goods:** None. **Health options:** A few things for vegetarians. **WiFi:** Yes.

Original Pancake House

Old School

It's like Mickey Mantle is still hitting homers.
8601 SW 24th Ave. (SW/Inner) ~ 503-246-9007 ~
originalpancakehouse.com
Wednesday through Sunday 7 a.m. to 3 p.m.
$15–$20 (cash and checks only)

———————◆——●——◆———————

Maybe it's the tiny wooden booths. Or the community table. Or the regulars who, when the place opens, have a newspaper and their favorite dish waiting on their tables. Or the traditional, shared misery of waiting in the lobby.

All I know is I'm in love with the Original Pancake House, and I'm not alone. I also know that it's not of this era. It's like the *Prairie Home Companion* of Portland breakfasts, with its old-world charm that steadfastly refuses modern trends like credit cards and good coffee. Just ask folks about it sometime; you'll either get a crinkled nose and a comment such as, "What, wait all that time and pay all that money for *pancakes?*" Or, you'll get kind of a warm-glow smile and a story about eating there with Grandpa.

Pancakes and coffee will set you back about $15 with a tip. But these aren't your ordinary pancakes (warning: highly biased remarks ahead). For one thing, there are 14 kinds: buttermilk, buckwheat, potato, sourdough flapjacks (pause here while I enjoy a warm glow), 49er flapjacks, Swedish, blueberry, bacon, banana, Hawaiian, Georgia pecan,

 coconut, silver dollar pancakes, and wheat germ. There are also pigs in a blanket, sourdough French toast, strawberry waffles, Danish Kijafa Cherry

Crepes, and the twin signatures: the Apple Pancake (a steaming mass of Granny Smith apples and cinnamon glaze) and the Dutch Baby (a baked bowl shape of eggy pancake pleasure with whipped butter, lemon, and powdered sugar).

Plenty of other options are on the menu—another half dozen waffles and types of meat, seven omelets, oatmeal, cream of wheat—but that's like saying *A Prairie Home Companion* has comedy sketches and musical guests. Does anyone even remember those things? I don't, and I love that show.

My friend Craig and I consider it a special occasion to go there, mainly because of the prices. But that adds a certain flair to the occasion: we're deciding where to go, then the Pancake House comes up, and we get all excited, like a couple of little kids. Deciding what to have is an excruciating ordeal for me, because half my mouth is filled with sweet teeth, and to pick one kind of pancake is to eliminate so many others. I usually get the sourdough flapjacks, which are so sweet I catch a buzz off them. Throw in a side of bacon, coffee, and a tip, and I've had myself a $20 smile-fest.

That's a lot, I don't deny it. I am also thoroughly biased and consider $20 worth it every now and then. And the OPH is a chain, but the one on Barbur is the *original* Original Pancake House, opened in 1953. From there, a chain of some 100 places has blossomed across the country. And none other than the James Beard Foundation gave it an America's Regional Classics award. You can argue with me and thousands of other Portlanders if you'd like, but I don't see how you can disagree with James Beard. Or the sourdough flapjacks.

Wait: Nearly constant, and up to 45 minutes on weekends. **Large groups:** No. **Coffee:** A "special blend." **Other drinks:** Hot chocolate, tea, juice, and, believe it or not, buttermilk and Postum! **Feelgoods:** The website says it uses "93 score butter, pure 36% whipping cream, fresh grade AA eggs, hard wheat unbleached flour, and our own recipe sourdough starter." **Health options:** You don't have to eat it all. **WiFi:** No.

Overlook Family Restaurant

Old School

Working classy.

1332 N Skidmore (N/Inner) ~ 503-288-0880

Daily 5 a.m. to 9 p.m.

$7–$10 (all major cards, no checks, ATM on site)

The first thing I heard about the Overlook was that it was "a place for contractors and alcoholics." Considering this remark came from a good friend who's a contractor and a recovering alcoholic, it wasn't an insult—though it hardly captures everything the Overlook is about.

When I got around to checking out the breakfast, two people from the Breakfast Crew showed up: Tom, who said he used to go there when he was a contractor, and R, another recovering alcoholic. Coincidence? Well, it was also the only time in the research for this book—almost 150 breakfasts over two years—that professional basketball was ever discussed. The Overlook is a bedrock, working-class, fill-you-up restaurant with staff who are total pros, more food options than just about any place in town, and the ability to handle kids and large groups. And you can damn near eat yourself to death for $10.

I walked in and saw one of those classic dessert cases right inside the door. I counted 11 cakes, eight pies, two puddings, and a custard. We sat down at a table with brown-and-white coffee mugs, and above us were a Keno screen and a high-definition TV showing Fox News (this ain't your lefty Portland).

And the menu! One online reviewer joked that it had won several literary awards. Eggs Benedict, eight omelets (including taco), eight farm-style breakfasts and eight specialties. Pancakes, plain and Belgian waffles, and four kinds of French toast. Two versions of steak and eggs are $9.50 (top sirloin) and $10.50 (New York Steak), including toast, jam, and pancakes or hash browns. And heck, for $2.25 they'll cover anything with their sausage gravy, thick with big chunks of sausage. I could go on.

Tom, for old times' sake, was wearing a Carhartt shirt and ordered the Monte Cristo: a triple-decker French toast sandwich with grilled ham, cheese, and egg that came with a serrated steak knife stuck through it. We called it the Sandwich of Death. I got the cinnamon roll French toast, a mess of sweetness I could barely finish. R got the half order of biscuits and gravy and marveled that anyone would ever eat the whole one.

We talked sports and jobs and women. Other diners were families, older couples, businesspeople with notebooks, somebody who may have slept outside the night before, and some kids from the University of Portland who looked like they were on an anthropological field trip. And, yes, some contractors.

Don't miss the lounge, by the way. I was there at 9 a.m. and the waiter was serving a couple of highballs to two guys watching golf on one of the many televisions. The lounge is lifted straight from the 1960s—and I don't mean the hippie 1960s, either. I'm talking about caged-in gas fireplaces with seats branching out from them, wood paneling, green seats, slot machines, and faux stained-glass windows.

So, that first report on the Overlook wasn't all wrong or all right.

Wait: Maybe a little on weekends. **Large groups:** No problem. **Coffee:** Boyd's. **Other drinks:** Stash Tea, milkshakes, cocktails in the bar. **Feel-goods:** Uh, no. **Health options:** Egg substitute available. **WiFi:** No.

Paddy's

Weekend

Food from a place built for drinking.
65 SW Yamhill St. (Downtown) ~ 503-224-5626 ~ *paddys.com*
Weekends 11 a.m. to 2 p.m.
$12–$14 (all major cards, no checks)

———————◆•◆———————

If you're under 30 and/or work downtown, you may have even been in Paddy's. Still, the chances are really good you didn't know they serve a weekend brunch, at least based on the scene when Alice, Kelly, and I showed up at 9:30 Saturday morning.

It's a long, open room with an antique bar down one side, and it looks like a place built for drinking (they claim to serve 500 spirits). It's not cozy, but it's serviceable, with lots of wood and high ceilings and a few big windows. The building dates to 1887, so it does have a classy, old feel to it.

The menu immediately led to questions: What's a boxty? Are the Clover Cakes really just regular pancakes cut in the shape of a four-leaf clover? Is fried soft shell crab an Irish treat? Who's ever heard of a Quail Eggs Benedict? Where is our server from? (Scotland, but we didn't care that he wasn't Irish.)

Kelly wanted a biscuit, but they were out. I wanted the Benedict, but they were out of quail eggs, which I'm told are quite rich. Kelly also wanted black tea, but they were out of that, too. Yes, an Irish bar was out of black tea at brunch. I am only reporting facts here. Again, I think Paddy's was mainly built for drinking.

Cautiously, Kelly ordered the oatmeal, which they had. Alice went with the corned-beef hash, and I went boxty, which the server said is Gaelic and "probably just means 'potato cake.'" I figure every culture has some form of "let's take the potatoes, the leftover meat, a veggie or spice, and grill it all up." Paddy's boxty has ham and onions, and it's "grilled to perfection," according to the menu. (The word *perfect* appears four time on the menu, leading me to wonder what's Gaelic for "hype.")

I was thinking, *This is kind of fun, It's nice to be here with two cool ladies,* and *I don't think the food is going to be very good.* My guess is Alice and Kelly were thinking the last part too, because as soon as we started eating, we all made that little, elevated *hmm* noise that means, "Hey, this is actually good." The corned beef, while no competition for Kenny and Zuke's, was tender and tasty. The oatmeal had a good texture and taste, though the latter was aided by butter, brown sugar, and cinnamon in a side dish.

As for the boxty, I think it's a good indicator dish for Paddy's. It's decent, a fun thing to say—"I'll have the boxty"—and it's only $5 for the "Pa" size ("Ma" is $3). So I got a meal and coffee for $7.50, with a little dose of culture and education from a foreign dude.

How did the boxty taste? Well, it's a potato cake with ham and onions. You pretty much know what it tasted like—just like you probably know what kind of place Paddy's is, even if you haven't been in there.

Wait: None. **Large groups:** Definitely. **Coffee:** Kobos. **Other drinks:** Full bar, Stash teas. **Feel-goods:** None. **Health options:** You can request vegetarian. **WiFi:** Yes.

Pambiche

New/Hip/Weekend
Music! Colors! Options!
2811 NE Glisan St. (E/Burnside) ~ 503-233-0511 ~ *pambiche.com*
Breakfast weekdays 7 to 11 a.m., weekends 7 a.m. to 2 p.m.
$10–$16 (Visa, MasterCard)

I am one of the few people in Portland who often doesn't really get Pambiche. I have always felt underwhelmed by their food—though I completely understand that I may just be an ignoramus. In fact, there's no doubt I am, especially when it comes to experience with Cuban food. All my "expertise" comes from the fact that I've been to Miami a couple times and eaten it there. My reaction was always a big *wow*. I love the bistek, the sandwiches, the coffee, everything.

Then I go to Pambiche, and the bright Caribbean colors are there. The music is there. The voodoo priestess is there with her cigar. And the food makes me go . . . eh. Seems like it lacks zip.

Clearly, this is a minority opinion. People love Pambiche, and I don't think they're nuts for it. Although the Spanish names sound exotic, what you're often getting is a Cuban twist on something you're used to seeing: Huevos a la Cubana, for example, is a couple of fried

eggs with your choice of meat (or vegetarian) plus rice, black beans, avocado, and a side of yummy, sweet fried plantains. The Torrejas con Frutas is advertised as "Cuban toast," thick-sliced baguette thoroughly soaked in creamy egg batter, grilled in sweet butter, topped with toasted almond slices, and served with a pile of tropical fruit. All very well done. But the capper for us was the cane syrup, made in-house.

It's lighter than maple syrup in both flavor and texture, but somehow even sweeter, and it just blew our minds. Folks at our table were wondering where to get it, how to make it, everything.

Interesting and traditional Cuban dishes also abound. Pisto Manchego is a pile of chorizo, smoked ham, creole pork, shrimp, potatoes, asparagus, pimentos, and *petits pois* with an olive oil *sofrito* sauce. (A similar, meatless version, the Revoltillo a la Jardinera, features roasted peppers—but it's darn near the only option for vegetarians.) The Tamal en Hoja (creole pork in red sauce, encased in corn, yucca, and plantain masa) was a favorite as well.

But there's one thing that's becoming more and more clear to me: their sweet stuff rocks.

Start with a $5 basket of pastries. The best of them is the fruit-filled and sugar-coated *empanaditas*, which on any day may have mango, guava and cheese, pineapple, papaya, or *dulce de leche*. And we also fought over the Toronja Pound Cakes (grapefruit). Just *saying* the rest of them gets me worked up: semisweet coconut bread with ginger and pineapple, cream muffins with chunks of mango, sweet potato spiced cake with guarapo icing, sweet bread filled with peanuts and baked in caramel. This lineup changes regularly, but they're all amazing. Wash them down with Café Cubano and you'll be ready to fight a revolution.

Maybe I'm just all about the coffee and sweets at Pambiche. No harm in that. It's a cool place, and having a favorite for sweets, caffeine, colors, and vibe is a good thing. Especially if it moves me toward the majority opinion—and away from being an ignoramus.

Wait: Not bad, with plenty of cover outside. **Large groups:** Get there early. **Coffee:** Their own special blend. **Other drinks:** Fabulous fruit smoothies and shakes, espresso, fruit juice, and sugarcane lemonade. **Feel-goods:** None in particular. **Health options:** Lots of meat? Low on carbs? **WiFi:** No.

Papa Haydn

Weekend/Classy

Faded glory, youthful beauty.
701 NW 23rd Ave. (NW) ~ 503-228-7317 ~ *papahaydn.com*
5829 SE Milwaukie Ave. (Sellwood) ~ 503-232-9440 ~
Sundays 10 a.m. to 3 p.m.
$14–$17 (all major cards, no checks)

How many times have you driven down Northwest 23rd Avenue? Hundreds? How many times have you gone by Papa Haydn and been wowed by the youthful beauty of the evening crowd? How many times has someone said to you, "That place has amazing desserts"?

Now, how many times have you actually eaten there? Did you know there's one in Sellwood? And did you know both locations serve Sunday brunch?

If you said "Often" and "Yes," I am convinced you're in the minority. In fact, I lived here for years before I went in there at all, and made it more than a year beyond the publishing of this book before I had a clue they serve brunch. But I am in my 40s and don't make much money. I'm pretty sure this means I'm too old for the dessert crowd at Papa Haydn and too young and poor for the brunch scene.

I went to the one in Sellwood and found it to be a lovely place with old-fashioned food and the feel of a country club. And trust me, I grew up going to country clubs. The average age of the clientele was pushing 60, the music was Sinatra and Crosby, the tablecloths were white and pressed, the staff was young and very polite, and they served quiche. They even have the nice garden patio and everything.

As for the food, I can tell you two things. One, nobody has ever said to me—and I'm known as the Portland Breakfast Guy—that I should check out brunch at Papa Haydn. Maybe that's the age thing. The other is that just about every online review I could find said some variation of "Great desserts; otherwise forget it."

I thought the food was pretty good, actually. I had a strata, which is sort of an eggy bread pudding, like a frittata but fluffier. It had sausage and fennel in it, and we all agreed that it was tied for Best Dish with Jerry's garden omelet, which had a fine, smoky flavor mainly due to some mushrooms.

The rest of the menu (which changes pretty regularly) is straightforward Portland brunch stuff: biscuits and gravy, pancakes, Dungeness crab omelet, a few Benedicts, French toast, Monte Cristo, smoked salmon omelet, and a waffle. We thought the griddle stuff didn't live up to the place's reputation for sweets. The waffle was quite firm—dry, really—but with enough syrup and fruit compote, it was decent. The accompanying fruit was not terribly fresh. Some baked goods that came out were tasty: blueberry muffin, brioche buns, a selection of cheese sticks.

All of this reminds me of visiting Grandma. She's old and sweet, but she ain't exactly cutting edge, and you like going to her place because you liked it as a kid, and you're polite toward her, so you don't mention—or care, maybe—that her food isn't really that great anymore. Maybe it never was. But back then you had less experience with good food, and besides, it was Grandma. And it still is.

Wait: Maybe a little, but they take reservations. **Large groups:** With notice. **Coffee:** Stumptown. **Other drinks:** Espresso, wine, beer, and cocktails—the Bellini is very popular. **Feel-goods:** Local ingredients. **Health options:** A few things for vegetarians. **WiFi:** Wouldn't be polite!

Paradox Café

Hip/Veggie

The hippies took over the diner!
3439 SE Belmont Ave. (SE/Belmont) ~ 503-232-7508 ~
paradoxorganiccafe.com
Weekdays 8 a.m. to 9 p.m., Saturday 8 a.m. to 9:30 p.m., Sunday 8 a.m.
to 3 p.m. (hours change seasonally)
$8–$11 (all major cards)

———————◆·◆———————

I wasn't particularly kind to Paradox in the first edition of this book.
I kind of covered my ass by making fun of myself and saying that I
might just be an idiot. And I hung it on various friends, reporting that
they all shrugged at the food. But the truth is, I thought it was a dirty
place with bad food. I just didn't know if it was me, them, or vegetarian food.

Well, now they have expanded, cleaned up, and improved on the
food considerably. They also have AC and take cards, which is nice.

The website used to state the cafe's philosophy as "wholesome common meals at a fair price . . . seasonal organic produce, organic grains,
local and organic tofu and tempeh, free range eggs and hormone free
meats . . . local co-ops . . . breads, sauces and desserts are mostly dairy
and egg free . . . maple or fructose for our sweeteners." Now it just says,
"Great food prepared fresh for your mind and body." Let's hear it for
simplicity!

The place opened in 1993, and I suspect it was one of the first mostly
vegetarian places in town. As the *Willamette Week* has said, "Customers
learned to expect a little grease here, a little filth there (but) cheap and
easy comfort food."

The 2010 menu offered eight savory items plus a pile of sweets and
sides. The savories include down-home options like a scramble with
seasoned potatoes or brown rice, topped with steamed vegetables and
your choice of one egg, tempeh, or tofu. For $1, you can also get this
"curry style," which is mixed with Asian curry sauce, raisins, and
toasted nuts. There's also Holy Frijoles (tostada with chili, topped with

egg or tofu), Country Comfort (a basic combo with biscuit and almond gravy), a burrito, and the Spit Fire Scramble (Mexican chipotle sausage, caramelized onions, sweet red and jalapeño peppers scrambled with seasoned tofu, and spinach, served with a dollop of sour cream and seasoned potatoes.) They say they can "veganize" anything that's not already vegan.

I had the Paradox Benedict (herb and onion bread with veggie sausage, your choice of tofu or egg topped with fresh tomatoes and "Tree Hugger hollandaise sauce" served with seasoned red potatoes), which was probably too salty but at least had some action to it, and was quite filling. The taters were awesome. My friend had the corn cake special, with bananas and walnuts in the cakes and strawberries on top. Outstanding.

By the way, neither of us finished our meal. Add two cups of coffee and a nice tip, and we got out of there for $27.

So maybe Paradox is just a little neighborhood place with a lot of cheap, healthy food, much of which happens to be vegetarian and vegan. And now that it's bigger, cleaner, and better, I'm happy to have good things to say about it.

Wait: Medium on weekends. **Large groups:** No more than six, I think. **Coffee:** Stumptown. **Other drinks:** Large variety of natural juices and sodas. **Feel-goods:** Local ingredients, free-range eggs, hormone-free meats, seasonal produce, organic Mountain Rose Herbs. **Health options:** Many dishes are vegan, vegetarian, gluten-free, dairy-free, etc. **Wi-Fi:** Yes.

Pattie's Homeplate Cafe

Mom & Pop/Old School

1947, downtown, somewhere in America.
8501 N Lombard St. (N/Outer) ~ 503-285-5507
Monday 8 a.m. to 6 p.m., Tuesday through Saturday 8 a.m. to 3 p.m.,
Sunday 9 a.m. to 3 p.m.
$6–$8 (all major cards)

———————————◆•◆———————————

I used to go by this place on the #75 bus all the time on my way to play disc golf in Pier Park. I would see tables outside and read something about a soda fountain, and I'd think, "Man, I need to go there."

I looked around on the web for breakfast places on North Lombard Street, and I wound up at the John Street Café, on the other side of the street—and in another decade. The John Street is much more *New York Times*, flowers, original art, and sour buttermilk pancakes. A fine place (see page 152)—and *not* what I was looking for that morning.

So I walked across the street, and when I entered Patti's, four guys at the counter stopped talking, looked up at me, gave me the head-to-toe, then went back to their coffee. I felt like I was on the road!

Patti's is in the middle of downtown St. Johns, and when you walk in, you couldn't be farther away from what many people think of as Portland: jogging paths, urban planning, peace marches, lattes, and

so on. Some of the folks in Patti's look like they make it down to Portland only once a year or so and couldn't imagine why they'd go any more than that.

Whole families were coming in, three generations at a time. Men with canes. Women in slippers. People speaking Spanish. A referee in uniform, people asking which game he was working that day. Camouflage hats, flannel shirts, and Cat Diesel baseball caps.

The food is precisely what you would expect, and then some. Contemplate the words *home plate café*. I sat at a table with a laminated Coke tablecloth and had scrambled eggs with ham, hashbrowns (the grilled strip variety), crisp bacon, and pancakes. I ordered orange juice and got a bottle of Langers. I asked for maple syrup and got a bottle of Aunt Jemima.

The food was good, filling, and not pricey. While I ate, I watched the server greet people with lines like, "Well, it's a regular family reunion in here today!" I watched the man behind the counter cook while trading barbs with the old guys. I looked at the store in back and saw wigs, yarn, picture frames, bird feeders, costumes (in March), costume jewelry, fish lures, plastic flowers, you name it.

My favorite moment was when a young Portland couple came in. He had a thin figure, sideburns, and thick-rimmed glasses. She had matching workout clothes, a bike helmet, and a newspaper. They looked at each other briefly, and so did everybody else. They surveyed the scene, made a loop through the store, talked in hushed tones near the toy section, then casually strolled out—and across the street, I'm sure. Probably rather wait in line at John Street than cross the cultural divide.

They don't know what they missed.

Wait: Can't imagine. **Large groups:** Call ahead for more than eight **Coffee:** Folgers. **Other drinks:** Old-fashioned hand-packed milkshakes, juice by the bottle. **Feel-goods:** The folks. **Health options:** Juice in bottles! **WiFi:** Yes.

Petite Provence

Weekend/Classy

"Our server is from Marseilles, and he's hot!"
4834 SE Division St. (SE/Division) ~ 503-233-1121 ~
provence-portland.com
1824 NE Alberta St. (NE/Alberta) ~ 503-284-6564 ~
Breakfast daily 7 a.m. to 2 p.m.
$13–$17 (all major cards)

———————◆ • ◆———————

"I would go 10 miles for these pastries; they're better than sex."

I won't divulge the name of the person who uttered that remark (her boyfriend might read this), but I will say it was typical of the Breakfast Crew's trip to Petite Provence. It was Beth who let me know that our server was from Marseilles, then added, "and he's hot!"

Yes, things got a little saucy for us at the fancy French place. In fact, just about every review I've read or heard includes something like, "The place was lovely, and my server was really cute and had a French accent."

People just seem to be in love with this place. Consider what the *Portland Tribune* had to say: "The perfect croissants are so light they nearly float; the buttery layers puff up against the flaky crunchy crust . . . and it's hard to get out of there without a pound cake, pumpernickel baguette or cutely decorated meringue." *Willamette Week* slipped past love and into lust, calling the *croque monsieur* sandwich "almost pornographic . . . oozing with Gruyère, butter and creamy béchamel." The *Tribune*'s writer was also smitten by the "authentically snarky French-speaking staff" and their "silky accents." I'm just sayin'.

All the pastry delights will be waiting for you right inside the door, as will gilded mirrors, gold leaf, Impressionist art, lantern-style light fixtures, and of course the fleur-de-lis motif all over the walls and tables.

But it's still an American place, with its reasonable prices, large portions, and a big menu. At the low end, around $9, are the Berry French Toast and the Risotto Cakes and Eggs.

The menu includes three hashes: corned beef, salmon (with smoked and cured salmon and a lemon dill sauce), and Latin (chorizo, onions, cilantro, and sour cream); notable omelets include the open-faced Colette and a blue cheese–shrimp. For sweets, the multigrain pancakes come with banana-pecan sauce, and the French toast is studded with berries. Crepes are available during the week only.

The items we ate almost sent us into lovers' tangles. The La Provence Omelet with sausage was perfectly light and fluffy despite being loaded with sausage; the hollandaise on the Benedicts wasn't gooey like it is in a lot of places, but "light with some bite," as someone chuckled. My friend Cheryl had pancakes with a crème brûlée sauce that tasted like honeysuckle and had the consistency of eggnog; I shamelessly dipped my multigrain pancakes in it, and when I wanted more, I started lightly stroking Cheryl's arm.

By then, Cheryl's boyfriend was giving me a look, so I switched to other passions: a run past the pastry counter for something to go. Hmmm, shall it be the cheese brioche, the almond brioche, the chocolate croissant, the Napoleon, the meringue cookie, the mousse cake, the orange éclair. . . .

Wait: Long on weekends after about 9 a.m. and sometimes even during the week. **Large groups:** With notice. **Coffee:** Nossa Familia Coffee. **Other drinks:** Espresso, Italian sodas, lemonade, beer, and wine. **Feel-goods:** You can flirt with French cuties. **Health options:** C'mon—it's French! **WiFi:** No.

Pine State Biscuits

Old School/Mom & Pop

Y'all come visit and have some biscuits!
3640 SE Belmont St. (SE/Belmont) ~ 503-236-3346 ~
pinestatebiscuits.com
2204 NE Alberta St. (NE/Alberta) ~ 503-477-6605 ~
Daily 7 a.m. to 2 p.m.
$8–$10 (Visa, MasterCard)

———————◆•◆———————

When you're talking to Kevin Atchley, one of the owners of Pine State Biscuits, it's clear that he's a restaurant guy through and through. He politely gives credit to previous mentors, compliments all his vendors, and lovingly describes the eight-month process he and his partners went through with their "chef and foodie" friends to get just the right biscuit recipe. And then he'll drop something like this on you: "See that cabinet over the door, how it's facin' the kitchen? We're gonna put a TV set in there, and y'all ain't gonna know we're watchin' ACC basketball!"

Yes, Atchley is just as much a North Carolinian as he is a Portland foodie, and he and his partners—Brian Snyder and Walt Alexander, all Pine State transplants and NC State Wolfpack fans—have given the Portland breakfast scene something it never had before: a genuine biscuit kitchen.

Take this mix of old-style Southern goodness and modern restaurant professionalism, throw in some Portland foodie sensibility, and you have Pine State Biscuits. They built a following at the Portland Farmers Market with golden Creamtop Buttermilk Biscuits served with sausage or mushroom gravy, thick-cut bacon, fried chicken, eggs, grits, and preserves.

Such was this following that within two weeks of the "soft" opening, the Belmont location was already doing the same amount of business as at the market: about 500 biscuits daily; but as Atchley says, "now we won't run out." Especially since they opened another location on Alberta Street in 2010. There, they won't run out of seating, either, with about 50 seats including an outdoor section. They also intend to serve alcohol there.

Both locations are perfectly positioned to take advantage of the neighborhood feel; Belmont gets a little commuter rush, too. Just don't think of it as a regular restaurant. Each location is designed as a Carolina-style biscuit shack, with only a few tables. The idea is to eat it quick and keep moving, or just get something to go.

So, what's in this fabulous biscuit, anyway? Of course, Atchley won't tell. But he will say there's no shortening at all. There is some butter, but all the flakiness comes, he says, entirely from baking technique. "We decided to do something a little more health oriented. We use very, very fresh ingredients, all perishable and sourced as close to home as possible. The inspiration is from North Carolina, but the ingredients are all from right around the greater Portland area."

To further tempt us, Atchley offers sweet tea and Cheerwine (a super-sweet cherry soda from North Carolina), and he occasionally features country ham. "When all the true-blood North Carolinians come in and visit with us," Atchley says, "the first thing they say is, 'When are y'all gonna do country ham?'"

Country ham is a heavily salted, cured bacon Atchley admits is an acquired taste; what he has, on occasion, is ham from Johnson County, North Carolina, which has about 40 percent the usual salt content of a "real" country ham. "It's more of a domestic prosciutto," he says. Still, to many Portlanders it will seem awfully salty; that, of course, is what the sweet tea is for.

Wait: Long on weekends. **Large groups:** Maybe at the Alberta location. **Coffee:** Stumptown. **Other drinks:** Sweet tea and Cheerwine soda, hand-crafted chocolate milk made by a local chocolatier. **Feelgoods:** Everything's local and fresh. **Health options:** Does "no shortening in the biscuits" count? **WiFi:** No.

Podnah's Pit

Old School/Weekend
Git yer Texas on!
1469 NE Prescott St. (NE/Alberta) ~ 503-281-3700 ~ *podnahspit.com*
Breakfast weekends 9 a.m. to 1 p.m.
$9–$12 (all major cards)

———————◆━●━◆———————

Podnah's Pit doesn't look like much, inside or out. And the menu, especially at breakfast, is as simple and to-the-point as the décor is. But Podnah's is a serious attempt to capture the simple, profound magic of Texas-style barbecue.

Podnah's doesn't actually serve barbecue at breakfast, but here the emphasis is as much on *Texas* as on *barbecue*, and besides, barbecue isn't just a style of cooking or a sauce; it's a state of mind and a way of life. Like Podnah's Pit, it is utterly non-ornamental and is entirely about substance. I once experienced a slightly teary moment of peace at a Formica Podnah's table, sipping iced tea and chewing a piece of brisket while Dolly Parton sang "Smoky Mountain Memories."

I'm not alone in this experience. Among the volumes of positive comments about Podnah's on the Internet, the one must-read is the Food Dude's rapturous soliloquy at *portlandfoodanddrink.com*. In describing childhood summers in Maypearl, Texas, he weaves together images of hay bales, ceiling fans, raising a calf, losing his virginity, a living room he wasn't allowed to use, "impossibly red tomatoes," and watching his grandmother make "perfect chocolate pies with a meringue that always cried a little; she said they were angel's tears."

There are no pancakes or waffles, but there's plenty of food—until the kitchen runs out. You can get biscuits and gravy for $5.50; add a couple of eggs for another $1.50. Or you can get just a biscuit with jam for $2.25 (or 3 for $6). The biscuits are, according to the *Oregonian*, "the best biscuits in town—at once buttery, tall, flaky and tender, with a subtle crispness around the edges." You can get them with grits, ham, and two eggs for $8.75—in fact, I recommend you do.

A little farther up the fanciness scale is a yummy smoked trout hash ($9.25 with two eggs), and more basic is a taco with potatoes, egg, and cheese for $5.25. If you get it, add chorizo for another $1.50 and plan on taking a nap soon afterward. The house-made salsa is available on the taco, too, and isn't to be missed. There will also be the occasional pot of *menudo* (a spicy soup), *migas* (a Tex-Mex classic with peppers and cheese and tortilla), and maybe some *kolaches*, Czech fruit-filled pastries that for some odd reason are huge in Texas.

Even now, sitting at my computer, I think back to a moment at Podnah's Pit. It was early on a Saturday morning and I was there with my friend Steve, from Missouri. We were filling up before doing some work around his house. I was having the hash, and he was happily working on a burrito. We weren't talking much, because there wasn't much to say, and when Tony Joe White started singing "Polk Salad Annie," Steve half-closed his eyes, stopped chewing for a second, dropped his head a little, and started groovin'. I slouched a little deeper into my chair, felt the warmth radiating from my stomach, reached for some more tea, and let myself drift down South for a spell.

Wait: A little. **Large groups:** No. **Coffee:** Self-serve Stumptown. **Other drinks:** Orange juice, mimosas, and red beer (Tecate beer mixed with tomato juice). **Feel-goods:** It's all smoked in-house; cage-free eggs. **Health options:** Uh, no. **WiFi:** No.

¿Por Qué No?

Weekend

Food from Mexico, everything else pure Portland.
4635 SE Hawthorne Blvd. (SE/Hawthorne) ~ 503-954-3138 ~
porquenotacos.com
3524 N Mississippi Ave. (N/Inner) ~ 503-467-4149 ~
Weekends 11 a.m. to 3 p.m.
$12–$14 (Visa, MasterCard, no checks)

———————◆•◆———————

No place is more Portland than ¿Por Qué No? It occupies prime real estate on two very-Portland streets: Hawthorne and Mississippi. Both locations are quite literally crawling with hipsters. They are bright and colorful and perhaps just weird enough to suit our city's unofficial motto: "Keep Portland Weird."

It's also very serious about food, community, and sustainability. The owner got the idea for a taqueria on a trip to Mexico; after opening on North Mississippi in 2005, he created a bike corral out front, and in 2010 fulfilled a goal of offering health insurance to employees. He also takes his staff on overnights to Mount Hood and the coast.

A second location opened on Hawthorne in 2009, and according to an article in the *Oregonian*, the tables are built from salvaged wood, the barstools from used rebar, the bar front and patio fence from reclaimed doors, and the benches straight out of the Hawthorne Theatre.

To all this classic Portland-ness, Portlanders have reacted in two predictable ways: adoration and argument. The former will be apparent if you check out any local media outlet or just try to get into the place. You order at the counter and wait for your food at a table, and both of those experiences may last a while.

At brunch, you can order off the regular menu, and there are always specials, but the basic menu is Chilaquiles (tortillas in ranchero sauce with eggs and a side of beans), Huevos Rancheros, Huevos Mexicanos (egg–bean–pico de gallo–cheese scramble with guacamole and chips), and Tamale with Eggs.

As for the argument, I refer you to (as of summer 2010) 316 reviews on *yelp.com*, a visit from virtually every blogger in town, and a long, often bitter discussion on *portlandfood.org* that ventures into sociology, economics, Mexican culture, and the authenticity of their food.

Ah yes, authenticity: this is a big deal with ¿Por Qué No?, and its detractors. Their website says, "We have traveled from the Pacific Coast of Mexico to the mountains of Oaxaca to share the flavors & the essence of what we found." They also take an annual food trip to Mexico. And yet a lot of folks say it isn't authentic Mexican. I think that means that either folks ate something in Mexico that wasn't like ¿Por Qué No?—the Food Dude at *portlandfoodanddrink.com* said it reminded him more of Hermosa Beach than Mexico—or they say it can't be authentic because the place is clean and owned by white people, and the food is fresh, healthy, mildly spiced, and as cheap as a taco truck. (*Willamette Week* did a story in 2005 with the headline "The $2.50 Taco"—and now they're priced at $2.75 to $3.50.)

There's no reason to think any place could live up to all this discussion, be it pro or con. But if you want a taste of Portland culture and Mexican food, and maybe want to get into some heated discussion about both, get in line at ¿Por Qué No?

Wait: Can get long. **Large groups:** No. **Coffee:** Courier. **Other drinks:** Horchata, seasonal fresh juices, Jarritos soda, Mexican Coke with real sugar, beer, and margaritas. **Feel-goods:** They are all about sustainable and local. **Health options:** Good vegetarian and vegan options. **WiFi:** No.

Po'Shines

Mom & Pop/Old School

At the intersection of food, church, and community.
8139 N Denver St. (N/Outer) ~ 503-978-9000 ~ *poshines.com*
Monday through Thursday 7 a.m. to 3 p.m., Friday 7 a.m. to 10 p.m.,
Saturday 8 a.m. to 10 p.m.
$11–$13 (all major cards, no checks)

When I first ate at Po'Shines, I wrote on my blog, "I may have found my next neighborhood." Kenton, centered around Interstate and Denver, has all the markings of the "next thing": old but nice homes, pedestrian-friendly streets, parks, a Max station, and a little commercial strip of a few blocks with some empty places for businesses to set up. And it's got a breakfast place.

Kenton still has that grass-roots feeling, as well, epitomized by Po'Shines, which is part restaurant and part nonprofit, both of them run by a church. Here's what their website has to say:

> *Much of our profit goes back into the cafe and to our youth training program. As a part of the Teach me to Fish Organization we provide training and counseling to youth and young adults of our community who are in need of such services as job skills, life skills and GED preparedness. All of our regular employees volunteer their time, including our Chef and our Management Staff.*
>
> *Our mission is simple: feed the community and feed it well.*

When I had the CEO and manager on my podcast, it became the finest half hour of my broadcast career. They were polite and reserved until, a few minutes in, I asked the CEO (also the minister next door at Celebration Tabernacle) about the food, and when he started in about sweet potatoes, catfish, and peach cobbler, his manager and (and nephew) shook his head, smiled, and said, "Oh, we're goin' to *church* now!" From then on, those two preached the gospel of soul food.

To see what they're talking about, get the Bayou Breakfast Burrito with blackened catfish. Not many places in Portland have catfish (and the Po'Shines folks won't say where they get it), but when it's good, fresh, and blackened, eating it can be a religious experience. I also once had chicken and waffles: three briny full wings fried with a little something spicy in the dark crust, sitting next to a pair of sturdy waffles that held up while I was eating the chicken and after I slathered them with syrup.

You can also get grits, fried okra, a creole omelet, chocolate or blueberry or plain pancakes, cornmeal waffles, a Down Home Pork Chop, and Chef Lorenzo's Down Home Louisiana Scramble, which is hash browns, bell peppers, onions, and diced tomatoes with your choice of bacon, ham, or sausage, topped with two scrambled eggs, cheese, and country gravy. Mercy!

The Southern flair is legit (the CEO/minister is from Louisiana), and so is the hospitality. The whole time I sat there, the staff was greeting customers like old friends, and there was some kind of little meeting happening among four people at a table. (When I drove by again the next day, the same four people were sitting at the same table.) There's a small kiddie area, a couple of sofas, jazz posters on the wall, and the biggest gumball machine you'll ever see.

Plan on spending a little time when you eat at Po'Shines—not that they're slow, but because you just might want to settle in for a spell and visit with those nice folks.

Wait: Maybe on weekends. **Large groups:** With notice. **Coffee:** Gourmet Sumatra. **Other drinks:** Juice, sweet iced tea, and house drinks including green tea and juice, and hibiscus sweet tea. **Feelgoods:** They just might save your soul. **Health options:** Decent vegetarian options. **WiFi:** Yes.

Prasad

Hip/Veggie

Too much loveliness.
925 NW Davis (NW/Pearl) ~ 503-224-3993 ~ *prasadcuisine.com*
Weekdays 7:30 a.m. to 11 a.m., weekends 9 a.m. to 11 a.m.
$10–$12 (all major cards, no checks)

———————◆•◆———————

I confess that sometimes I feel a little piggish when I go to Prasad. This is despite the absolutely charming staff, who have told me they go out of their way to make folks like me feel comfortable.

Prasad, you see, may be the single healthiest spot in all of the Portland breakfast scene. In fact, it's not even *of* the Portland breakfast scene. It's a visitor from the world of health, fitness, and spirituality. It just happens to serve excellent breakfast food during the morning hours (as well as its lunch menu starting at 9, by the way.)

Consider their mission statement:

> *Prasad is an offering of sustainable organic cuisine to nourish and heal the mind, body and soul. Here to honor our earth, community and one another, we gratefully utilize the precious ingredients of dedicated farmers, fostering change to provide a future of health, love and respect for all.*

And it's in the lobby of Yoga Pearl, which means it is without question the only breakfast place in town with little signs on the tables asking you to be mindful (read: quiet) because there's yoga and meditation going on.

So, the reason I feel piggish is that I've never come anywhere near a yoga class, and my diet is more a force for world destruction than any kind of healing. Whenever I eat at Prasad, I feel like a grateful visitor in their world . . . and I try not to flirt too much with the beautiful young women who run the place.

In fact, I had them on my podcast; they were the only guests to ever show up drinking kombucha. The owner, Karen Pride, is a restaurant lifer who went to culinary school and by her late 20s was in

Portland running a food cart at Northeast 15th and Alberta. When the old Blossoming Lotus place opened up in the Pearl, she pounced. "It's all so natural," she said on my show. "It's just the right spot, and everything happened the way it was meant to happen."

That in-the-flow attitude, combined with her travels, Eastern philosophy, and time as a vegan all show up in the menu at Prasad. Almost everything is vegan and gluten-free because she sees her role as helping people heal themselves through food.

Hence, there's gluten-free bread, from local baker New Cascadia, served with butter or jam; zucchini hummus, cucumber, and tomato; sprouts and avocado; or almond butter and fruit. There's a Chipotle Tempeh Scramble with black beans, spinach, tomatoes, carrots, zucchini, and avocado, served with green chili sauce, red rice, and toast. There's also a Chili Scramble with roasted garlic chili, chipotle tempeh, dark greens, spinach, avocado, scallions, quinoa, garlic tahini sauce, and toast. The best seller is the gluten-free oatmeal (from Bob's Red Mill) served with dried figs and currants, brazil nuts, fresh fruit, vanilla, cinnamon, and maple syrup. I don't often get oatmeal, but I do often dream of Prasad's.

The oatmeal is indicative of how I get over feeling out of place at Prasad. It's all about relaxing, being happy, and peaceful, and eating well. Anybody can dig that.

Wait: A little. **Large groups:** No. **Coffee:** Stumptown organic cold press. **Other drinks:** Foxfire teas, ginger tea, chai, and amazing smoothies. **Feel-goods:** Everything! **Health options:** Everything! **WiFi:** No.

Prescott Cafe

Mom & Pop/Old School

Home cookin' in a place from the '40s—literally.
6205 NE Prescott St. (NE/Outer) ~ 503-287-8495
Weekdays 7 a.m. to 2 p.m., weekends 6 a.m. to 2 p.m.
$8–$10 (Cash and checks only—but they've got a cool old-timey register!)

———————◆•◆———————

When Jean and I got to the Prescott Cafe and sat down, the first thing I read on the menu was, "We use real butter, real cheese, and fresh grated real potatoes." And I thought, "As opposed to what?" And then I remembered shopping at New Seasons Market, feeling overwhelmed by the French, Portuguese, and English Gruyères and Camemberts and what-the-hell-ever . . . so now I'm thinking the message of Prescott Cafe is, "That ain't real cheese—and neither is that soy stuff. We use *cheddar*. Like from Tillamook."

In fact, the whole place says, "We don't mess around—sit down, relax, and we'll go back and cook you some food."

The Prescott has white lace curtains, every version of Trivial Pursuit cards on the table, the specials written on an RC Cola chalkboard, items like a 2 x 2 (eggs and pancakes) and pig in a blanket and corned beef hash and a *six-egg* omelet. It's the United States of Generica,

straight out of black-and-white television, cash only, and served quick with a smile.

Sometimes you want to be impressed. Other times you want to be fed and you want the server to bring you a pair of gigantic tasty biscuits and say, "You want honey, honey?"

While we were testing each other's trivia knowledge, I noticed a picture of the place from the 1940s, back when it was just one room. The server said it used to be called Mary's Fine Dining. She turned to a guy sitting alone in a booth and said, "Bill (not his real name), did you used to eat here back in the '40s?" He looked like he could have fed his kids here back then, and his response of "No, I'm only 40!" drew a laugh from several tables. I noticed I was the only guy in the room under 60 and not wearing a plaid shirt.

The menu had things like linguiça (a kind of sausage) and eggs, and three-egg omelets with shrimp or crab or otherwise-unspecified "seafood." See a pattern? Eggs and meat and potatoes. The Working Man's Feed is three eggs, meat, hashbrowns, biscuits, and gravy. Strawberry waffles when strawberries are in season, which is something I admire. You aren't supposed to have strawberries in January.

Is the food good? Well, that depends on what you like. Jean said she liked it because it's what she grew up with. My fried eggs were perfectly round and still had little pockets of butter and grease on them—literally just like Mom used to make. My hash may have come from a big can. The huge blueberry pancakes came with a slowly dissolving pile of whipped butter and squeeze bottles of maple and blueberry syrups.

I didn't see one thing I couldn't have made at home. And that either is, or isn't, the point. The Prescott Cafe is the kind of place where you just relax, feel at home, and eat.

Wait: Never seen one. **Large groups:** With some notice. **Coffee:** Old school. **Other drinks:** Tea. **Feel-goods:** Real cheese! **Health options:** Some vegetarian items. And real potatoes! **WiFi:** Check back in 20 years.

Rose's Restaurant and Bakery

Old School

A Portland tradition or a lesser replica?
838 NW 23rd Ave. (other locations in Sherwood, West Linn, and Vancouver) ~ 503-222-5292 ~ *eatatroses.com*
Breakfast weekdays 9 a.m. to 11 a.m., weekends 8 a.m. to 2 p.m.
$10–$15 (all major cards)

━━━━━━━◆━●━◆━━━━━━━

When longtime Portlanders talk about Rose's, their eyes almost mist. It was a legend on Northwest 23rd Avenue starting in 1956 when Rose Naftalin founded it. Seems like everybody has a story about eating at Rose's: first bite of corned beef or first date or, in the case of former Senator Mark Hatfield, the site where he proposed to his wife. That was the old Rose's. When these longtime Portlanders talk about the new Rose's, misty eyes often turn to crinkled noses.

I moved to Portland after the old Rose's closed. The new Rose's looks to me like a quiet, friendly place that serves a deli-style breakfast: kosher salami omelets; scrambles with lox, corned beef, or smoked salmon hash; cinnamon roll French toast; and blintzes. I find none of it to be exceptional in any way, though the prices seem to be inflated a bit by the location.

In a bigger sense, what Rose's looks like to me is a brand somebody is trying to take global. It started as a neighborhood place with a family-style atmosphere where everyone ate well and had fun. Rose retired in 1967, the place closed in 1993, and everybody agrees it was a sad thing.

The new owners developed a new business plan, as stated in the *Portland Business Journal*: "(develop) Rose's as a growing regional chain . . . open as many as eight restaurants and lounges between Seattle and the California border. Eventually, the duo want to expand Rose's to the East Coast."

Before I get to what the community seems to think of the place on Northwest 23rd Avenue (not exactly its original location, by the way), I'll tell you ahead of time that I don't see what all the (mostly negative) fuss is about. It's not the best food on the street, but it stays open, and there's rarely a wait.

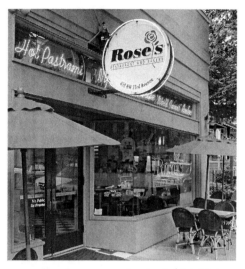

Of course, it may be there's no wait because a lot of people can't stand the place. A reviewer for *Willamette Week*, after paying homage to the old Rose's, went on to trash the new one with lines like "there was no evidence that an actual chicken had come anywhere near the insipid (chicken soup)" and the "meat loaf looked like that mysterious 'Swiss steak' they used to serve at the school cafeteria." Well.

One online reviewer suggested the same thing I would: forget about the past and judge the place on its own merits.

In the back of the restaurant on 23rd, there's a Rose's sign hanging in a corner. I asked the server if that was the original sign from the old place, and she said no, it's a replica one-fourth the size of the original.

A lesser replica, hanging over the whole scene, not as prominent or as bright as it once was, but still there. Seems fitting to me.

Wait: Not much. **Large groups:** Yes. **Coffee:** Farmer Brothers. **Other drinks:** Stash Tea, espresso, Italian sodas. **Feel-goods:** None that they claim. **Health options:** Egg beaters and whites for $.99 **WiFi:** No.

Salty's

Weekend/Buffet/Classy

Seafood extravaganza with a view.

3839 NE Marine Drive (NE/Outer) ~ 503-808-1998 ~ *saltys.com/portland*

Sunday 9:15 a.m. to 1 p.m.

$34.99 all-you-can-eat buffet; $5 more for champagne brunch; $10 off before 10 a.m. $1.50 per year of age for children 12 and under (all major cards)

Big. That's what Salty's is, and big is what you'll get: a big time, a big belly, a big bill, a big marketing plan, and a big view. The weekend brunch at Salty's can hardly be called breakfast, although breakfast items are in abundance (along with everything else). An experience is what it is.

You drive past the yacht clubs and the Portland airport to a big building on the shore of the Columbia River. You offer your car to the valet service (free, but you should tip). You walk into a buzzing scene of staff greeting you and running around with trays of food, and people surrounding buffet tables looking like animals released to the feed trough.

The place feels like a factory, but it borders on elegant. It's also very structured. Our young server greeted us immediately and offered beverages. When two friends joined us unexpectedly, he said the same things to them, word for word. Salty's also has a newsletter, chef blogs on its website, brochures touting its classification as Nation's Best Sunday Brunch by *msn-citysearch.com*, and live music three nights a week.

As for the scene, you'll see old folks dressed up, entire families, and young people shuffling in wearing sweatpants. It doesn't matter; it's all about stuffing a pile of food—most of it from the ocean—down your gullet. Here's the list of what was being served when I went:

Peel-and-eat prawns, Dungeness crab, salmon lox, seafood seviche, clams and mussels, fresh oysters shucked to order, omelets, crepes, pastas made to order, Belgian waffles, fresh fruit, vegetable and cheese trays, array of seasonal salads, bacon and sausage, country potatoes, biscuits and gravy, teriyaki salmon, prime rib and baked ham, Salty's world-famous seafood chowder, coffee, juice, soda, tea, desserts made from scratch, apple dumplings, breakfast breads and pastries, and a fountain of cascading liquid chocolate.

Yes, there *is* the fountain of cascading liquid chocolate. You haven't been indulgent until you've stood with a heaping plate of food in one hand, holding your marshmallow or strawberry under four feet of molten chocolate with the other hand, and giggling like an eight-year-old.

Nothing at Salty's will be the best version you've ever had. But it would be hard to cook that stuff ahead of time, feed hundreds of people, and have it taste consistently excellent. (I read one online review that said the food was "about on par with a nice hotel banquet.")

My girlfriend and I once spent $15 on fresh crab at a little market in Florence, and then ate the whole thing on a blanket at Sunset Beach. That we will remember as a wonderful meal in a romantic setting. Salty's, I think, we will recall as an over-the-top, special-occasion spectacle with good friends, very friendly service, a comfortable setting, and a fantastic view.

Wait: Almost none if you make a reservation. **Large groups:** Absolutely. **Coffee:** Starbucks. **Other drinks:** Espresso (à la carte), build-your-own Bloody Marys, bottomless mimosas, champagne, and juices. **Feel-goods:** You don't have to eat for about two days afterward. **Health options:** In a place with a four-foot chocolate waterfall? **WiFi:** Yes.

Sanborn's

New/Classy

Real cooking, real casual.
3200 SE Milwaukie Ave. (SE/Powell) ~ 503-963-8000 ~
sanbornsbreakfast.com
Wednesday through Sunday 8 a.m. to 2 p.m.
$10–$16 (Visa, MasterCard)

At some point in this town—at least, if you're researching breakfast places—your mind starts to fill up. You reject new information the same way you'd wave off a short stack when you're already loaded down with an omelet.

So it was when a friend named Robb said I needed to check out this place called Sanborn's. Actually, what he said was, "It's the *shizzle* for breakfast." This made me doubt Robb's credibility, as did the place's location at Southeast Powell and Milwaukie. Hardly an area one associates with fine dining.

Undeterred, I headed down there, and as soon as I walked in, I remembered how foolish geography-based restaurant reviews are. I was confronted with a classy-looking place that also seemed completely casual, and best of all, no line whatsoever at 10 a.m. on a Saturday. In fact, a little Internet research revealed that hardly a word has ever been written about the place: one glowing review in *Willamette Week*, to be exact.

Ah, the mysteries of Portland breakfast.

So, how does this sound? You slide into a comfy booth in a spacious, natural-light restaurant. A pleasant server (one is the owner's daughter who runs the front-of-house staff) brings you a French press of coffee (that's a $5.99 option; a regular cup is $1.99) and hands you a menu full of delicious-sounding meals at perfectly reasonable prices, with half orders available on everything except potatoes.

It's heavy on baked goodies, with two waffles, sourdough French toast, and five kinds of pancakes ranging from $6.29 to $8.49: buttermilk; buckwheat; sourdough (from a genuine 1847 Oregon Trail starter); blueberry with powdered sugar and blueberry compote; and potato with diced green onion and egg, served with sour cream or house-made applesauce. Then you cruise over

to the Specialties section of the menu and see the German Pancake with whipped butter, lemon, and powdered sugar; the Apple Pancake with sliced apples caramelized in sugar and cinnamon; seasonal pancakes; and the Mango Pancake with sliced mango caramelized with sugar, ginger, lemon, and orange peel.

Stop and read that last dish again. This place is a serious restaurant!

I went for the Build-Your-Own Omelet section (any two ingredients in a three-egg omelet for $10.99, another $0.89 each for more ingredients) and got one with chorizo, feta, and peppers. There were 15 other ingredients to choose from, and you can get the same deal in a scramble for $9.29.

What came out was as surprising as the rest of the experience: a massive omelet in which the eggs had been whipped, then stuffed with the ingredients, folded over, and baked. I was stunned. And soon I was stuffed.

Sanborn's is also casual and friendly (and even a little odd: for some reason, every price ends with a nine). And it's not crowded. And it's at Powell and Milwaukie. Who knew?

Wait: A little on weekends. **Large groups:** With notice. **Coffee:** Bridgetown. **Other drinks:** French-press coffee, mochas (!), and teas; individual teas, hot cider, six juices, milk. **Feel-goods:** None that are touted. **Health options:** Egg substitute or whites available on omelets and scrambles. Veggie sausage an option. **WiFi:** No.

Sapphire Hotel

New/Classy

Come in and get some, sweetie.
5008 SE Hawthorne Blvd. ~ 503-232-6333 ~ *thesapphirehotel.com*
Brunch weekends 9 a.m. to 2 p.m.
$13–$16 (all major cards)

———————◆●◆———————

The Sapphire Hotel, which isn't a hotel, is clearly going for an evening vibe at all hours, with kind of a vintage angle. With the hanging lampshades, throw cushions on the benches, vaguely Asian artwork, and nine fancy cocktails on the menu, they're all about being cozy and intimate. Obviously, this would be more effective when the sun isn't shining.

And speaking of, um, intimacy . . . not only does their website claim that the place used to be a brothel, they even have a flashing neon "RED" light up in the corner. In fact, their website takes the whole thing to a romantic extreme:

> *The Sapphire Hotel was originally a turn of the century seedy hotel in Portland Oregon inhabited by sailors, travelers and ladies of the night. They rented rooms by the week, night or by the hour and spent long days and evenings in the lobby drinking, laughing, eating, talking and kissing.*

Sounds downright sweet, doesn't it? It's not like there were "hookers" and "vagrants" and "cheating husbands" screwing there; just sailors and ladies of the night kissing. So the Sapphire definitely hits all the comfy/luxury/sexy buttons, and even during the day, I have to say, it works pretty well.

Might as well run through some of those cocktails. Their calling card seems to be the Alotta Mimosa, which is $10 all-you-can-drink, available at brunch only. (A single is $6.) There's also a Bellini, Bloody Mary, a Bloody Mick (the Mary plus a bacon salt rim, a drizzle of Worcestershire, and a steak garnish), a Gin Fizz, and the Elixir, with

New Deal vodka, muddled with cucumber and lemon and mixed with MonaVie's blend of açaí berry and 19 other fruits. Damn!

By the way, did I mention the sexy vibe? The evening cocktail menu offers such drinks as the Other Woman, Eve and Apple, and the Naughty Toddy.

I wanted a cappuccino, but there are no espresso drinks here. You're welcome, though, to head next door to Albina Press and bring something in.

The brunch menu has some interesting things going on, at least in name. I had a Benedict with cremini and oyster mushrooms. Alice had the Salmon Corn Cakes, which were about the size and shape of falafel patties, served with stone-ground mustard aioli; for another buck it could also be a Benedict. Steve went with the Sweet Potato and Yam Frittata (with smoked Maasdam cheese, spicy Sriracha sour cream, kale, and chard,) and it occurred to me that for all the confusion between those two tubers, I've never seen them served together. One wonders who can tell which is which.

Honestly, I wasn't blown away by the food. But I can get jaded. It was cooked well, looked great, and I wasn't disappointed, but nothing really popped to me. Steve and Alice both liked it very much, and by the time we left, the place was quickly filling up.

I did enjoy the experience and would recommend it for a relaxed, no-line, solid brunch along Hawthorne—especially if the old timey/vintage/brothel vibe is your gig.

Wait: Maybe a little. **Large groups:** With notice. **Coffee:** Stumptown. **Other drinks:** Foxfire French-press teas, Ginger Brew, and plenty of cocktails; espresso next door. **Feel-goods:** They "make every effort to use only local, organic produce and natural, free-range beef and eggs." **Health options:** Egg whites available on omelets and scrambles. **WiFi:** Yes.

Sckavone's

Weekend
Still there, still in the family.
4100 SE Division St. (SE/Division) ~ 503-235-0630 ~ *sckavones.com*
Weekends 8 a.m. to 2 p.m.
$11–$13 (Visa, MasterCard, no checks)

———————◆•◆———————

Since I am the author of a breakfast guidebook, there are two questions I get all the time, neither of them easily answered. One is what's my favorite place, and the other is where a person can go for brunch without a long line.

I am somewhat ashamed to admit that whenever I answer either one, I always forget about Sckavone's. In fact, I'm willing to bet that unless you live near the place, you don't even know it exists. And sometimes I think the folks who run it like things that way.

It's been open since 2006—meaning it should have been in the first edition of this book—and yet I rarely run into anybody who's been there. It's just a little neighborhood place with, as the website says, "No pretense, just really good food served by nice people in a great space."

It's a space with a great history, as well. Nick Sckavone came from Italy to Southeast Portland in 1908. He led a labor action against the *Oregonian* at age 15, and at 17 he formed a club of neighborhood baseball teams, and there's a field in Westmoreland named for him. In 1930, he opened a drugstore at Southeast 41st and Division, and in 1980 his grandson took it over.

It still has every bit the look and feel of a neighborhood place—and the original counter—as well as the complete absence of a wait when I visited on a Saturday at 10 a.m. We left close to 11, and there was still no line.

We tried the corned beef hash (crispy and excellent, eggs poached just right), the smoked salmon Benedict (good sauce and fish, muffin still crispy), and the French toast, which really was more like apple pie, with cream cheese icing and cinnamon and chunks of apple. It wasn't really French toast, as far as I'm concerned, and it was too big to eat the whole thing, and too intense to have solo, but it was good. If you have a group of four or more, have everybody get something savory and get one order of the French toast as the table sweet. I think if you ate the whole thing, you'd have to run around the block to burn off the energy . . . and then take a nap.

Other folks had omelets, including a veggie with a big chunk of avocado on it. Portions were large, coffee was good, we all agreed the food was excellent, and seven of us got out of there for about $85 with tip. Actually, I think one person didn't order, so it was the usual $12 or so per person, with coffee and tip.

I really had no idea about this place, and I should have. But if you're looking for a combination of comfort, a chilled-out vibe, and quality, check out Sckavone's. It's just your basic neighborhood place, and it has been for 80 years. Kind of makes a guy want to move to the neighborhood and sit at that counter all the time.

Wait: None that I've seen. **Large groups:** Yes. **Coffee:** K&F. **Other drinks:** Tea, Italian sodas, milkshakes, and floats. **Feel-goods:** None they tout. **Health options:** Veggie sausage. **WiFi:** No.

Screen Door

Weekend/New/Classy

Southern soul meets Northwest style.

2337 E Burnside St. (E Burnside) ~ 503-542-0880 ~
screendoorrestaurant.com

Brunch weekends 9 a.m. to 2:30 p.m.

$10–$18 (all major cards, checks)

I was all ready to make fun of the Screen Door. I'm from the South, you see, and when a restaurant outside the South calls itself Southern, I tend to load up the sarcasm cannon. Waiting for my friends at the Screen Door, I saw Swiss Chard and Bacon Frittata, Goat Cheese Scramble with Roasted Red Peppers, and Bananas Foster French Toast on the specials board. "Good luck finding any of *that* in the South," I thought.

Maybe it's not a Southern place, in the stereotypical sense. It's a Portland restaurant with a Southern theme. And, as it turned out, that was just fine with all of us.

Still, the sarcasm cannon almost went off when I saw something called Garden Grits, with spinach, grilled tomatoes, onions, and provolone, and Farm Grits with ham, poached eggs, and provolone. I thought, "That's not how you do grits!"

I emailed this news to some of the prime Southern ladies in my life. Here are some of their responses:

My mom, Marjorie, in Memphis: "Well child, I just can't imag-ine all these names they thought up for grits! Cheese grits is a standard brunch dish here, but with cheddar, for Pete's sake! If I ordered regular grits—which a menu would never need to say, cause grits is grits—I would just put a heap'a butter on it. Mercy!"

My sister-in-law, Lela, in Memphis: "Having been born in Alabama, raised in Tennessee and schooled in New Orleans, I've yet to meet the self-respecting grit that would interact with Provolone."

My sister, Lucy, in Maryland: "Provolone is great on a turkey sandwich but definitely NOT on grits. I may have left the true South but there are just some things you don't fergit." (Yes, she typed *fergit*, but she was going for the effect. I think.)

Dee, a family friend in Atlanta: "All that gussied up grits on the menu is just for those poor Northwesterners who don't know any better."

So the South didn't exactly rise up in favor of this grits thing, nor for the Screen Door's Praline Bacon, which is very sweet and covered with pecans. And I didn't have the heart to tell the ladies about the Tofu Hash.

But I had to email everyone back and say, "I hate to tell y'all, but this place was *good*, and the regular side grits have cheddar in them." Indeed, the Breakfast Crew was entirely impressed, from my Crabcake Benedict to the waffle smothered in fruit and whipped cream to the Alabama Scramble with ham, green onions, and pimento cheese. The menu is full up (as my grandma would have said) with modern twists on old faves: a mushroom omelet with morels and fontina cheese; Brioche Vanilla Bean French Toast; a puff pastry filled with eggs, caramelized onions, fontina, tomato, and thyme cream.

Two objections come through in most of the Crew's reactions to the Screen Door: the place is way too loud, and it feels a little overpriced. I told the Southern ladies the dinner menu included hush puppies at $5.75 and fried chicken for $14.75; their responses were unprintable.

I don't think there are too many places in the South like the Screen Door. But I think maybe that's the South's loss.

Wait: Legendary; no cover outside and a small area inside. **Large groups:** Yes. **Coffee:** Stumptown. **Other drinks:** Fresh juice and a wide range of cocktails. **Feel-goods:** Produce and meats from local vendors. **Health options:** Organic ingredients. Tofu for $1.50 or egg whites for $1. **WiFi:** No.

Seasons and Regions

Weekend

It's all about the fish.
6660 SW Capitol Hwy. (SW/Outer) ~ 503-244-6400 ~
seasonsandregions.com
Breakfast weekends 9 a.m. to 2 p.m.
$12–$16 (all major cards)

———————◆•◆———————

Seasons and Regions is a restaurant that practically nobody in the Portland breakfast scene has ever heard of. For one thing, it's on Southwest Capitol Highway, hardly the center of our culinary world. Since breakfast is served only on weekends, it's hardly the signature offering. If you were to drive by, you would probably think, "Gee, it looks like an old Dairy Queen or something." And that's precisely what it was; the drive-through window is still there, in fact.

So what is served? One word: seafood. Even on the weekend brunch menu, the bounty of the sea dominates. There's Crab Cake Benedict, Nova Scotia Benedict with house-smoked salmon, and Hangtown Fry with fried Willapa Bay oysters, eggs, bacon, spinach, and mushrooms topped with freshly grated Parmesan. There's Smoked Salmon Hash, Smoked Salmon Scramble, and the all-out Tillamook Scramble: three eggs scrambled with salmon, bay shrimp, Pacific cod, mushrooms, onions, spinach, tomatoes, and Tillamook cheddar. The prices are downright reasonable as well: the Tillamook Scramble is only $8.90.

Seasons comes off as a semi-serious place. And that's not a slight: the website boasts "Fresh Northwest seafood and shellfish, transformed into world class creations and served by friends." Many of the patrons are local regulars. There's a full bar, and the food falls somewhere between diner and cutting edge. They have down-home stuff like the Mexican Chorizo Breakfast Burrito and an apple waffle, and "fine-dining" stuff like garlic-parmesan cream sauce sauce on the Florentine Benedict and Northwest Omelet. Just about everything comes with rosemary potatoes (crispy outside, soft inside); light, fluffy rosemary scones; or both.

As you may imagine, a former Dairy Queen is not exactly an
architectural must-see. I happened
to eat there with three women (not
braggin', just sayin'), and they said
it "looks like a dude decorated it."
Trivial Pursuit cards were on the
unfinished wood tables along with
salt and pepper shakers shaped

like slot machines. Grapevine-shaped lights hung from a black ceiling that said "evening dinner," but the yellow walls said, "daytime
cheery." Faux picture windows "looked out" at lovely scenes that were
not Capitol Highway. A year-round outside seating area is covered by
a tent and has overhead heaters.

The owners (two dudes, by the way) met while working at
McCormick's Fish House & Bar in Beaverton, and critics would say
Seasons is just a local version of that chain. In a 2002 *Portland Business
Journal* story, the owners said they aim for a wide breadth of options
based on what's currently available, so you'll see a revolving menu and
different specials depending on the time of year.

My friends and I enjoyed our meal, especially because we didn't
have to wait at all on a Saturday morning. Seasons and Regions seems
to put more effort into dinners, but there's a lot to be said for a down-
home laid-back breakfast place with fresh seafood and just a hint of
fanciness without being over-the-top expensive.

Wait: Perhaps a little. **Large groups:** Better outside. **Coffee:**
Tully's. **Other drinks:** Kobos espresso, mimosas, Bloody Marys.
Feel-goods: Most ingredients are local, including from the owners'
farm. **Health options:** Egg substitutes available; gluten-free and vegetarian menu now available. **WiFi:** No.

Simpatica Dining Hall

Weekend/New/Classy

A serious place—and seriously good.
828 SE Ash St. (SE/Inner) ~ 503-235-1600 ~ *simpaticacatering.com*
Brunch Sunday 9 a.m. to 2 p.m.
$13–$16 (all major cards, checks)

Most of us diners are aware of only the normal world of restaurants—the ones with signs outside, private tables and food that's familiar. But there's another world of restaurants: it's a parallel universe of experimentation and innovation, and it's on a higher plane, like the New York fashion world is to the local mall. Most of us eat in the mall; the Serious Food People eat in New York.

Simpatica Dining Hall is of the Serious Food World, and it was born in a Portland restaurant movement that is simultaneously innovative and old-fashioned: family-style suppers featuring the creations of highly trained chefs and made from local ingredients. It started as invitation-only suppers among friends served in backyards or local restaurants. Three of the guys (two are owners of Viande, a specialty meat company) created a catering company that eventually started hosting events in the basement of the long-lost Pine Street Theater. This is Simpatica, where reservations-only fixed-menu dinners are served a couple of nights a week with brunch on Sundays.

Still, you sort of have to know where it is. A small line forms outside the nondescript building (with only a small sandwich board announc-

ing its presence) just before 9 a.m. every Sunday, with people doing crosswords and reading magazines to kill time. Seating is still family-style, so if you're a party of two, you'll be seated across from each other and next to another party. This leads to much cross-party conversation and menu discussion.

Despite the mildly underground vibe, it is a very serious restaurant. But neither the prices nor the attitude is worrisome. And, keeping to the old-is-new spirit that makes family dining from local farmers something revolutionary, the menu at Simpatica is really just all your breakfast favorites, a little fancied up and done very, very well. I had French toast, for example, with a smoky orange marmalade and Chantilly cream. At one point I was wiping up a combination of real maple syrup, cream, and marmalade with a piece of bacon, and I officially reached the top of both the fat intake scale and, not coincidentally, the pleasure scale. Another time I had a crab cake Benedict, and after one bite actually felt sad that it would have to end.

Other offerings I have seen on the ever-changing menu include a classic Eggs Benedict with ham; crepes filled with butternut squash or bacon, asparagus, and *crème fraiche*; an andouille and prosciutto hash; and lunch items like a much-raved-about cheeseburger and a Philly cheesesteak sandwich. All the meats are outstanding, as you would expect from guys who own a meat company; vegetarians will probably have to stick to the sweet stuff.

We counted four servers who stopped by our table at some point, all efficient and thoroughly knowledgeable about the entire menu. Substitutions were easy, and when other friends happened in and joined us, their orders were taken, and somehow the food all arrived together.

Among the many pleasures of living in Portland, one has to count the existence of young chefs like those who run Simpatica.

Wait: Can get long; get there when it opens if you're in a hurry. **Large groups:** Tough. Reservations for parties of eight or larger, maxed out at 20–25 people for groups. **Coffee:** Stumptown. **Other drinks:** Steven Smith teas, cocktails. **Feel-goods:** Everything is local. **Health options:** Not much for the vegetarians. **WiFi:** No.

Slappy Cakes

Kiddie/Veggie

"Let them eat—and cook their own—cakes!"
4246 SE Belmont (SE/Belmont) ~ 503-477-4805 ~ *slappycakes.com*
Monday through Thursday 8 a.m. to 2 p.m., Friday through Sunday
8 a.m. to 4 p.m.
$11–$13 (all major cards, no checks)

———————◆•◆———————

If you live in or near Portland, there's almost no chance this is the first you'll hear of Slappy Cakes. I can't think of a place that got more buzz when it opened, and for a simple reason which you already know about: You cook your own pancakes there. And you can get a Slappy Screw, but I'm getting ahead of myself.

I suppose the owners figured "cook your own" was about the last niche available in the Portland breakfast pantheon, so in 2009 Slappy Cakes opened in a neighborhood that didn't already have a breakfast joint, and the fire was lit.

It's a gigantic space, actually an early-20th-century garage, and they filled it with a combination of orange and fuchsia that puts you somewhere between art deco and the cheesy '70s. They also scored a collection of amazing, twisted orange vases at an estate sale.

Giant paintings of pancakes add to the festive air—as does an outrageous cocktail menu, all made with locally distilled spirits. This is where you'll find the Slappy Screw, with Lovejoy Vodka, organic orange juice, and house-made ginger syrup. It's one of seven cocktails which, along with three champagne-based Bubbles are all available from opening time at 8 a.m. One owner came on my radio show and said they sell "whiskey for breakfast" mainly to nurses getting off the graveyard shift. Uh, right.

There is a kitchen-created menu here (chicken fried steak, huevos rancheros, a few Benedicts, etc.), which answers a common question: why the hell would I pay them so I can cook my own pancakes? Well, they'll cook them if you like, but what's the point? Anyway, you're paying them to provide the batter, do the prep work, and clean up.

And it really is fun to cook the cakes on each table's Japanese teppanyaki grill (made in Germany, by the way). The staff spreads rice oil on the griddle, and you order (for $5 or $6) a little eight-ounce squeeze bottle filled with one of five batters: buttermilk, ginger, vegan whole grain, gluten-free, and a rotating seasonal option; I've seen peanut butter, carrot-cardamom, and pumpkin. Yes, I've been in a few times. And yes, you can make your cakes in whatever shape you want.

Then there are the mix-ins, which are $1 or $1.50 each. It's a heck of a list, with variations on chocolate, butterscotch, fruit, nuts, and creations such as lavender honey, lemon curd, and orange ginger marmalade. And that's just the sweet stuff! The savory list includes bacon, sausage (regular or veggie), peanut butter, cheddar/blue/goat/vegan cheese, roasted mushrooms, and chopped scallions. Organic maple syrup is $2.

The best plan seems to be to order one or two batters—either as an appetizer or just as the sweet alternative—and get something savory from the menu. Nobody seems too impressed with what the kitchen creates, and nobody seems to care, either. I think that's because they're too busy cooking their own pancakes and maybe enjoying a Slappy Screw.

Wait: Long on weekends. **Large groups:** With notice. **Coffee:** Stumptown. **Other drinks:** Espresso, Foxfire Teas, Columbia Valley organic juices, beer, wine, cocktails. **Feel-goods:** Local, seasonal, organic produce, plus a garden out back. **Health options:** Gluten-free batter and plenty of stuff for vegetarians and vegans. **WiFi:** No.

Stepping Stone Cafe

Hip/Mom & Pop

Northwest Portland really does *have a neighborhood place!*
2390 NW Quimby St. (NW) ~ 503-222-1132 ~ *steppingstonecafe.com*
Monday and Tuesday 6 a.m. to 7 p.m., Wednesday and Thursday
6 a.m. to 10 p.m., Friday 6 a.m. to 3 a.m., Saturday 7:30 a.m. to 3 a.m.,
Sunday 7:30 a.m. to 10 p.m.
$10–$14 (all major cards)

———————————◆•◆———————————

My first apartment in Portland was on Northwest Quimby Street,
back in 1996. I had just stumbled into town from a fishing season in
Alaska, and on one of my first lonely mornings, I started walking
toward Northwest 23rd Avenue, the only street I knew. On the way I
passed a little corner diner with five people sitting in it. I heard laugh-
ter and smelled bacon. I couldn't resist.

I walked into Stepping Stone Cafe and immediately found myself
taking, and then giving, a bunch of crap from the guy working there.
I was fresh off a fishing boat, more than capable in such pursuits, and
I immediately fit in. For the next six months, until my fishing money
ran out and I had to move to a hovel in Southeast, I ate at Stepping
Stone several times a week, and the legendary, cranky staffer became
something of a friend—until one day, according to published reports,
he relapsed into his drug habit and was banned from the premises.

Those were different times, and today Stepping Stone is friendlier,
although the official motto remains: You eat here because we let you.

Now I live in Northwest again, and Stepping Stone still feels like
my local place. Yes, even fashionable Northwest has a little neighborhood diner. It's not flashy like Meriwether's, or sophisticated like
Besaw's, or faux sentimental like Rose's. It's just a diner, and has been
for more than 50 years, since the block across the street (now town-
houses) hosted a garage for the streetcar.

The menu is probably similar to what the old streetcar guys ate:
chicken-fried steak, ham, Tillamook cheddar, five scrambles, and
10 omelets, although they probably didn't have sundried tomato basil

chicken sausage or an omelet with spinach, portobello, feta, and artichoke. The menu has also expanded to include three kinds of French toast, Belgian waffles, and cheese blintzes. The cinnamon sweet roll is still insane (they used to joke that if you eat 10, you get a free angioplasty), and now it's been sliced up for French toast.

There's still a slight edge of funkiness about the place, like the dismembered action-hero dolls that move up and down when the doors open, and the chain-pull toilet in the men's room, where a Help Wanted sign hung for years. But it's also extremely down-home, with checkered tablecloths, red vinyl chairs, immensely charming booths, and pictures of friends (called Stepping Stoners) on the wall.

You won't see high-heeled ladies sipping mimosas; more likely a musician just waking up and doing a crossword or, God bless him, some hungover, stoned kid in a corner booth staring blankly into his coffee.

I'm not that kid anymore, but I still feel at home at Stepping Stone. And now that it's become entirely cruelty-free, you can too.

Wait: Long on weekends, almost entirely outside. **Large groups:** Yes. **Coffee:** Portland Roasting special blend. **Other drinks:** Cocktails, great milkshakes, hot chocolate, cocktails and beer. **Feelgoods:** Nothing jumps out. **Health options:** One tofu scramble. **WiFi:** Yes.

SubRosa

Weekend/Classy/Kiddie

A friendly neighborhood joint.

2601 SE Clinton (SE/Division) ~ 503-233-1955 ~ *subrosa.textdriven.com*

Weekends, 8:30 a.m. to 1 p.m.

$12–$14 (Visa, MasterCard, no checks)

———————◆•◆———————

There is a common theme in people's reactions to SubRosa—mine included. It goes something like this: I used to go by there all the time, and it looked like a nice, inviting place. And it's in a great location. So I always wondered about it, and then one day I was having brunch with some friends, and all the usual places were crowded, so I thought, *Hey, let's check out SubRosa.*

There is more common ground to the reviews. While it isn't an all-out kiddie place, all agree it's kid-friendly—and small. If you want a quiet place for a romantic chat, this isn't it, at least not at brunch. Another agreed-upon point: the service is excellent and friendly, and the place is cozy, making everybody want to love the place.

After that, opinions vary.

I can say this: I took a group of eight people there, and I called way ahead to give notice. They reserved the community table for us, and the Crew hardly ever had a better time. I just love seeing friends form different parts of my life meet each other, exchange stories, and laugh out loud. The sun was bathing us through the big front window, and most of us were there for two full hours. And I can honestly say—and most of the Crew would agree—that the closest thing to a disappointment in the whole experience was the food.

Okay, that's harsh. But there's another common theme in folks' reaction to SubRosa, something along the lines of, "It's just a little neighborhood place, nothing fancy." Pretty much everybody in the Crew shrugged when I asked about their food, though we all agreed that the bread, potatoes, and French toast were outstanding, as were the service and the setting. Then we talked about how much fun Crew breakfasts are.

For the record, a couple of folks thought it was great. Also, one person said it was the worst she'd ever had. Do with that as you will. I think you'll find a similar mix among any number of people who've been there.

It really is a charming little place, calling itself "authentic Italian with a Midwestern sensibility." And to their credit, they are very upfront about letting the ingredients speak for themselves. So it's not like they claim to be something they aren't. Also, they only do brunch on weekends, and I assume the rest of their food is better—only because they've been open awhile, and people say nice things about them. And it really is in a sweet spot, right at the corner of 26th and Clinton.

If it tickles your fancy, you will love SubRosa. And if you're one of those people—especially if you live nearby—I'd say you have a sweet little brunch place on your hands.

Wait: Maybe a little. **Large groups:** With notice. **Coffee:** Nossa Familia. **Other drinks:** Espresso, juice, Bloody Marys. **Feel-goods:** None they tout. **Health options:** Limited veggie options. **WiFi:** No.

Sweetpea Baking Company

Weekend/Veggie

Heaping, healthy happiness.
1205 SE Stark (SE/Inner) ~ 503-477-5916 ~ *sweetpeabaking.com*
Sunday 9 a.m. to noon
$10 all you can eat including coffee, $1 for orange juice (all major cards, no checks)

———————◆◆———————

I get all giddy when I think about Sweetpea Baking Company. For one thing, "Sweetpea" was my older sister's nickname for me when I was a kid—and I can't believe I'm putting that fact in a book. Also, I may or may not have a thing for women in aprons covered in flour. Um, let's move on.

I follow Sweetpea on Twitter, and nobody sends out happier tweets. One Sunday brunch was announced as: "Brunch! biscuits and gravy, seitan, kale, potatoes, grits and peach crisp!" The next tweet was: "Did you know that our biscuits are made with magic?" I always get this image of some baker stepping away from the oven to bang out a quick tweet, overcome with joy at the vegan baking revolution.

This particular corner of that revolution—which has established a solid toe-hold in the vegan/cruelty-free mini mall where Sweetpea resides—started in the kitchen of one Lisa Higgins. She started vegan baking as a hobby, then placed some items in local stores, then expanded to a wholesale business, then this retail spot in 2008.

It has kept the family feel. Another brunch announcement included crepes because Lisa's mom was in town celebrating her birthday. According to the website, Mom wanted crepes "filled with aspara-gus and drizzled with béchamel, with sides of potatoes, scramble, etc. Crepes with fruit, chocolate sauce, and whipped cream for dessert!"

Another fun tweet: "Vanilla berry Nothin' Muffins and GF-SF (gluten-free/sugar-free) cinnamon swirl coffee cake for breakfast. Plus coffee. Lots and lots of coffee."

Brunch is only a few hours a week but merits inclusion here because it's the only all-vegan brunch, and one of the few all-you-can-eat options. It is most casual, if a little tight. There are a handful of tables, and you might say it lacks ambience from a decoration standpoint (concrete doesn't warm the soul). What it does offer is a roomful of happy vegan and non-vegans chowing down on menu items described as: "Biscuits, baked tofu, stacked w spinach & tomatoes, covered in hollandaise sauce. With potatoes, kale, & oregon berry crisp." Or maybe: "Breakfast Tacos! I've spiced it up quite a bit, and it is very gluten-free friendly. Dulce de Leche Cake is the dessert."

A scant $10 gets you all can handle of this, including Stumptown coffee, and another dollar brings orange juice. Fill up at the counter and grab one of the few seats; you might need to share a table with strangers. So if you're looking for that hang-out-all-morning place, this isn't it.

Another fun tweet: "It's a dreary day, but it's happy in here—Danishes are fresh outta the oven. Cherry, jam, maple cream and fresh strawberry!" I'm giggling again.

Did I mentioned the doughnuts? Saturday is doughnut day at Sweetpea. They're 75 cents each, and one recent day included raspberry glazed, vanilla glazed, chocolate coconut, chocolate raspberry, and Boston cream.

Okay, my sugar habit is howling now. It's time for "Sweetpea" to make a run for Sweetpea.

Wait: Getting a seat can be the tough part. **Large groups:** Not the best place. **Coffee:** Stumptown. **Other drinks:** Townsend's Tea, espresso. **Feel-goods:** The whole place. **Health options:** Gluten-free and non-allergenic options, too. **WiFi:** Yes.

Tasty n Sons

New/Hip

A long, fine journey continues.
3808 N Williams (N/Inner) ~ 503-621-1400 ~ *tastynsons.com*
Daily 9 a.m. to 2 p.m.
$10–$15 (all major cards, no checks)

The short version of this story is that a guy with a lot of restaurant experience lived in a neighborhood that didn't have a breakfast place, so he opened one. But saying John Gorham has a lot of restaurant experience is like saying Brandon Roy plays basketball. And calling Tasty n Sons a breakfast place is like calling U2 a band.

So here's a little more background. Gorham grew up in a restaurant family and always wanted to be a chef; he was working in kitchens before he finished high school. He then hit the road, working the kitchen circuit—golf courses, ski resorts, etc.—and did some traveling in Europe. He worked at the landmark Cafe Zenon in Eugene in 1993, where he discovered the joys of buying direct from farmers. He also knew a Malaysian woman married to a Chinese man who opened a casino in western Africa, and he helped open a restaurant there while also working as a pit boss in the casino. He is, by the way, a great storyteller.

In the late '90s, he wound up in Berkeley and in the extended family of Chez Panisse chefs; he helped open an Italian place there, then came back to Oregon in 2001, where he opened another Italian place, Fratelli. But soon after that, his long-time desire to run his own place started to blossom, and he got a chance to buy Viande, the meat counter inside City Market on Northwest 21st. He did that in partnership with Ben Dyer, who he'd worked with at Zenon, and since neither one wanted to run a meat counter, they together started a Sunday evening supper club (served at Bridges Cafe) called Simpatica—now housed on Southeast Pine Street and described elsewhere in this book.

Still with me? I love these kinds of restaurant stories. Turns out Simpatica's most popular nights were the tapas meals, and in fact *USA*

Today called their tapas night "the No. 1 meal in the world." That, Gorham says, was it; he sold out, bought a ticket to Barcelona to study tapas kitchens, and came home to start Toro Bravo. The lesson from this style, as he put it on my podcast, was that "family style was the way to go. Please bring it all at once, put in the middle of the table, and we're gonna feast."

And *that* is what happens at Tasty n Sons. It's the culmination, so far, of a local genius's career. The menu changes regularly, based on what's in season and what the crew feels like cooking; when I asked him to describe the food, the first thing he mentioned was the chocolate potato doughnut with *crème anglaise*. He also mentioned the yams with toasted cumin, glazed in maple syrup. And the frittata with (when I asked) fava beans, olives, confit green beans, caramelized onions, and feta, served in the cast iron pan.

I could go on. But you need to go on over there. Get a crew together, feast, and be glad you're in John Gorham's neighborhood.

Wait: Crazy on weekends. **Large groups:** Yes, and they take reservations for parties of six or more. **Coffee:** Stumptown. **Other drinks:** Steve Smith teas; local, fresh-squeezed orange, grapefruit, and cranberry juice; soda; wine, beer, and cocktails. **Feel-goods:** Local ingredients abound. **Health options:** Vegetarians and vegans could do well. **WiFi:** No.

Three Square Grill

Weekend/Classy

Wait, I thought this was a strip mall . . .

6320 SW Capitol Hwy. (SW/Inner) ~ 503-244-4467 ~ *threesquare.com*

Sunday 9 a.m. to 2 p.m.

$13–$15 (Visa, MasterCard, no checks)

———————◆·◆———————

There are a few adjustments you're likely to go through when brunching at Three Square Grill.

It starts with the location, which is in a strip mall next to a dry cleaner. When somebody told me to check the place out, I thought they meant Baker and Spice, an amazing bakery a few doors down. It never occurred to me there was a real restaurant there.

When you walk in, you may be surprised by the size and semi-fanciness of the place: white tablecloths in a strip mall! And you'll likely be a little creeped out by the Giant Lady. Even if I hadn't called your attention to it, you would not miss the massive portrait of a woman who looks more than a bit like Lucy Liu; she appears to be watching everyone in the place from a kind of throne over the dining room. Both servers I asked about it chuckled, as if I was far from the first person to do so.

The next surprise may be the rest of the art collection, which ranges from impressionistic to kiddie. But once you get the menu, probably from a noticeably young server, the surprises will stop. You'll see egg dishes like a pork–scrambled eggs sandwich on a biscuit with redeye gravy, a morel omelet, a chili omelet, Hangtown Fry, huevos rancheros, crab cakes and eggs, and baked eggs with lamb.

There's also Our Famous Smoked Salmon Hash, which suggests this really is a neighborhood place; they may have the only smoked salmon hash in Hillsdale. (Vegetarians can go for a roasted vegetable hash.) They do shrimp and grits, bagels and lox, berry French toast, and a "many-grained" Belgian waffle. Sides include collard greens in "pot likker," and if you want lunch, there's a burger and a Caesar salad.

Now, look back over that list. It's all over the place, right? I should mention that the menu changes weekly—the dinner menu changes daily, in fact—so you might not see all these things when you visit. But this gives you an idea. I count Southern, West Coast, East Coast, Mexican, Northwest, Jewish deli, Southern again, and Italian.

Many, many reviewers use the phrase *comfort food* to describe the menu at Three Square. Frankly, I think that phrase means as little as *hangover food*, and in both cases I'm not sure it's entirely a compliment. What I think they're saying here is that Three Square Grill is trying to just be a neighborhood place, not a fancy cutting-edge place. Critics think that they charge too much for bland food, but fans say it's, well, comfortable. Besides, if you don't think it has enough pop, they also make a host of hot sauces and pickled items you can add to it.

It's not that the food isn't trying to be serious. They were written up in *Bon Appétit* back in 2002. Around the same time, they were praised by the *Portland Tribune* and the *Oregonian* for striking a balance between homey and foodie. In the end, maybe the biggest surprise is that little ol' Hillsdale has its own semi-serious restaurant.

Wait: Maybe a little. **Large groups:** With notice. **Coffee:** Bella Selva. **Other drinks:** Espresso, juice, sodas, mimosas. **Feel-goods:** A lot of the food is made in-house. **Health options:** Decent for vegetarians. **WiFi:** Yes.

Tin Shed Garden Cafe

New

These hippies are kind of grown up—and they can cook!
1438 NE Alberta St. (NE/Alberta) ~ 503-288-6966 ~
tinshedgardencafe.com
Breakfast daily 7 a.m. to 3 p.m.
$11–$13 (Visa, MasterCard)

————————◆•◆————————

Mushroom-rosemary gravy. Somehow that wraps up the Tin Shed perfectly—that, plus when the weather's nice, there are so many people waiting out front and drinking self-serve coffee that they put up benches so people could be comfortable.

In fact, when you travel east from MLK Boulevard, the first major indication you have arrived on the Alberta scene is about 35 people milling around outside Tin Shed. And the Shed is a perfect intro to the scene. It's popular, inventive, and works very well, on its own terms.

Once you get inside—and it may be an hour on weekends—the feel that's always struck me is grown-up hippie, or as a fellow former Southerner put it, "kinda weird, but good." He was referring to the brie and green apples on top of his Sweet Chix scramble (with chicken-apple sausage, sweet onion, basil, and roasted red peppers). But he might as well have been talking about the light fixtures with forks on them, the artwork, or even some of the people eating breakfast.

The crowd is Alberta Arts + late-rising horn-rimmed hipster + just-bought-a-house young adult, all watched by curious pseudo-tourists from other parts of town coming over to check out the galleries and shops.

Tin Shed is a monument to what has happened on Alberta. As late as the mid-'90s, Alberta was a place that showed up on the local news every month or so—with police lights flashing. But it was cheap to live there, so artists moved in. Then came coffee shops, galleries, and the Last Thursday art walk. Eventually, people started noticing all the cheap, older houses around the neighborhood.

Flash forward a few years. Folks are sitting in the Tin Shed's garden patio eating French toast made with sweet-potato cinnamon bread; scrambles with portobello mushrooms, sun-dried tomatoes, spinach, and goat cheese; and the Tim Curry: tofu, roasted garlic, yams, zucchini, mushrooms, and sweet onion in a coconut-curry sauce served over a bed of spinach and topped with toasted peanuts, raisins, and avocado.

Kinda weird. Also damn good.

And then there's the potato cake. It's what the place is known for, and as a signature it's an appropriate choice. The Shed potato cake is somewhere between hashbrowns and potato pancake—golden brown outside, soft in the middle, semi-mashed and semi-stringy—and served by the hundreds each day, either as a side with sour cream and green onions or underneath a scramble with bacon and eggs and cheddar, or sausage and gravy, or spicy sausage, peppers, onion, and eggs. Mmm.

In other words, the signature potato cake is just right: it's got variety, it's unique, and folks love it, kinda weird or not. And that's all you need to know about Tin Shed.

Wait: Long, mainly on weekends, mostly outside. **Large groups:** One big table seats eight. **Coffee:** Their own Tin Shed Blend from Portland Roasters. **Other drinks:** Numi Tea, espresso, cocktails. **Feel-goods:** Free-range eggs, and for a small fee you can get pure maple syrup. **Health options:** Vegetarian, vegan, egg whites, tofu. **WiFi:** No.

Toast

New/Mom & Pop

One man's quest, a neighborhood's gain.
5222 SE 52nd Ave. (SE/Outer) ~ 503-774-1020 ~ *toastpdx.com*
Brunch daily 8 a.m. to 2 p.m. except Tuesday 9 a.m. to 2 p.m.
$9–$20 (all major cards)

———————◆—•—◆———————

The way Donald Kotler sees it, every neighborhood needs a great breakfast place. So when he and some old restaurant friends wanted to open a place, it made sense to do breakfast in his own Woodstock neighborhood. Apparently, the neighborhood agreed: the day Kotler opened Toast in August 2007, a 45-minute line lasted for two hours. It's been hopping ever since.

Kotler's other goal was to keep it simple—on the menu and in the space. "We wanted to take food and bring it back to its simplest form, not overprocessing it or covering it with overly lemony hollandaise sauces, but letting the true flavors of the food stand out on their own."

Toast's appearance is also clean and simple, with bamboo tables and comfortable chairs. The room's history is a little more interesting: it used to be Bad Ass Video, purveyor of porn, and the name lives on in the Bad Ass Sandwich (fried eggs, bacon, and goat's milk cheese on toast served with a potato *rosti* for $8).

One more thing about the space ties in with Kotler's plan for the food: Toast is *small*—what you can see is all there is—meaning food can't be kept for very long. So everything is fresh, and much of it (like jams, peppers, baked goods, and sausage) is made in-house. He's even got some herbs growing out back.

A lot of the food is from local farmers and vendors (ask to see a list of suppliers), and Kotler has created a menu that is, as he puts it, more brunch than breakfast. You can get a burger at 8 a.m., for example. And there's beer and half a dozen cocktails. You'll find granola (called Hippies Use Front Door) and oatmeal, and a sweet onion tart called the Occasional Hedonist, with a poached egg, fresh herbs, and a light Hollandaise sauce. You can get steak and eggs, a Benny and the Mets (house made English muffin, ham, two poached eggs, hollandaise and a rosti), and a chicken breast with eggs over easy.

Portions and prices (most less than $10, except for the steak) are quite reasonable, and everything I've had was tasty—never flashy, never awe-inspiring, but there's a lot to be said for fresh ingredients cooked well. And the vibe, as you might expect from such a local place, is extremely welcoming and friendly. I'm also a sucker for anyplace that welcomes you with a little scone: the day I was there, it was cinnamon and raisin.

Toast is wide open not only to changes ("We want to be a restaurant that says yes," says Kotler) but also to suggestions: at first there was no bacon on the menu, but enough diners said they wanted it that there's now nitrate-free bacon.

What else would you expect from your little neighborhood brunch place?

Wait: Can get long on weekends. **Large groups:** Call ahead; expanding fall 2010. **Coffee:** Courier. **Other drinks:** Tazo Tea, beer, wine, cocktails, juice. **Feel-goods:** Everything's fresh and local, natural. **Health options:** Pork and ham are nitrate-free. Tofu is on the menu and can be prepared to taste. **WiFi:** No.

Tom's Restaurant

Old School

A bit of small-town America in the big city.
3871 SE Division St. (SE/Division) ~ 503-233-3739
Monday through Saturday 7 a.m. to 9:30 p.m., Sunday 7:30 a.m. to
9:30 p.m. Some dishes only available until 2 p.m.
$9–$13 (Visa, MasterCard)

Back in 1991 I hiked a bunch of miles on the Appalachian Trail. One day during a break, I was having the Trail Burger at the Smoky Mountain Diner in Hot Springs, North Carolina—a town of a few hundred where the A.T. goes right down the middle of Main Street. At the table next to me were two old-timers wearing tractor-related baseball caps, and when a car drove down the street, the two of them stopped talking and watched it. The car made a left turn down one of the few streets in town, and one old-timer said to the other, "Now, where's *he* goin'?"

I told that story to somebody awhile back, and the very next day I was eating breakfast at Tom's Restaurant with my friend Trisa. We were catching up on mutual friends and old times when she looked out the window at the traffic on Southeast 39th and saw her sister making a left turn! I guess that could have happened anywhere, but the fact that it happened at Tom's seems somehow to fit the place perfectly.

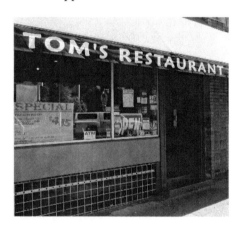

Chances are you know exactly what kind of place Tom's is, even if you've never been there. Such restaurants are in the blood of Americans, even if some folks wouldn't walk into such a place. They go by names like Diner and Family Restaurant, and they serve cheap, basic fare to longtime regulars and new folks alike. They also tend to have customers who stick around for decades.

Tom's has all of that as well as the type of menu you'd expect: biscuits and gravy, waffles with strawberries and whipped cream, omelets that hover around $7 (only the Feta and the Taco are different from any other place), and Breakfast Nos. 1 through 7 that mix various combinations of meat, eggs, pancakes, toast, and hashbrowns. There's also French toast, pancakes, a couple of items for the kids, juices, and fruits, and generally a special or two for less than $5. And the other side of the business is a sports bar where you can shoot pool and watch the games on TV.

What's funny about Tom's is reading people's reactions to it on various Internet sites. (And for what it's worth, I doubt that many of Tom's regulars write reviews online.) I often wonder if all these reviewers are eating in the same restaurant. I've seen one that said Tom's has the best gyros in town (seems a stretch) but admitted, "It isn't the prettiest place to eat." Another complained about bad cooking but admitted the service was prompt and "the waitress was super nice." Yet another included such words as *puke* and *gag* and *icky poo* three times . . . but liked it for people watching.

Do you feel like you're seeing Tom's from completely different angles? And do you feel like you've seen Tom's a million times while driving by but have never gone in? And do you feel like you don't even need to?

Well, I think you should anyway.

Wait: Perhaps on the weekends. **Large groups:** Yes. **Coffee:** Boyd's. **Other drinks:** Fresh-squeezed juice, tea, hot chocolate, milk, pop, full bar. **Feel-goods:** Not much in the food, but the server will treat you like family. **Health options:** You don't *have* to get the homemade cinnamon roll. **WiFi:** Yes.

Tosis

Mom & Pop/Old School

Not of the Portland you probably know.
6120 NE Sandy Blvd. (NE/Hollywood) ~ 503-284-4942
Monday through Saturday 6 a.m. to 9 p.m., Sunday 7 a.m. to 9 p.m.
$7–$10 (Visa, MasterCard)

For most people I know in Portland, a breakfast at Tosis would be like visiting another world.

Here's one reason: Tosis is a place where the church crowd goes. It may be the only place in this book that can make such a claim. My Southern soul is profoundly soothed by the sight of a restaurant full of well-dressed old people eating after services are over.

Another reason: on several occasions I've been in Tosis when an older guy walked through the door and a nearby table full of similarly old guys erupted into calls like "Why, they'll let anybody in here" and "Oh, look out, here comes trouble."

But the biggest reason Tosis is dear to my heart is captured perfectly in the person of my dear friend Craig: fisherman, guide, author, French toast connoisseur, lover of old-school coffee, and occasional grouch. Craig used to live near Tosis and got me to go there because it had, he said, plain coffee, great French toast, and rude service. He turned out to be right on two counts: the service is actually quite nice, but if staffers are having a bad day or you're on their nerves for some reason, they're honest enough not to pretend otherwise.

At Tosis, you can sit and talk with your friends, or mind your own business, or work a crossword, or read the paper, or get in and out in about 20 minutes. You cannot sip a latte and surf the Internet. Tosis has flowers, coat racks, Formica tables, and cheesy paintings—in short, all the decorative charm of a cheap motel. And God bless the diners and cheap motels!

To Craig, who I can picture slumped in a booth going on about his daughter or fishing the Klamath Basin or theology or Frank Zappa, the appeal of Tosis is captured perfectly in its French toast, which, he wants the world the know, is perfect. But to understand that, you must understand that when I tell Craig about having French toast made with challah or brioche, or I regale him with tales of caramelized bananas at Screen Door or chopped pecans at Cadillac, he usually rolls his eyes and lets out an obscene, cranky version of "Man, that stuff ain't French toast!" By *French toast*, Craig means white bread that's been soaked to yellow in egg and milk and *perhaps* a little vanilla, then fried, covered in powdered sugar, and served six or eight pieces on a heavy, white oval plate, with a plastic pitcher of maple syrup, a mug of plain coffee, and a bowl full of creamers. Then leave him the hell alone unless he runs out of java.

If you worked at it or tipped really well (which you should), you could probably manage to spend $10 at Tosis, though it would defeat much of the purpose of going there. That purpose is to strip away all the pretense that so often comes with food these days, hit the reset button, relax, and just go have some damn breakfast.

Wait: Maybe around noon on Sunday. **Large groups:** Not so much. **Coffee:** Boyd's. **Other drinks:** Iced tea, juice, soda. **Feel-goods:** It's cheap! **Health options:** Someplace else. **WiFi:** If they ever get it, Craig and I will stop going.

Trébol

New/Weekend/Classy

Monumental Modern Mexican.
4835 N Albina Ave. (N/Inner) ~ 503-517-9347 ~ *trebolpdx.com*
Brunch Sunday 10 a.m. to 2 p.m.
$13–$17 (all major cards)

———————◆•◆———————

Mexican brunch, although accurate, doesn't begin to describe what Trébol is about.

Everything about it says "more than a place to eat." The space is impressive, with high ceilings, big windows, and massive mirrors on the walls. The website, which includes Mexican rock music and impressive, flashy graphics, touts Trébol's state-of-the-art composting, oil recycling, eco-friendly cleaning products, and relationships with local farmers. There's also a list of upcoming events: the Tour of Tequila, for example (featuring 75 kinds) and Santo Sundays, when you can watch cheesy Mexican adventure films featuring a pro wrestler named Santo (with his mask on) who fights bad guys and saves people. It's even weirder than it sounds.

The menu seems much more predictable, at least at first glance. Names like Soup of the Day, Shrimp Cocktail, Guacamole, Chorizo with Egg, Tamale with Fried Egg, Flautas, and a Torta of the Day don't spin your head. Other items, like Chilaquiles (a soupy egg dish with fried tortillas) or Grilled Quail with Peanut Mole, hint at greater Mexican ambitions.

And it's those greater ambitions that really set Trébol apart. To the Breakfast Crew, it's an impressive place with fun-loving staff and great food that, we had to confess, seemed a little expensive ($8 for organic guacamole?). I had the Torta, with a cornmeal pita topped with layers of black beans, grilled flank steak, greens, cheese, and a spicy sauce that on first bite was a blow to my senses but then settled in wonderfully. I loved it, even if it seemed small for $10 and didn't come with anything else.

The rest of the Crew had nothing but praise for the Huevos Rancheros, the vegetarian Posole soup, and the tamale; the same was true for the Bloody Maria, made with tequila and house pickles on the side. Some things seemed odd to us. For example, one of the Santo movies was on, so we'd occasionally look up at the big TV screen over the bar—and a TV over the bar is a little weird on its own in a serious restaurant—and we'd see Santo talking with scantily clad women, overly dramatic young men, people in space suits, another wrestler in a blue mask, and so on.

These things did cause us to pause and ponder. So did the owner/chef's announcement that Trébol had been named one of the 10 Best Mexican Places in the U.S. by *Bon Appétit*. I thought, "Really?" How does someone even come to such a conclusion?

At any rate, local reviewers are more mixed. The *Mercury* said it was "inconsistent and overpriced." The *Oregonian* said the food was improving but the service was over-eager. *Willamette Week* liked it, but the folks at *portlandfood.org* leaned toward "I don't get it."

All I can say is that if a serious restaurant serving Mexican food for Sunday brunch sounds good, Trébol just might be your cup of tequila.

Wait: None. **Large groups:** Yes. **Coffee:** Self-serve Stumptown. **Other drinks:** Several versions of Bloody Marys and mimosa, plus over 100 kinds of tequila. **Feel-goods:** Ingredients are local, seasonal, and organic. **Health options:** Good vegetarian options, and they sometimes serve fruit and yogurt (for $8). **WiFi:** No.

Utopia Cafe

New/Hip/Veggie

Grown-up hippie, or hippie grown-up?

3308 SE Belmont St. (SE/Belmont) ~ 503-235-7606

Breakfast weekdays 7 a.m. to 2 p.m., weekends 7:30 a.m. to 2:20 p.m.

$9–$14 (Visa, MasterCard)

———————————◆·◆———————————

"Not as hippie as I expected."

That's the first line in my coffee-stained handwritten notes from a trip to Utopia. I don't recall whether it was good news or bad. I guess I was expecting something a bit more airy from a place called Utopia.

I was probably just being cranky. When I entered through the very cool old-timey screen door, though, I saw a long black bar, Formica tables, lovely wood floors, high ceilings, fused-glass art on the walls, and faux stained glass. It was all very clean and modern, and not a bit rustic. "This is nice," I thought—as if *hippie* and *nice* couldn't possibly coexist. Just being cranky, I'm sure.

Out came the menu, and it was pure Portland: eight scrambles ranging from Garden (with goat cheese) and no-egg Tofu (with tomato, onion, zucchini, mushroom, basil, and garlic) to the Baja (with chorizo) and the Camp (with bacon, mushrooms, and red and green peppers)

And they'll sub tofu for eggs or meat for no charge.

I was eating with two women who called themselves the Candida Sisters because they both had issues about eating sugar and wheat, and they had no problem finding stuff they could eat. And substitutions were easily made.

So here's the thing about Utopia. The first time I went, I came home with no notes at all; chalk that up to eating with two women. The second time, I was in the neighborhood and wanted to try the

Brioche French Toast. It was amazing and bountiful. I still didn't have good notes on the place, so next time I got the Bacavo Scramble with bacon, tomato, avocado, and blue cheese crumbles. It, too, was amazing. Again, I took almost no notes.

For some reason I could not get a handle on the Utopia Cafe. So, I decided to see what other writers had to say. Among all the Internet praise, I found this from the *Portland Mercury*: "There's no angle on the Utopia Cafe. It's not a good place to take Grandma, it's not great for a date, it's not healthy, it's not vegan, it doesn't have great ambiance and they don't allow dogs. It's just really good food."

So it wasn't just me! Then I found this in the *Willamette Week*: "Utopia offers a breakfast dish I have never seen before, and it strikes a very satisfying note: hot wild rice . . . a mix of long gray and black grains, thoughtfully served with raisins, hazelnuts and brown sugar."

Really? Utopia has that? Well, I dragged out the menu, and by golly it does. It's right under the From the Griddle section, which explains why I never made it that far. I also saw Fried Cornmeal, cooked on the grill and served with warm syrup. Somehow I missed that, too. Clearly, I need to go back—a pattern I have no intention of ending.

Wait: Pretty long on weekends, with some space inside but little cover outside. **Large groups:** Yes, but no split checks for parties of five or more on weekends. **Coffee:** Portland Roasting, Utopia Blend. **Other drinks:** Espresso, Kobos loose-leaf tea, juice, milk, soda. **Feel-goods:** Lots of organic stuff. **Health options:** Plenty of vegetarian options as well as egg substitute and egg whites available for a small charge. And they can make any scramble vegan. **WiFi:** No.

Veritable Quandary

New/Classy/Weekend

Old-style class, new-style cuisine.
1220 SW 1st Ave. (Downtown) ~ 503-227-7342 ~ *veritablequandary.com*
Brunch weekends 9:30 a.m. to 3 p.m.
$15–$20 (all major cards)

———————————•———————————

Portlanders have been eating at VQ for almost 40 years. It's also a visual anchor, perched near the end of the Hawthorne Bridge, and it's been a popular lunch, dinner, and happy hour hangout for a generation or two. There's also been a long-running question: just what kind of place is it?

Is it a serious restaurant that wants to compete with the city's finest? Is it a casual lunch hangout? A happy hour where lawyers and downtown corporate types hit on one another? A tourist spot? A fancy bar? The answer to all seems to be yes.

My feeling is this: let's say there are three very general levels of restaurant. The low-end places are the cafés and diners of the world. The high-end places inspire foodie conversations about the presentation of the osso buco or the subtle mix of flavors in an *amuse bouche*. And then there's an area in the middle, whose inhabitants are trying to find a balance between casual and fine dining. I put VQ up at the top of this mid-section, where your Benedict is $14 and your Frittata with Wild Mushrooms and Oregon Black Truffles, Brie, and Fresh Chervil is $15.

I am probably over-thinking this thing. And over-writing it. It just seems like to foodies, VQ is a small step below their usual haunts, and to the other 80 percent of people, it's a fancy place that makes a fine start for a special cultural evening downtown. I do know that my good friend Mindie Kniss, the most frequent guest on my podcast, says VQ is her favorite place in town.

The staff, which trends to young and cute, is everywhere and extremely helpful. The seating options include a dark, elegant bar; a light, airy dining room with tall windows; the famed flower-adorned patio; and a super-cool wine cellar with one table for about eight.

262

The menu is grounded in everyday breakfast tradition but with foodie twists—and prices. For example, there's a sausage-and-egg plate that's actually house-made Italian sausage, two local unpasteurized eggs, potato cakes, and "Peppers & Onions Agro Dolce tossed with fresh Mozzarella, Arugula and Basil." When I went with my friends Bob and Judy, none of us knew what Agro Dolce was, and for $14 we decided we could get something more interesting anyway.

Bob got the Benedict, on house-made English muffins with house-smoked pork loin ($14), and he loved it. Judy had the Chilaquiles with Manchego, which the menu said was tortillas with chile sauce and scrambled eggs, guacamole, and *crème fraîche*. She also loved it. And I think it's the typical VQ brunch dish, because (a) it was really good, (b) it looked and sounded fancy, and (c) it could also, accurately, have been called Breakfast Nachos.

Now, am I saying VQ is trying to be something it isn't? The thought has occurred to me. Am I saying it is a serious restaurant trying to "keep it real"? I'd say that applies as well. What it seems to boil down to, though, is that whatever you're looking for in a slightly upscale brunch, it's probably a good idea to check out VQ.

Wait: Tends to form later in the morning. **Large groups:** Yes, especially if you can get the wine cellar. **Coffee:** Stumptown. **Other drinks:** Full bar, espresso, and fresh-squeezed juice. **Feel-goods:** Plenty of local ingredients and only local unpasteurized eggs. **Health options:** A few things here for vegetarians. **WiFi:** No.

Vita Cafe

Hip/Veggie/Kiddie

A veggie palace, a local hangout, a Portland institution.
3023 NE Alberta St. (NE/Alberta) ~ 503-335-8233 ~ *vita-cafe.com*
Breakfast daily 9 a.m. to 3 p.m., weekends 8 a.m. to 3 p.m.
$9–$13 (Visa, MasterCard)

When my college roommate was visiting from Dallas, Texas, he brought his wife, their three kids, his mom, and his wife's parents. The group collectively became known simply as the Texans.

My friends wanted to know how the Texans were liking Oregon, where I was taking them, and so on. And I knew before they came to town that I'd take them to Vita Cafe, a monument to what "my" Portland is all about: healthy food, community, grassroots neighborhood development, hipsters, hippies, leisurely breakfasts, outdoor dining, and local-sustainable-organic-vegetarian-vegan food.

The first charming moment came when the eldest Texan, after watching some of the human traffic stroll by on Alberta, asked me sincerely, "Paul, where does a woman with tattoos get a job?"

I'm pretty sure nothing like Vita Cafe or Alberta Street has ever happened in Dallas. The menu at Vita is a vast array of mostly vegetarian and vegan dishes. I wanted the Texans to see that organic, vegan

food can be both good and filling. They pored over the menu, expressing surprise at tasty-sounding dishes like a Greek, Mediterranean, Mexican, or Italian scramble, asking me, "And it's *vegan*?" It is if you get it with tofu or tempeh instead of with free-range eggs.

Then they asked what tempeh was, as well as tofu, jicama, miso, and TVP. And how you get milk from rice or soybeans. I didn't know, actually, but it's all explained in the Food for Thought section of the menu, which brings me to another of Vita's endearing qualities: it is by no means an elitist place. It's practically an advertisement for a food movement doubling as a kid-friendly restaurant and neighborhood hangout. There's a full bar and happy hour specials, and kids eat for a buck daily from 5 to 7 p.m. There's even a bocce ball court on the sprawling patio.

The best-known breakfast dishes are the corn cakes (including Mexican and Thai versions), the "Chicken" Fried Steak made with tempeh, and my favorite, the Tofurky Florentine, which is English muffins topped with slices of tofurky, spinach, vegan hollandaise (warning: it's brown), and either eggs or tofu. I'm not a vegetarian by any means, but I feel right at home at Vita; in fact, my favorite dessert in town is the super-sweet (and also vegan and wheat-free) carrot cake.

For me, the lasting image is sweet and wholesome. Late in the meal, with the kids romping on the patio with the not-too-hot sunshine streaming down, one Texan asked another with a slight grin, "How's your fake food?" Without even looking up from her rapidly emptying plate, Texan #2 just mumbled and gave two thumbs up.

Wait: A little on weekends, mostly outside. **Large groups:** Yes. **Coffee:** Stumptown. **Other drinks:** Smoothies, juice, cocktails, beer. **Feel-goods:** Free-range, sustainable, local ingredients; 1 percent of sales is donated to local social and environmental groups. **Health options:** Everywhere! **WiFi:** Yes.

West Cafe

Weekend/Classy/Veggie

All things to all people?

1201 SW Jefferson St. (Downtown) ~ 503-227-8189 ~ *westcafepdx.com*

Sunday 10 a.m. to 2 p.m.

$12–$14 (all major cards, no checks)

I go to the Unitarian church in downtown Portland, and West Cafe is right down the street. I've seen it for years, and the only people I ever knew who ate there were Unitarians. I always wondered: if nobody ever tells me, the Breakfast Guy, about a place that serves breakfast, what does that mean?

Well, here's what I think: if breakfast places were churches, the West Cafe would be Unitarian.

Understand, I love the Unitarian church. Yet there are some funny things about it, and Unitarians often make fun of themselves. For one thing, they are always trying to explain—to themselves and each other—who they are and what they believe. They are a little bit churchy, with a choir and a pipe organ, but real low-key, polite, non-flashy, and open to nearly everything. For example, the church hosts Buddhist meditation group and occasional pagan services.

And the West Cafe is . . . well, start with the name. What does that mean? Does it project anything to you? Northwest means something, Southwest means something, but just West? Next up is the décor. It's a perfectly nice place, a little bit fancy but not trying to wow you. It's . . . comfortable, aiming for class.

Reviewers have used phrases such as "A little something for almost every taste," "a long list of healthy creative entrees," and "sophisticated American food," whatever that means. Even their website says it's "simply inspired" and "casual but comfortable."

Next up is the crowd, which is slightly older than average—certainly when compared to, say, Cricket Café. The menu is a true brunch, with six starters, 11 breakfasts, 11 soups and salads, and a dozen or more sandwiches and wraps. Breakfasts range from the basic, like a skillet scramble, to the fancier, like poached eggs with crab meat and a roasted garlic-tarragon aioli. From "skillet scramble" to "tarragon aioli" pretty much covers everything, kind of like a Christian church with Buddhists in it.

As for the quality of the food, it's also non-flashy, non-wow, safe, and welcoming. And yes, I just said it wasn't particularly great. Then again, it wasn't bad. Most of my group thought our food was well done but uninspired. For example, we joked that the French toast was just like Mom made—literally.

The best things I tasted were the oatmeal pancakes (with a berry salad, candied hazelnuts, and dark, rich maple syrup) and a wild mushroom, spinach, chevre, and caramelized onion tart from the starter menu. The one bite I had of that tart was the highlight of the meal: like how the minister at my church occasionally says something that makes me look around at people as if to say, "Did a preacher just say that in church?"

So I'd say that if you're looking for a welcoming, friendly, community-oriented church to attend, check out the Unitarians. And if you're downtown on a Sunday looking for a decent brunch with no line, check out West Cafe.

Wait: None. **Large groups:** Yes. **Coffee:** Portland Roasters Vienna Blend. **Other drinks:** Numi tea, juice, mimosas, Bloody Marys. **Feel-goods:** None they tout. **Health options:** Numerous veggie options. **WiFi:** Yes.

Wild Abandon

Hip/Veggie/Weekend

Mmmm, red velvet!
2411 SE Belmont St. (SE/Belmont) ~ 503-232-4458 ~
wildabandonrestaurant.com
Weekends 9 a.m. to 2 p.m.
$12–$15 (all major cards)

———————————•———————————

Six of us once tried to come up with the theme of Wild Abandon. The mural on the wall says either Greek bacchanalia or Druid ritual. The dark red tones say New Orleans. The sculpted hands holding candles on the walls say freaky. The old-school country music says honky-tonk. Somewhere we sensed a thread in there; we just couldn't put our finger on it.

Then Michael, the owner, told us he calls the place "garage sale baroque." *That* was it! He explained that back in the '70s, his grandmother had a basement filled with frosted Mexican lights—he assured us that Grandma's was "*the* '70s basement"—and that was the feel he was going for. He got it. In fact, one of Grandma's original lights is on the right as you walk out to the big, beautiful patio. Look for the hole around back, where Michael accidentally hit it trying to toss a spoon into a bus tray.

He also said the building was the original home of Montage before that restaurant moved to its funky home under the Morrison Bridge. So the theme kind of continued, we thought. Before that it was a barber shop, and before that Michael said it was (no lie) Ginger's Sexy Sauna. Some guy once told Michael he had lost his virginity on the premises.

Michael calls himself "an old restaurant hand" and has given his funky-feeling place a selection of old-fashioned breakfasts and a casual ambience. Basic omelets and scrambles run about $8–10, three Benedicts (spinach, ham, and salmon) average $10, and vegetarians and vegans will find several options. In fact, Wild Abandon offers a Vegan French Toast made with soy milk, soy butter, and real maple syrup.

The Old Fashioned French Toast, like the restaurant, had a little something we couldn't put our finger on; we thought it might be rum, fitting the theme, but Michael said it was orange juice. I guess we were just getting carried away. By that time our conversation had turned to a wacky combination of Humanism, Alaskan fishing, our server's tale of coffee sampling (known as "cupping") to get the blend just right, and my trivia contest to see if anyone else could tell Marty Robbins from Hank Williams and Hank Snow.

Like the mood, we thought the food was just right: the Benedicts had a little crunch to the muffins, a light sauce, and some bite in the spinach. I had to defend my French toast from inquiring hands. There's a little Mexican flair to the menu, as well: Richard's Chilaquiles is an egg scramble with peppers, onions, cheddar, and fried tortilla strips, all topped with black beans, salsa, sour cream, and cilantro. Both, as well as the breakfast burrito, come with or without chorizo.

Mexican food, Marty Robbins, Grandma's basement, freaky hands holding candles, down-home food, cocktails, red velvet. . . . I'm telling you, there's a theme in there somewhere. I guess we'll have to keep going back to nail it down completely.

Wait: Not bad. **Large groups:** Maybe on the patio. **Coffee:** Bridgetown special blend. **Other drinks:** Good Earth tea, beer, wine, cocktails. **Feel-goods:** None in particular. **Health options:** Garden sausage, soy products including tofu, and an entire vegan section on the menu. **WiFi:** Yes.

Zell's Café

New/Classy

Relaxed elegance, Portland style.
1300 SE Morrison St. (SE/Belmont) ~ 503-239-0196
Weekdays 7 a.m. to 2 p.m., Saturday 8 a.m. to 2 p.m., Sunday 8 a.m.
to 3 p.m.
$10–$14 (all major cards, no checks)

———————————————◆•◆———————————————

Ah, back at Zell's. It's a weekday lunch, nothing like the weekend breakfast madhouse. I'm halfway through one of my two soft, buttery, and free scones, sipping apple cider, and soaking in the light that's streaming through tall windows and over luscious wood tables, chairs, and bar. It's an old pharmacy, drawers and soda fountain still intact, so folks have been sitting here in the sun for many a year.

I'm feeling rather savory today, and since I'm solo, there won't be any sweets. Well, other than this homemade raspberry jam and orange marmalade on the table. So I'll have to pace myself and leave some of that for the last few bites of my scone. I want some substance, which sadly rules out the French toast with honey oat bread, and the ridiculous German pancakes, for which I shall now have a moment of silence. Man, Zell's just cries out for a group of friends!

So let's check the specials. Today the German pancakes come with hot rhubarb or strawberries. (A buttermilk waffle comes with the same.) An asparagus-prosciutto-Asiago scramble: hmm, don't care for asparagus in the morning. Avocado-bacon-tomato omelet? Don't care for avocados that much. Portobello-spinach-tomato-Asiago omelet? Getting warmer. Reuben scramble with pastrami, eggs, Gruyère, and Dijon-mayo on rye with potatoes and kraut? Good gosh, that's our early leader! A gingerbread waffle with Oregon strawberries and whipped cream? See, that's not fair! I'd have the best 15 minutes of my life eating that, then need a nap. Why can't somebody else be here to order it so I can have a bite, or seven?

No, it's a savory day. Back to the menu. Two Benedicts, one with baked salmon. A salami scramble, an imported Gouda and ham scramble, a smoked wild salmon scramble. I'm getting depressed. I pick one; I eliminate all the others! Huevos rancheros, Greek omelet, corned beef hash. Wait: Gorgonzola-mushroom-thyme omelet? Folks, we have a winner! And, of course, two seconds after I make my decision, here's the server to pour water and take my order. Complete pros here, every time.

Now to just sit back and take it in. Moms are out with their kids. The two ladies by the window are clearly old friends. The couple by the register is definitely a first date. The group by the door is some kind of work team. The guy at the counter is just doing scones, coffee, and the paper. The clatter of dishes, the creaking wood floor, the subdued chatter of the crowd, the jazz—everything is in balance.

And bang-o, here's my food! A wrap-style omelet, just browned on the outside, some Gorgonzola oozing out the side. I take a bite and mmm, perfect. Somehow, it's firm and soft at the same time. The potatoes are lightly seasoned, and some smaller pieces got just a little crispy. Again, everything in balance.

Back and forth between the savory omelet, the crunchy potatoes, the sweet cider, the view, the sun, and the music. I manage to save one last little buttery bite of scone, too. I reach for the jam, at peace.

Mmm, Zell's.

Wait: Long on weekends, with a padded bench inside and some cover outside, as well as coffee and heaters. **Large groups:** Possible, but would add to the wait. **Coffee:** Kobos. **Other drinks:** Kobos loose-leaf tea, espresso, mineral water, Italian sodas, cocktails. **Feel-goods:** The request that everyone refrain from using cell phones! **Health options:** Tofu or egg whites available for $0.50. Morning Star patties and soy milk are available. **WiFi:** No.

Breakfast Carts

by Brett Burmeister

The Big Egg

N Mississippi at Skidmore in Mississippi Marketplace
Wednesday through Friday 8 a.m. to 2 p.m., Saturday and Sunday
9 a.m. to 2 p.m.
thebigeggfoodcart.blogspot.com

This bright yellow cart is in Mississippi Marketplace, a developed cart lot in North Portland. It's owned and managed by two great ladies, Gayle and Elizabeth, who always serve up your share of smiles along with your food.

The Big Egg specializes in breakfast sandwiches and wraps, yet with some unique flare. For example, the Portlander is made with two eggs, cheese, fresh chives, and country dijon mustard and served on a brioche from Grand Central Bakery down the street. Their version of the Monte Cristo Sandwich comes with eggs, black forest ham, and Gorgonzola. All that is stuffed between two pieces of crunch vanilla cardamom French toast slices and heavily dusted with powdered sugar.

The Big Egg is a great place to take the family for a weekend breakfast with covered seating. Vegetarian options also available.

The Ruby Dragon

N Mississippi at Skidmore in Mississippi Marketplace
Tuesday through Sunday 10 a.m. to 6 p.m.
therubydragonpdx.blogspot.com

Located in a wonderfully appointed cart hand built to resemble a small cottage, the Ruby Dragon is one of the only carts in town that serves a vegan breakfast. Tyler, the owner, is a long-time vegan who wanted to offer tasty, hearty vegan food with an ethnic flare.

With ingredients like quinoa, yams, nuts, fresh fruits and vegetables, you can't go wrong in finding a flavor profile you will enjoy. Quinoa is a grain out of South America that has been making inroads into the American diet due to its ease of preparation and unique texture. Similar to a couscous or bulger, you can use it to make an assortment of other items. The quinoa pancakes served here are made from fresh ground quinoa flour and hemp seeds and topped with real maple syrup, blueberries, and walnuts. Other days, the same pancakes may come with chocolate and walnuts mixed in.

Another breakfast item they serve up is Yammies—sliced yams sautéed with onions, garlic, cashews, and a touch of spice. If you plan on staying, they serve their dishes on bamboo plates to minimize waste. As close to a restaurant as a cart can get.

BrunchBox
SW 5th Ave. at Stark
Monday and Tuesday 8 a.m. to 4 p.m., Wednesday through Friday 8 a.m. to 7 p.m., Saturday 10 a.m. to 4 p.m.
brunchboxpdx.com

BrunchBox is known for their killer hamburgers, including the YouCanHasCheeseburger, a seasoned quarter-pound patty between two grilled cheese sandwiches. Yep, one heck of a burger. But they also serve breakfast—one of the few downtown carts that do, and they're located right on the MAX tracks at the transit mall.

When they opened, they introduced Portland to fresh homemade English muffin sandwiches with eggs and sausage. These arent your typical McMuffins or those things they try and pass off in the corporate deli. This muffin, along with the eggs and sausage and some veggies, melts in your mouth as you make that walk down the street.

In 2010, BrunchBox introduced fresh bagels to the options for your breakfast bread. These guys know what they're doing and have pride in what they serve.

Perierra Crêperie
SE 12th and Hawthorne in the Cartopia pod
Tuesday through Saturday 8 a.m. to 3 a.m., Sunday 9 a.m. to 3 a.m.
facebook.com/perierra

Dustin Knox, the owner and operator of Perierra Crêperie, decided Portland needed some truly authentic tasting crepes. Before opening his cart, he traveled to France to learn the art of crepe-making for six months. That experience, coupled with the desire to make a superior product, makes Perierra Crêperie a destination spot for Portlanders morning, day, and night.

A crepe is like a thin pancake wrapped around either sweet or savory fixins. At Perierra, you can get a lemon and sugar or a nutella and banana crepe, or hop to the savory side and pick up a ham and Gruyere or a Mozzarella, soprasetta, basil, and red pepper crepe. All of them are decadent.

While the crepe itself is paper thin, the ingredients are put on prior to the crepe finishing, so they can wrap it all up in a triangle. The cheese or the chocolate or both have some time to melt while the outside of the crepe gets toasty brown and crunchy.

Pair any of these crepes with a strong cup of coffee or one of their smoothies and you have a wonderful start to the day. But make sure you swing by Cartopia on a weekend late night. It's a cart scene unlike any other, and if you decide crepes aren't your thing, you can hit other carts for fried pies, Belgian fries, barbecue, pizza, or just some excellent people-watching.

bloop! Oatmeal
SW 3rd Ave. and Washington Ave.
Monday through Friday 7 a.m. to 10 a.m.
bloopoatmeal.blogspot.com

When I was a Captain Crunch-eating youngster, my parents couldn't even get us to eat homemade oatmeal we helped create. Why did it take until my adult years to discover a love for oats in the morning? If it's healthy and tasty, it makes sense.

bloop! makes sense in another way, too: it's a partnership with a lunch cart. This approach utilizes the most of what the physical cart has to offer. bloop! is the handiwork of Nat and Kat, a couple of youthful souls who believe the city needed an alternative to what has become the standard fare for breakfast.

My childhood memories of oatmeal usually include tons of sugar in order to choke it down. As an adult, I have come to enjoy oatmeal but sometimes don't make the time in the morning to cook it at home. bloop! comes to the rescue with freshly made whole oats mixed with toppings including fesh fruit, nuts, and homemade spice blends. Peanut Butter Banana Dreams includes oats, almond milk, peanut butter, banana, almonds, agave drizzle, and cinnamon mix—a great warm start to any day, especially a winter morning in Portland.

Buddha Bites

SW 4th Ave. and Hall Blvd.
Monday through Friday 9 a.m. to 4 p.m.
buddhabitespdx.blogspot.com

Buddha Bites' menu of homemade, locally grown and sourced goodies plays into Portland's ever-growing culture of getting back to the basics.

They are also riding another wave by offering gluten-free options. Many people are discovering intolerance to gluten these days, and there aren't many breakfast options for them. At Buddha Bites, they'll find tasty French toast with gluten-free cinnamon raisin bread or Naan bread with local fresh eggs, chipotle black beans, and cheddar cheese. The texture of the Naan—an Indian style flatbread—works great with the spicy black beans and a runny egg.

Buddha Bites prides itself by creating healthy food that you won't normally find at either a cart or a restaurant. Their dishes makes you feel at home. Coffee, tea, chai, and housemade kombucha available daily.

FlavourSpot

N Lombard St. between Denver Ave. and Greeley Ave., N Mississippi Ave. and Fremont St., SW 3rd Ave. and Ash St.
Lombard: Weekdays 6:30 a.m. to 2 p.m., weekends 8 a.m. to 3 p.m.
Mississippi: Monday through Saturday 9 a.m. to dark, Sunday 9 a.m. to 3 p.m.
Downtown: Weekdays 8 a.m. to 2 p.m., weekends 10 a.m. to 2 p.m.; Friday and Saturday 11 p.m. to 3 a.m.
flavourspot.com

Back in 2006, FlavourSpot became the first cart in town to offer the dutch burrito. What's a dutch burrito, you ask? Basically a waffle wrapped around some goodies. In so doing, they revolutionized how Portland saw the waffle by taking it off the plate and putting it in your hands.

I distinctly remember my first waffle burrito from the Spot. It had fresh-picked strawberries sliced up with whipped cream. As I bit into it, the crunch of the waffle mixed with the sweet fruit, and the airy cream forced me to sit down and chew slowly. I wanted to take it all in, as I knew this couldn't become a regular haunt—especially because they also serve Ovaltine, a childhood favorite.

FlavourSpot has expanded their waffle empire to three carts, including a downtown cart with a grill to serve up eggs and bacon with that sweet treat.

Parkers Waffles

1805 NE Alberta St.

Daily 8 a.m. to 2 p.m., Thursday through Saturday 8 p.m. to 2 a.m.

parkerswaffles.com

Parkers Waffles sets itself apart in a few ways. It was the first waffle cart option for downtowners, and it isn't just a breakfast joint; they have waffles with items like pulled pork, scrambled eggs, and fresh spinach. Try an egg scramble with pesto, onions, tomatoes, and mozzarella, or maybe a waffle with sausage gravy. If you're a sweet tooth, go for the lemon and blueberry: house-made lemon curd with blueberries topped with whipped cream and lemon zest, a wonderful mix of both tangy and sugary flavors.

Parkers has been known to offer specials incorporating items from other carts in the lot like a Philly Cheesesteak waffle or a seasonal waffle featuring Oktoberfest sausage with kraut and deli mustard.

Moxie Rx

N Mississippi Ave. at Shaver St.
Friday through Monday 9 a.m. to 4 p.m.
moxierx.com

Take a vintage cart, build up an enclosed area out of reclaimed housing parts, adorn the walls with recycled signs, handmade items, and maybe a rusted cupcake tin . . . and you have a special brunch spot that has captured Portland's heart.

Moxie Rx is an elixir of tasty items to sate your soul. Their menu focuses on breakfast items such as pastries, egg sandwiches, pancakes, cookies, smoothies, and fresh-made juices. Take the Swell Fried Egg Sandwich with prosciutto, provolone, peppers and basil; partner that with one of their Cure Alls—fresh-made juices with veggies like beets and kale—and you won't need to eat for a while. You may, however, head back for another, anyway.

Moxie is a popular weekend spot on North Mississippi, the perfect way to start a day of shopping or people-watching. It even has enclosed seating for those not-so-sunny days.

Pepper Box

NE Martin Luther King Blvd. at Graham St. in Dreamer's Marketplace
Wednesday through Friday 8 a.m. 2 p.m., weekends 9 a.m. to 3 p.m.
facebook.com/PepperBoxPDX

Take a sous chef from a couple of North Portland's best restaurants in the past 10 years, let him follow his dream, and you have the makings of a great cart. Jim Wilson, who designed the brunch menu at now-closed Roux, took his culinary experience and New Mexican roots and combined them to open a cart focusing on breakfast tacos and quesadilla sandwiches. Start with a freshly handmade flour tortilla, then fill it with a potato and cheese scramble, and top it with hot green chili sauce, and you have a solid meal that will satisfy you through lunch. Meat choices include homemade chorizo and baco,n or you can keep it veggie with slices of avocado. The red and green chili sauces are spicy yet flavorful mixed with the egg creation. That first bite with fresh tortilla will keep you coming back for more.

Since 2009, Brett Burmeister (aka dieselboi online) has been one of the main people behind foodcartsportland.com, the definitive online resource for news about, and profiles of, Portland's amazing food cart scene. He also contributed (as did the author of this book) to the 2010 book Cartopia: Portland's Foodcart Revolution.

He's lived in Portland all his life and been a blogger since 2003. He works downtown and says he likes to "evangelize" food carts, so the author asked him to provide a wrap-up of carts that serve breakfast. He can be reached via the website.

A World of Breakfasts

by Nick Zukin

My wife wanted breakfast. I don't eat breakfast. But wives have a way of convincing husbands to do things they'll be better off for doing, even if those things seem stupid at the time. Sometimes it's through gentle coaxing—a soft caress of the neck, a loving hug coupled with puppy dog eyes. This wasn't one of those times. We hadn't been married long, but we'd been married long enough for me to understand the seriousness of that insistent, sugar-starved stare. We were having breakfast.

It was our first trip outside the United States together and only my second trip farther than 50 miles across the southern border. We had decided on Puerto Vallarta, described as a good mix of tourist Mexico and "real" Mexico. I didn't know what to expect from breakfast in Mexico, but I knew that breakfast had always been my least favorite meal, a meal built on starches, such as pancakes and waffles, soiled with sugary toppings, more like second-rate dessert than what I considered food. And eggs.

We found a little cafe serving *desayunos*—what they call breakfast—and sat down. Except that most dishes included eggs, almost nothing was familiar. There were *chilaquiles, platanos fritos, huevos con chorizo,* and a dozen other dishes you won't find at your local IHOP. I did know chorizo, spicy Mexican sausage, so I ordered it with scrambled eggs. My wife got *molletes.* The eggs were light and fluffy, mixed with the complex, chili-red ground pork, served with a side of rice, lard-enriched beans, and corn tortillas fresh off the griddle. I sat there making chorizo and egg tacos, spooning smoky chipotle-tomatillo salsa into each one. I felt like I'd met my true love and wanted to ask her where she'd been all my life. My wife's molletes consisted of a split French loaf, toasted and smeared with refried beans, topped with ham, chorizo, and cheese, cooked in an oven until the bread began to crisp and the cheese melted. It was served with a salsa mexicana, a mixture of fresh tomatoes, onions, chilies, and lime.

That meal changed my breakfast habits. Since then, breakfast hasn't been a meal I've avoided, but a meal I've sought out. In Thailand, every morning was met with a bowl of *khanom jiin*, a noodle curry topped with fresh vegetables and herbs. In Malaysia, I'd rush to a roadside stand to get *nasi lemak* before they sold out. The coconut-infused rice with peanuts, fried anchovies, hard-boiled egg, and spicy *sambal* is one of the treats I miss most from my travels. From Mexico, I miss the morning tamales. I especially long for the stand outside one of the subway stations in Mexico City that served tamales leftover from the day before fried until crispy on the outside and oozing cheese and chilies on the inside. Pancakes? I don't need no stinkin' pancakes.

■ ■ ■

Touring the world of breakfasts doesn't have to mean cashing in the rest of your airline miles and buying a plane ticket for far-off lands. Well, not that far-off. You *will* have to get to the outskirts and suburbs of Portland.

Latin America

Start with the semi-familiar morning munchies of Mexico and Latin America called *desayunos*. There are no better *desayunos* in Portland than at Autentica (see page 44). The quality of ingredients, the quality of preparation, the diversity of the menu, and the pleasantness of the patio make it the best in town. However, they only offer weekend brunch.

Your next best bet is in Portland's tastiest suburb for Mexican food, Hillsboro. Taqueria Hermanos Ochoa's is open every day offering standard south-of-the-border breakfast items like huevos con chorizo (eggs with spicy sausage) or *huevos rancheros* (eggs with tomato salsa). You'll get a side of rice and luscious refried beans, plus a pile of corn tortillas for wrapping up everything on your plate. Add a little of one of their fiery salsas if you have a penchant for the piquant.

Another good bet, also on the west side, is Chavita's in Beaverton, serving Mexican and Salvadoran favorites. You can get chilaquiles, fried tortilla strips mixed with chili sauce, with or without eggs. It's both very simple and very delicious. In addition to coffee, they also serve *champurrado*, a corn gruel flavored with chocolate and sipped from a cup like other hot drinks. It's better than it sounds. Nothing will warm you from the inside on a drizzly Oregon morning like champurrado.

If you want desayunos a little closer in, La Superior has a location in St. John's that also serves American-style breakfasts. Get the kid a waffle and enjoy chilaquiles, *huevos a la Mexicana*, or even a breakfast burrito with chorizo and egg.

For a lighter meal on the run—or just as an alternative to picking up doughnuts for the office—try one of the *panaderías* (Latin bakeries). The Portland area's best is La Espiga Dorada on Tualatin Valley Highway in Aloha. In addition to the sweet breads (*pan dulce*), such as the colorful, sugar-crusted rolls called *conchas*, or the *churros*—long, crisp doughnuts tossed in cinnamon and sugar—are savory items, such as breads filled with cheese and jalapennos. They even serve a roll stuffed with chipotles and ham. Another good option is Yesenia's in both Hillsboro and East Portland on Powell Boulevard. Try one of the *empanadas* (hand pies) filled with spiced pumpkin, apple, or Bavarian cream.

Speaking of pan dulce, the Cuban restaurant Pambiche (see page 200) makes one of the most heavenly baskets of pastries in Portland, available every morning as part of their excellent desayunos menu. Like Autentica, their breakfasts may surpass the rest of their repertoire.

Asia

Next stop: the Orient. Grab some friends or family and find yourself in exotic Hong Kong by way of one of Portland's several dim sum houses. Dim sum is China's answer to tapas, except it's meant to be served with tea instead of booze. You choose from dozens of dishes by checking names on a card or pulling them straight from carts wheeled around the room. The best dishes go fast, so you have to have an eagle eye. Being shy only leaves you hungry.

Each plate or steamer basket has three or four of the same items, which is why any respectable dim sum house will mostly consist of larger, round tables where food and conversation is easily shared. Common dishes include: dumplings, such as *siu mai* (open-topped steamed pork dumplings) or *har gau* (steamed pork and vegetable dumplings); buns, such as *char siu bao* (barbecue pork buns); rolls, such as the familiar fried spring rolls or the less familiar *cheong fun* (steamed rice noodle rolls often filled with meat or vegetables); and various fried items, such as deep-fried shrimp. For those with a sweet tooth, custard-filled tarts will satisfy the most persnickety patron. If you want a story to tell the grandkids, try the stewed chicken feet. They look terrible, they're a lot of work, but they actually taste darn good.

Portland's best dim sum can be found on or near Southeast 82nd Avenue. The best of the best is at Ocean City Seafood Restaurant. The runner up in the dim sum department is Wong's King Seafood with its original location on Southeast Division Street and a newer location near 217 in Beaverton. Either restaurant will be a wonderful introduction to a frenetic, banquet-style Chinese brunch.

For a more solitary and soothing Chinese breakfast, the noodle houses, such as Good Taste or Kenny's, serve *jook* (aka, congee), Asia's version of oatmeal or grits. It's a rice porridge with a pasty texture not immediately agreeable to the American palate. You may want to add some butter, brown sugar, and cinnamon. I'm sure it would be good that way. But the Chinese take a distinctly savory approach. Common choices for mix-ins include sliced pork, assorted seafood, roast duck, and ash-black preserved duck egg. If you like yours spicy, you can add hot pepper oil found next to the soy sauce on the table. The rice-thickened soup is rarely over $5 even with a cup of coffee. It's very filling, easy on the belly, and warms from within for hours.

The most common ethnic breakfast around Portland, though, is something food lovers know well—just not as a beginning to their morning. It's *pho*, the great Vietnamese-French fusion beef soup. Perhaps the best can be found at Pho Oregon on Northeast 82nd Avenue, though the replacement for its original location on Sandy Boulevard, Pho An, offers a beefy bowl just as fragrant with cinnamon, ginger, and star anise.

A spicier cousin to pho available for breakfast at several shops around Portland is *bun bo hue*. This soup is bold, bold, bold. The noodles are thicker and more toothsome than pho. The meats are more mysterious, including things like congealed pork blood. The salad plate includes more exotic choices, too, such as banana blossom. And the soup is both sweeter and spicier. Three Portland restaurants specialize in this soup, and choosing between them is an impossible but enjoyable task: Bun Bo Hue on Southeast 82nd Avenue just south of Woodstock, Ngoc Han Bun Bo Hue on Southeast 82nd Avenue just north of Division Street, and Bun Bo Hue Minh just east of Southeast 82nd Avenue on Division Street.

For those who can't make up their mind what to eat, there's HA&VL, perhaps the best breakfast spot in Portland. Each day they make one soup, maybe two on the weekend, a different soup each day, which they often sell out. Especially good is their *bun rieu*, a vermicelli noodle soup with fish balls, ground pork, and ground shrimp in an orange, tomato-infused broth.

And while sandwiches are exclusively a lunch-time meal here in the United States, in Vietnam they're also popular for breakfast. For this reason, the bánh mi shops generally open early. There's nothing better than driving through Best Baguette at Southeast Powell Boulevard and 82nd Avenue, grabbing a fresh-squeezed juice and French roll stuffed with grilled marinated pork, pickled veggies, jalapeños, and cilantro on the way to the airport for a morning flight.

Next time you're complaining about a 45-minute wait in the rain for a table at your neighborhood cafe on a Sunday morning, remember that there's an entire world of breakfasts in Portland with no line, where the food has twice the flavor for half the cost.

Chinese & Asian
Bun Bo Hue (7002 SE 82nd Ave., Portland)
Bun Bo Hue Minh (8560 SE Division St., Portland)
Good Taste Noodle House (8220 SE Harrison St., Portland)
HA&VL (2738 SE 82nd Ave., Portland)
Jin Wah (8001 SE Powell Blvd., Portland)
Kenny's Noodle House (8305 SE Powell Blvd., Portland)

Ngoc Han Bun Bo Hue (8230 SE Powell Blvd., Portland)
Ocean City (3016 SE 82nd Ave., Portland)
Pho An (6236 NE Sandy Blvd., Portland)
Pho Oregon (2518 NE 82nd Ave., Portland)
Wong's King Seafood (8733 SE Division St., Portland)

Mexican & Latin
Autentica (page 44)
Chavita's (18385 SW Alexander St. Beaverton)
La Espiga Dorada (18370 SW Tualatin Valley Hwy., Beaverton)
La Superior (2727 N. Lombard St., Portland)
Tortillería y Tienda de Leon (16225 NE Glisan St., Portland)
Yesenia's (6611 SE Powell Blvd., Portland)

Nick Zukin is the Zuke in Kenny & Zuke's (see page 158) and creator of the local food sites, PortlandFood.org and Extramsg.com. He likes food.

Out on the Road

Sure, it's a book about breakfast in Portland, but we occasionally venture out, right?

Get mad if you want, but I have skipped right over the suburbs. Here's an introduction to some of my favorite places to stop for a bite when headed to or from mountain, lake, trail, or beach.

Camp 18 on Highway 26 It's about . . . well, 18 miles before 101. You have probably driven by it and thought it was a logging museum. It is. It's also a restaurant with outrageous portions and a Sunday buffet (10 a.m. to 2 p.m.) that's off the charts. It's an excellent way to feed up for, or recover from, a hike up nearby Saddle Mountain. But mainly, it's a monument to the logging industry and to wood carving. They have all sorts of machinery and photos, a Loggers' Memorial, hand-carved doors that are four and a half inches thick and weigh 500 pounds, and a central rafter that's 85 feet long and 25 tons—one piece of wood! So put away your liberal anti-logging bias, go wallow in history, and chow down. *camp18restaurant.com*.

Charburger in Cascade Locks You could *not* open a place like this today. Forget the purple goo on the marionberry pancakes; I think the PC police would burn you down if your mascot was a little feather-headed Indian boy named Chief Char. But this place has been open for 50 years, owned by the same guy, and is a monument to the old days. By that, I mean the arrowheads and gun collection and logging photos, and also the food. It ain't fancy, or even very good. They've got a pizza omelet on which I still await a report. There's also a Sunday Buffet ($17.95, reservations required, 10 a.m. to 2 p.m.) with beef, chicken, salmon, seafood, link sausage, bacon, fettuccine, Belgian waffles, biscuits and gravy, to-order omelets, and a fruit and dessert bar. All this, and probably the best view of any place in this book.

Columbia Gorge Hotel in Hood River When most of us think about Hood River, we picture windsurfers and snowboarders and Full

Sail brewing. This place is more like Grandma. It dates back to 1921, with a little break for new owners in 2008 and 2009, and its website claims it has entertained "movie stars like Clara Bow, Rudolph Valentino and Shirley Temple (and) presidents like Roosevelt and Coolidge." Now their main attraction is a Sunday brunch ($19, 9 a.m. to 2 p.m., reservations strongly recommended) where you choose one of eight entrées and then have at a buffet. They still do the famous thing with "honey from the sky," they still have a waterfall and an amazing view, and they still play jazz for an older, well-dressed crowd. *columbiagorgehotel.com.*

Huckleberry Inn in Government Camp I confess a deep and abiding love for this place. Whether it's huckleberry pancakes before a hike or huckleberry pie after, it almost doesn't feel like a day on Mount Hood unless I sit down at their wooden booth or counter and load up on carbs. They also have a fine old-school cheeseburger. And it used to be the Greyhound station, which brings a whole new level of people-watching. In an ever-growing and modernizing Government Camp, "the Huck" is an old-time institution. They put huckleberries in ice cream, pie, pancakes, bonbons, lip balm, tea, preserves, and milkshakes. They also make their own doughnuts and have the largest pile of butter you'll ever see. *huckleberry-inn.com.*

Joe's Donuts in Sandy All right, I said no doughnut places in the book. Whatever. Not only that, but I've never even *had* a doughnut at Joe's, the place you've driven by at the far end of Sandy, with the red and white cinder blocks. Wait: is an apple fritter a doughnut? I don't know, and I don't care. I just know that even for a sugar addict like me, that apple fritter is a limit-pushing orgy of sweetness. A third of the way through one, I am in heaven. Two-thirds, I'm thinking about leaving the rest for after the hike. After a kind of blackout, I suddenly have no more fritter, my head is spinning, and my ears are ringing. People have all kinds of strong opinions about Joe's, but I do recommend you try the place, at least once. Well, I recommend the fritter.

Otis Café on Highway 18 at the Coast It's hard to think of a place with a size-to-reputation ratio to match Otis. They got written up in the *New York Times* in 1989, and they've been media darlings ever since. They're also loved by regular folks, who try to out-write each other with childhood memories, odes to the small-town diner, and gasps at the portions. Mainly, the tiny café (it's been there since the '20s) is known for the German potatoes, a pile of hash browns topped with green onions and white cheddar cheese. It's $5.50 for a softball-sized pile; $7.25 for a football; $1.25 each for sausage, vegetable, ham, bacon, and mushrooms; and $0.75 each for "as many eggs as you please." Also, check out the molasses toast and all the various pies. And be sure to visit the tiny bathroom; you weave through the kitchen and wait in the room where they bake the pies. That is some good stuff back there! *otiscafe.com.*

Skamania Lodge in Stevenson, Washington First, though I wish it were different, this isn't a place for people with a mania for ska music. If they had any sense, and maybe less class, they'd schedule a Ska Mania festival. Instead, what they offer is a Sunday Champagne Brunch (9 a.m. to 2 p.m., reservations suggested) that is an epic eating experience: eight starters, eight salads, a build-your-own omelet station, a carving station with five meats, seven entrées and a plethora of desserts. It's a spectacle. It's also $28.95 plus tax and gratuity (kids are $10.95 or $16.95). You'll want to make reservations, go for a big hike in the Gorge beforehand to earn it, and find a spot for a nap afterwards. *skamania.com.*

Timberline Lodge on Mount Hood Don't let this business about the Farmers Market Brunch fool you. That's a mostly lunch deal that starts at 11 a.m. Go for the breakfast buffet, which I have my own name for: the Hiker Hoedown. It runs from 7:30 to 10 a.m. on weekdays, and until 10:30 a.m. on weekends, and it's $8.95 for the continental (fruits, pastries, and cheeses) and $13.95 for the full buffet. At any of those hours from July until October, look around for scruffy, perhaps still filthy, people behaving somewhat strangely. Chances are they have been out on the trail for a few days or weeks, and you might see them worshipping at the orange juice machine, pacing back and forth in front of the waffle iron, making architectural wonders out of bacon and sausage, and generally making the most of the all-you-can-eat feature. Otherwise, you'll be eating breakfast in a 1930s-era lodge at 6,000 feet elevation on Oregon's highest mountain. Highly recommended. *timberlinelodge.com.*

On Facebook, Twitter, iPhones, the Web, and Internet Radio

This used to be about books.

But by the time I put this edition together, I had started a breakfast podcast, I had worked on an iPhone app, and Facebook and Twitter were in the process of taking over the world. Here are a few words, then, about online resources.

First, the app: it will work on iPhones (iPad coming soon), and there will be a free (with ads) and not free (without ads) version. It's called, of course, Breakfast in Bridgetown.

Next, the podcast: It airs live every week on *cascadia.fm*, and you can subscribe to the podcast in iTunes. There's also a list of all the shows on my website, *breakfastinbridgetown.com*.

Instead of cluttering up the book with Facebook links and Twitter's @nonsense, I instead offer all the Facebook, Twitter, and website links you can ever stand at my site. Go there and click Restaurants on the Web, Facebook, and Twitter.

Another way is to go to my own Twitter page (I'm @pdxbreakfast-guy) and look for my Breakfast Places list.

Other websites of note—and usefulness in writing a breakfast book.

- *extramsg.com:* Nick Zukin's great blog
- *foodcartsportland.com:* Brett Burmeister's hub of food cart world
- *goodstuffnw.com:* Food writer Kathleen Bauer specializes in farmers markets
- *lizcrain.com:* Local food writer and author of *Food Lover's Guide to Portland*
- *pdx.eater.com:* News and commentary
- *portlandfood.org:* Sprawling discussion of all things Portland food
- *portlandfoodanddrink.com:* The Food Dude's great review and news site
- *stumptownvegans.com:* Terrific site for vegans, occasionally talks breakfast

About the Author

I've always wanted to do interesting things, visit interesting places, meet interesting people, and then tell folks about them. As a teenager I found out that writers get *paid* for doing those things, and my life's trajectory was set.

I started as a sports writer at the Southern Methodist University *Daily Campus* because I wanted to sit in the press box at football games. I also had a sports-desk job at the much-missed *Dallas Times Herald* for three wonderful years.

After college I screwed around and traveled for a few years, then retreated to my hometown of Memphis and another fantastic sports-desk job at the *Memphis Commercial Appeal.* I also got hired at the weekly *Memphis Flyer* and wrote for every section of the paper: sports, news, book and film reviews, editorials, you name it. Good times!

And then in the mid-1990s I found the twin promised lands of freelance writing and travel writing. That was when I cut loose from the docks of life and set myself adrift; I've held exactly one "real" job since. Along the way I've also hustled for money at an amusement park, a temp agency, a landscaping company (briefly), restaurant kitchens (more briefly), Alaskan fishing boats, social service nonprofits, FedEx, and an insurance company—yes, cubicle and all. Those are the jobs I can remember, anyway.

I moved to Oregon in 1996 because it's about 4,000 times cooler than Memphis. I have written two hiking guidebooks, both published by Menasha Ridge Press of Birmingham, Alabama: *60 Hikes within 60 Miles of Portland* (fourth edition, 2010) and *Day and Overnight Hikes on Oregon's Pacific Crest Trail* (2007). I also revised Menasha's *Best in Tent Camping: Oregon*, which came out in 2009.

I published this book myself through a small publishing company I created called Bacon and Eggs Press. Future editions and more titles are on the way. For the price of a cup of coffee, you can pick my brain about publishing all you want. I can talk you into or out of it.

I also host a breakfast radio show/podcast on *cascadia.fm*, and I blog fairly often at *breakfastinbridgetown.com*.

I hope my writing gives you pleasure and makes you hungry.

The Author's Favorites

There is one question that *everybody* asks me: "What's your favorite place?"

There really is no such thing. I have favorite diners, favorite fancy places, favorite dishes, favorite ways to show off Portland . . . you get the idea. And I don't do ratings in the book, anyway.

Still, everyone asks, so I forced myself to list my 12 favorites. Note that I didn't say "the 12 best in town." These places (listed alphabetically, by the way) all have some combination of good food, good memories, a vibe that I dig, and cute servers.

Two disclaimers: I invested exactly four minutes in putting this list together, and if you ask me in person, I probably won't remember what's on here.

Besaw's because it's in my neighborhood, it's casual and classy, and the staff and food are both solid.

Country Cat if only for that fried chicken/pecan spoonbread thing. Dang!

Genies because it has my favorite (aka the best) Benedicts in town.

Helser's for half-price early treats, the clean and simple vibe, and my crush on the staff.

Kenny and Zuke's for the pastrami and root beer. Yes, in the morning.

Original Pancake House because it's so 1950s, and deciding which pancakes to order is pleasurable torture.

Pine State Biscuits for a couple of country ham biscuit sandwiches on the way to a hike.

Po'Shines for blackened catfish and a good mission.

Sanborn's because it's so great and nobody seems to know about it.

Simpatica because it's the best breakfast food in town and makes me feel good about Portland.

Stepping Stone because it was my original regular place, and 12 years later, it still is. And because of the Thursday Night Boys.

Zell's is the one place I make sure out-of-towners eat.

Breinigsville, PA USA
13 November 2010
249288BV00004B/10/P

9 780979 735011